The Circulation of Anti-Austerity Protest

Bart Cammaerts

The Circulation of Anti-Austerity Protest

palgrave
macmillan

Bart Cammaerts
LSE
London, UK

ISBN 978-3-030-09935-0 ISBN 978-3-319-70123-3 (eBook)
https://doi.org/10.1007/978-3-319-70123-3

Softcover re-print of the Hardcover 1st edition 2018

Cover illustration: Bowornsak Jhanpet / EyeEm

Printed on acid-free paper

This Palgrave Macmillan imprint is published by Springer Nature
The registered company is Springer International Publishing AG
The registered company address is: Gewerbestrasse 11, 6330 Cham, Switzerland

Acknowledgements

Writing this book was a long journey with many challenges and difficult moments. It was an ambitious project and its outcome is not perfect, just like life itself. Many people—loved ones, friends, and colleagues—helped me in this endeavour. In particular I wish to express my gratitude to my ex-partner Steph Newell for her relentless support and the productive discussions we had; and to Manon for being my loving daughter. I also want to thank Lance Bennett, Nick Couldry, Lillie Chouliaraki, Ellen Helsper, Sonia Livingstone, Peter Lunt, Robin Mansell and Shani Orgad for reading chapters and providing insightful comments, constructive feedback and helpful suggestions—in doing so they improved the book enormously. I also thank the anonymous reviewers of the manuscript, as well as participants in seminars and workshops where I have presented my work in recent times; all your critiques, comments and suggestions have also contributed to making the book into what it has become.

I am also thankful to the LSE, as well as the Department of Media and Communications, for their financial support (Research Infrastructure and Investment Funds—RIIF) to fund the survey and the focus groups. Finally, I am also incredibly grateful to Ariel Shangguan, Yuanyuan Liu and Kullanit Nitiwarangkul for their help with the content analysis, and to Brooks DeCillia for his help with the statistical analysis.

Contents

List of Figures

List of Tables

CHAPTER 1

Introduction

'They Cut, We Bleed'
(anti-austerity slogan)

In September 2015, Jeremy Corbyn, a veteran left-winger, won the UK Labour Party leadership election convincingly on a distinctly anti-austerity agenda, despite having pitted himself against the establishment candidates. The result surprised many observers as well as many in the Labour Party, who asked themselves how a somewhat scruffy 67-year-old self-proclaimed socialist had achieved such popularity, especially among young people, in such a short period of time.

A large part of the answer to this question stems from seven years earlier, when the capitalist financial system experienced a near-systemic collapse resulting in an economic crisis that hit not just the poor, but above all the middle classes and, in particular, young people. Two years after the 2008 crash, and after a series of massive state interventions, including the nationalization of financial institutions in order to save the global capitalist system, the UK's centre-left Prime Minister, Gordon Brown, was voted out of office and replaced by a Tory/Liberal Democrat coalition government led by David Cameron. A few months into that government's term, the new Tory Chancellor of the Exchequer, George Osborne, announced that the UK government would start cutting public spending by a massive £83bn—£7bn of which would have to come from cutting welfare benefits. 'Austerity Britain' was born (see HM Treasury 2010). A few days before

B. Cammaerts, *The Circulation of Anti-Austerity Protest*,
https://doi.org/10.1007/978-3-319-70123-3_1

this, it was announced that a long-running dispute between the mobile operator, Vodafone, and Her Majesty's Revenue and Customs (HMRC) had been settled through what was described by some as a 'sweetheart deal'. Investigative reporting revealed that Vodafone had been able to cut its tax bill from approximately £6bn to £1.3bn (*Private Eye* 2010).[1]

This glaring injustice provided the impetus for the launch of an anti-austerity movement in the UK. A group of friends who gathered in the Nag's Head, a pub located in Islington in north London—coincidentally (or not), Jeremy Corbyn's constituency, were sufficiently incensed by this contradiction that they decided to take action to focus the public's attention on tax dodging and aggressive tax avoidance, by juxtaposing them with the government's austerity agenda. It was obvious to this group that there were sensible alternatives to austerity, but the government clearly did not want to consider them:

> We were just a group of friends having a drink together. It certainly wasn't a political meeting but we got chatting about the cuts—like people all over the country. Every time we talked about the cuts, it kept coming back to the story about Vodafone and the £6 billion. Later in the evening, when we were all a bit tipsy, we decided to blockade a Vodafone store. (David Wills, quoted in Messenger 2010)

After the exchange of a few emails in the wake of their discussions in the north London pub, the group decided to plan some direct action. First, they set up a Wordpress weblog called 'Their Crisis', which contained a call for an 'anti-cuts direct action':

> The cuts have come and we need to get to work opposing them fast. This Wednesday we will take direct action against a target to expose the lies that these cuts are necessary or fair. The target has to stay secret until Wednesday morning but we need as many people as possible to join us ... See you on the streets! (Posting on 24/10/2010: https://theircrisis.wordpress.com/)

A day before the planned protest, a twitter account called '@ukuncut' was created and people were asked to 'meet 9:30 AM at the Ritz—look for the orange umbrella #UKuncut'. About 65 people showed up on Wednesday, 27 October; most were strangers to one other, and some were undercover police officers (see Lewis et al. 2010). It was only at this point that the target of the action was revealed: the flagship Vodafone store on Oxford Street, which was subsequently occupied and blocked. A day after this first direct action, a new Wordpress weblog and a Facebook group called 'UK Uncut' were set up, and the first post on the Facebook page was a link to a Google Maps page showing all the Vodafone stores in the UK.[2]

After this first action, the numbers and scope of the group grew exponentially. One week later, Vodafone shops on the high streets of Leeds (Thursday, 28 October); Weymouth and Hastings (Friday, 29 October); York, Glasgow, Edinburgh, Leicester, Portsmouth, Bristol, Birmingham, Oxford, Manchester, Liverpool (see Fig. 1.1), Brighton, and several

Fig. 1.1 UK Uncut protest outside Vodafone, Church Street, Liverpool, 12 December 2010

locations in London (Saturday, 30 October); Nottingham (Tuesday, 2 November); Glasgow again (Wednesday, 3 November); and Newcastle (Thursday, 4 November) had been targeted and successfully shut down by activists aligning themselves with the hashtag #UKuncut. Later, retail chains such as Top Shop, several banks, Starbucks, the chemist chain Boots, and the luxury department store Fortnum and Mason were occupied, named and shamed for their dodgy tax-regimes.

UK Uncut's direct actions are illustrative of the productive and connective roles that social media platforms such as Twitter and Facebook can play as powerful mobilizing and organizing tools, bringing together like-minded people who are willing and eager to take action (see Bennett and Segerberg 2013). They appropriated smart-mob tactics mediated through distributed networked communication technologies, bringing together 'people who are able to act in concert even if they don't know each other' (Rheingold 2002: xii). The activists were asked to show up in a particular place, at a given time, to demonstrate togetherness with a touch of street theatre. Referring to a 1960s artist-activist collective, Beckett (2011: np) called their actions 'witty and creative neo-Situationalist agit-prop'. Relevant in this context is that the direct actions of UK Uncut were aimed mainly at shops, 'normal everyday place[s] where financial exchange and profit-making happens' (McKay 2011: np).

At the same time, traditional media, such as flyers and posters, were also important to UK Uncut. On their blog, the protesters posted a set of flyers denouncing tax dodgers. These were 'print ready' and were made for activists organizing actions to hand out to the shopping public. A letter addressed to the employees of the shops UK Uncut targeted was also distributed. It explained that UK Uncut's actions were not directed at them, but at their employers and the government: 'We … do not aim to intimidate you in any way' (UK Uncut 2010).

All this activist enthusiasm and the somewhat spectacular direct actions that UK Uncut and its growing number of activists organized throughout the country attracted growing mainstream media attention, with all broadcasters and most newspapers reporting on their actions, and in doing so also touching on the problematic nature of tax avoidance by corporations and rich individuals.

As is apparent from this introductory account of the genesis of the UK's anti-austerity movement, media as well as communication tools and the various mediation practices they afford were, in several ways, central to and of crucial importance in the constitution and development of this movement. Mediation practices were central in the setting up of the movement, for internal communication among the activists in terms of mobilizing for and coordinating direct action, for communicating the aims and goals of the activists, for self-representing and depicting the actions, and for how the mainstream media represented UK Uncut's actions and reproduced the activists' messages.

In recent years, the study of the various roles that media and communication play for activists and social movements has moved centre stage. To a large extent, this can be explained by the emergence of digital media and communication technologies such as the internet, mobile phones, and social media applications, and how they are seen to be essential tools for activists to mobilize and to communicate independently across time and space. These digital technologies arguably have extended the activists' repertoire of contentious action (Costanza-Chock 2003; Rolfe 2005; Chadwick 2007; Van Laer and Van Aelst 2010; Cammaerts 2012). Many scholars, however, continue to stress the crucial importance of mainstream media for activists and social movements in reaching beyond the like-minded and in increasing the public legitimacy of their struggles (Gamson and Wolfsfeld 1993; Rucht 2013; Cammaerts 2013).

Media and communication matter, in a variety of ways, for social movements, and ultimately for the strategies of social change that activists enact. In this book I show how they implicate symbolic struggles over meaning through the dynamic interplay between hegemony and counter-hegemony. Media and communication are also central to the communicative practices of activists aimed at disseminating their societal critiques and movement aims, and their efforts to mobilize for direct action. Political struggles and contentious actions are, however, not only fought on the street, but also in the public sphere, in the mainstream media, and online as well as offline. A focus on media and communication practices also brings public opinion into play and highlights the roles of those accessing, reading, and viewing news and social media.

Whereas media and communication has often been treated as a peripheral concern in social movement studies, I argue in this book that in fact they are central to the study of contentious politics today. Elsewhere I have argued that this increased centrality of media and communication in our everyday lives, and in contentious politics, constitutes a *mediation opportunity structure* for activists and social movements that is related inevitably to the political opportunity structure (Koopmans 1999), but that:

> there certainly is a case to be made for the distinct nature of the mediation opportunity structure as not only facilitative or instrumental, but also constitutive of direct action. It both enables and closes down opportunities for resistance and activists increasingly take this into account when surveying their repertoire of contentious action. (Cammaerts 2012: 129)

By mediation opportunity structure I mean the interplay between agentic opportunities and structural constraints in relation to media representations of protest and activism, communication technologies appropriated and used by activists, and the reception process which implicates non-activist citizens.

In an increasingly hyper-mediated and interconnected world, there is a pressing need for social movement scholars to incorporate insights from the media and communication studies field. Similarly, it is fruitful and essential to draw on social movement theories to understand the media and communication practices of activists, including their self-mediations, and the mainstream media representations of activism. Bridging what Downing (2008: 41) called the 'persistent divorce' in the social sciences between media and communication studies and other disciplines or fields is crucial if we are to understand how movement discourses and protest actions circulate through society and lead to social change.

The main aim of this book is to deepen our understanding of how protest circulates through society, and the consequences of that circulation process in the medium and long term. I develop a conceptual framework that encompasses the various 'moments' in which media and communication are implicated in protest and social change. The conceptual framework takes its inspiration from, and builds on the Circuit of Culture, which included five moments: production, representation, identity, reception/consumption, and regulation (Johnson 1986; Du Gay et al. 1997). My framework is comprised of four core moments, which together I designate as the *Circuit of Protest*. The moments in this circuit are:

- the *production* of movement discourses, frames and a collective identity (addressed in Chap. 3);
- a set of *self-mediation practices* of the movement (addressed in Chap. 4);
- the mainstream media *representations* of the movement (addressed in Chap. 5); and
- the *reception* of the movement discourses and frames by non-activist citizens (addressed in Chap. 6).

In conclusion, in Chap. 7, I present insights into the mediation opportunity structure in the light of my analysis of these four moments, paying particular attention to the dialectic between enabling/generative and constraining/repressive factors at play. This provides a solid basis for assessing both the failures and successes of the anti-austerity movement.

In addition, this framework serves as a prism through which to address, and potentially reconcile, a number of long-standing tensions within the study of social movements including the tensions between the symbolic versus the material aspects of a political struggle, between a focus on processes internal versus external to a movement, and between an emphasis on agentic opportunities versus structural constraints. As such, the Circuit of Protest not only serves as a conceptual framework to structure this book, but also provides a conceptual model that can be used by others to analyse the mediation opportunity structure of a variety of struggles and mobilizations.

Empirically, I focus on what I refer to as the UK's anti-austerity movement, of which UK Uncut is a central component. In addition, the National Campaign Against Fees and Cuts (NCAFC), a radical student protest organization, and the Occupy London Stock Exchange (Occupy LSX) movement are also included in my analysis. There have been many influences on the messaging and tactics of the UK anti-austerity movement, such as the Arab Spring, the Spanish Indignados, the Occupy Wall Street movements, and others with transnational origins. In this book I limit my analysis to a consideration of factors that have been prominent in the UK context so as to enable in-depth analysis of the various ways in which media representations as well as independent communication practices of the anti-austerity movement have played a central role in the circulation of anti-austerity protest throughout UK society. In choosing the anti-austerity movement as the empirical lens through which to analyse these mediation practices, I also draw attention to the manifestation of a renewed and reinvigorated politics of redistribution in the wake of the 2008 financial, and subsequent economic, crisis.

In Chap. 2, media and communication are positioned within the conceptual apparatus of social movement studies, and social movements are similarly positioned within the fields of media and communication studies. The Circuit of Protest is elaborated and the methodological choices that were made to study the four moments of the Circuit of Protest empirically are discussed.

Notes

1. Unsurprisingly, Vodafone refuted the £6bn calculated by *Private Eye* (2010), describing it as 'an urban myth'.
2. See URL: https://www.google.com/fusiontables/DataSource?snapid=95114.

CHAPTER 2

Situating the Circulation of Protest

This chapter presents the book's conceptual framework. The aim is to theorize the way in which meaning and protest circulate through society. I propose the notion of a *Circuit of Protest*, inspired by the cultural studies model of a Circuit of Culture in order to make sense of the variety of ways in which media and communication facilitate or mediate social movements, their protest events and the social changes they aim to achieve.

The Circuit of Protest framework relates to and includes (1) the production of movement discourses and the discursive construction of a collective identity, (2) the internal and external communicative practices enacted by the movement; (3) mainstream media representations of the movement; and (4) the reception of the movement and the media discourse by non-activist citizens. The process of mediation is seen, conceptually, to connect the interrelations among several dimensions including the symbolic nature of a political struggle and its material aspects, alternative media practices and mainstream media representations, and the production of a movement discourse and its reception by those external to the movement. Furthermore, approaching mediation as a dialectic process also enables a consideration of both agentic opportunities and structural constraints, and their dynamic interrelationship. Mediation is thus understood as a 'fundamentally dialectical notion' which:

B. Cammaerts, *The Circulation of Anti-Austerity Protest*,
https://doi.org/10.1007/978-3-319-70123-3_2

> requires us to understand how processes of communication change the social and cultural environments that support them as well as the relationships that participants, both individual and institutional, have to that environment and to each other. (Silverstone 2005: 189)

In this chapter, media and communication are positioned theoretically first within some of the traditions in social movement theory. Second, social movements are considered in relation to theories in the media and communication studies field. Following this I outline the Circuit of Protest and justify the methodological choices that were made in the empirical part of my research on the UK's anti-austerity movement.

2.1 Positioning Media and Communication Within Social Movement Studies

Despite the pivotal roles of media and communication in contentious politics and in the emergence, development and sustainability of social movements, their importance is often downplayed and, as argued by Koopmans (2004) and Downing (2008), also undertheorized. This is not to say that social movement scholars ignore this area; there are some notable exceptions to the view that attention within social movement studies to the role of media and communication processes in relation to contentious politics is lacking (see, among others, Gitlin 1980; Snow and Benford 1988; Gamson 1992; Gamson and Wolfsfeld 1993; Melucci 1996; Ryan 1999; Scalmer 2002; Rucht 2004; Johnston 2009).

In the context of theories that aim to make sense of the phenomenon of the social movement, there are several approaches, each emphasizing different aspects and focusing on various levels of analysis. My review is not exhaustive but instead is designed to highlight four of these that are important in order to position media and communication within social movements' theoretical tradition:

1. resource mobilization;
2. political process;
3. cultural framing; and
4. network approach.

Some of these approaches start from contradictory assumptions or stem from a reaction against or a dialogue with another approach, but they each add insight. I suggest that, in their different ways, they contribute substantially to the understanding of the role of media and communication in contentious politics, but on their own they are insufficient.

2.1.1 Resource Mobilization Approach

The Resource Mobilization (RM) approach is concerned not only with why social movements emerge, but also, and especially, with how and in what way they are manifested. Unlike earlier approaches to collective behaviour (Blumer 1951; Park and Burgess 1966 [1921]), the RM approach does not consider social movements as a symptom of a sick society or as deviant and irrational responses to a set of grievances. Scholars within the RM tradition such as Oberschall (1973), McCarthy and Zald (1973), and Freeman (1979), argue, instead, that societal conflict and tension are a normal state of affairs rather than an anomaly that disturbs an otherwise harmonious society.

Social movements are positioned in this approach as rational actors pursuing shared and collective interests. It is argued that the existence of a set of grievances is, in itself, not enough for collective action to emerge. The ability of movements to mobilize a variety of resources, such as financial capital, people's participation and their gifting of time, the availability of charismatic leaders, skills, knowledge, information, popular support, etc. are deemed to be much more important than the mere existence of grievances (Freeman 1979). As a result, the RM approach focuses principally on the internal processes within social movements, on the ways in which movements are able, or indeed fail, to mobilize these resources. The main emphasis is on the organizational structures, on the quality of leadership and on the potential costs of participation.

In the RM approach to social movements, media and communication are regarded primarily as one (relatively important) resource among many others. As a tangible resource, communication infrastructures are essential to communicate internally; thus they are treated as organizational resources, but are also regarded as enabling communicative practices with a view to disseminating the aims and demands of a movement, and facilitating the mobilization for direct action. Taking the example of UK Uncut, which was outlined in the Introduction, the use of email and social media to coordinate direct actions and to mobilize is often examined, as well as, for example, the production of leaflets and flyers to outline demands.

Intangibly, media and communication practices are deemed to be particularly relevant to mainstream media representations, and above all to the influence that the media and mediation processes are considered to have over public opinion, which is considered to be an indispensable intangible resource. A RM approach tends to stress the importance and possibility of developing a well-thought-through media strategy that could potentially have a positive influence on the public perception of a movement. Thus an effective media strategy is said to enable a movement to punch above its weight (McCarthy and Zald 1973). For example, UK Uncut was a relatively small group of activists, but it managed to attract a great deal of mainstream media attention by creating protest spectacles and targeting high street brands, thereby succeeding in highlighting aggressive tax avoidance by big companies. Similarly, the student protests and Occupy LSX received ample, albeit not always positive, media coverage.

One of many critiques of the resource mobilization approach is that it neglects, or, rather, downplays, many macro external factors influencing the success or failure of a movement (Beuchler 1993). The ability or inability to mobilize resources, in itself, it is argued, is not sufficient to explain the rise or fall of a movement. There is a political and economic context outside a movement that has a considerable impact on the nature of the opportunities for, and constraints on, the movement's ability to mobilize and to achieve social and political change. There are also cultural and ideological factors that need to be recognized. Thus, social movements are part of a broader political process which influences their success or failure to achieve the social change they desire.

2.1.2 Political Process Approach

A Political Process (PP) approach emphasizes precisely these crucially important external processes that are understood to be situated outside the control of social movements. In this approach, these processes generally refer to the political momentum, the opportunities or the existence of external factors favourable to the aims and tactics of the movement, but it also refers to the structural constraints impeding social change and protecting the status quo (Tarrow 1994; Gamson and Meyer 1996; Koopmans 1999). Within the PP 'structuralist' approach, the external context, which may be economic or political, or a combination of the two, is called an opportunity structure. Thus, primarily in this approach there is an attempt to explain which structural aspects of the external world affect the development and success of a social movement.

The notion of an economic and/or political opportunity structure is contextual and spatial. This tradition seeks to accounts for different historical and political trajectories, for various protest cultures and for the distinct contexts in which limits and constraints on protest and social movements operate. In this view, the costs associated with different forms of protest and contestation are expected to vary from one locality to the next, and to change dynamically over time. Here, the intrinsic link between opportunity structures and repertoires of contentious action is a particularly noteworthy feature of the theoretical framework.

Activists are understood to select their tactics and strategies from a broad repertoire of contentious action (Tilly 1986). The metaphor of a repertoire points as much to the possible and the imaginable as it does to what is considered impossible, or to the constraints imposed on activists by both state and corporate actors. In different contexts, the repertoire is expected to vary, and over time to change, as new forms of action present themselves or are closed down. Thus, opportunity structures also are expected to influence the nature and extent of the repertoire of contentious action at the disposal of activists.

Within the PP approach, media and communication are regarded as part of the broader political opportunity structure, but they can also be seen as facilitating a repertoire of contentious action, and even potentially to constitute new repertoires. The mainstream media and their ability to influence public opinion, are considered to be a very important external factor for social movements, and to have a significant impact on their success or failure (Gamson and Wolfsfeld 1993; Oliver and Maney 2000; Koopmans 2004). Mainstream media resonance is deemed to be crucial for a movement's efforts to mobilize political support, to increase the legitimacy and validation of its demands, and to enable it to widen the scope of conflict beyond those who are like-minded. As Ryan (1991: 27–28) asserts, 'mass media remain a crucial arena in which social movements must vie for influence under difficult conditions and uncertain results'.

The centrality of the media's resonance to a social movement's aims in this approach has led to the recognition by some scholars of a distinct media opportunity structure, denoting the interplay between the agentic opportunities offered by and through the achievement of mainstream resonance and the structural impediments to achieving (positive) media resonance (Crossley 2006: 31). In the case of the anti-austerity movement, mainstream media resonance was mixed, as will be shown in Chap. 4, which examines mainstream media representations of the UK's anti-austerity movement.

Alongside the mainstream media, however, consideration should also be given to the self-mediation practices of activists. These communicative practices have to contend with an external context that creates opportunities for, but also imposes constraints on the activists. The state, whose pivotal role is emphasized frequently within the PP approach, is understood to act quickly to disrupt the production, distribution and accessibility of media and communication technologies—for example, through regulatory interventions or by licensing laws (Mansell and Raboy 2011). Historically, states have attempted to regulate the content that circulates on and through the media, using pre- as well as post-publication censorship regimes, for example (see, among others, Darnton 1982; Warf 2011).

In addition, private companies, inventors and designers—that is, those developing and making available new media and communication technologies—are also relevant actors in this context. At the same time, however, the users of these technologies have a degree of agency too in shaping media and communication technologies to fit their needs and everyday routines (Mackay and Gillespie 1992; Silverstone 1999). One of the first things that activists, such those of UK Uncut and Occupy LSX, do, for example, is to set up blogs or Facebook accounts, despite these platforms typically not being designed for protest per se, and susceptible to surveillance strategies.

Every new and emerging media and communication technology that has become available, whether print, audio recording, telecommunication, broadcasting or the internet, has been appropriated by activists to achieve various goals and aims linked to their struggles. In recent years, the internet and social media have caught the imagination of many scholars. This internet imaginary (see Mansell 2012) has led many researchers to refer to a new digital, electronic or internet repertoire of contentious action (Costanza-Chock 2003; Rolfe 2005; Chadwick 2007; Van Laer and Van Aelst 2010). Bennett and Segerberg (2013) have called attention to the emergence of a connective action repertoire which they characterize as combining a lack of clear leadership, weak organizational structure, predominantly personal action frames, and the centrality of network technologies. It is argued, also, that the technologies and the algorithms that drive the applications of these technologies are important factors in shaping collective action. In this regard, Milan (2015: 2) refers to cloud protesting as:

> a specific type of mobilization that is centered on individuals and their needs, identities, and bodies. It is grounded on, modeled around, and enabled by social media platforms and mobile devices and the digital universes they identify.

The PP approach to social movements has been critiqued over the years, especially because of the extent to which it emphasizes structural constraints and tends to neglect agency. While it tends to emphasize process, it assumes that too many variables are static, leading to Jaswin's apraisal that the PP approach should 'live up to [its] name' (Goodwin and Jasper 2004: 29). It has been argued, also, that the PP approach does not give sufficient acknowledgement—especially in its early incarnations—to the importance of culture, meaning making, and emotions in the constitution and sustenance of social movements. The PP approach relies, it is suggested, too much on rational 'cold cognition' to the detriment of 'hot' emotions and passions, which, more often than not, are the impetus for social movements and why people become active in them (see Ferree and Merill 2000).

2.1.3 Cultural Framing Approach

One of the early frameworks in which the role of culture and cultural factors in social and political struggles was acknowledged within social movement theory was a Cultural Framing (CF) approach. Introduced into sociology by Goffman (1974) frames were conceived as 'interpretative schemata', and framing strategies proved to be useful conceptual tools to highlight and analyse meaning-making processes and discursive practices enacted by elites, by activists, and by ordinary citizens who shape the framing process (Gitlin 1980; Snow and Benford 1988; Gamson 1992).

The CF approach is interactionist and constructivist, and is intended to bridge the processes internal to a movement with those external to it. Meaning-making, it is argued, operates simultaneously internally and externally to the movement, and is treated as a complex process in which a variety of actors are active. The CF approach implicates media organizations, journalism, representation and communication generally, considerably more directly than the other approaches discussed so far. The way in which 'media discourse' on social movements and on the issues they want to address shapes and influences 'public discourse' on those movements and issues is foregrounded in the CF approach (Gamson 1992).

However, in this approach, it tends to be assumed that media discourse is typically not fair or positive in its representation of social movements. Most often, mainstream media is expected to be adversarial, ideologically opposed and highly negative, focusing on violence and internal divisions rather than on the issues the movement wants to address. Gitlin's (1980) study of the 1960s US student protest movement is a case in point. Not all the media is negative about these movements, and media representations can shift over time from positive to negative or from negative to positive coverage (see Cammaerts and Jiménez-Martínez 2014 for an example in the case of protests in Brazil) and this suggests a weakness of this approach.

Alongside the media discourse in the mainstream media there is typically an activist discourse which relates to how social movement actors frame what their movement is about and articulate the nature of their struggle, how they discursively construct a 'we/us' or a collective identity as well as a 'they/them' with regard to their (ideological) enemies. By imposing moral and ethical frames, the social movement identifies the problem that needs fixing, solutions are presented, other related struggles are implicated, and people are mobilized. Hence, the framing practices of activists and their social movements provide the rationales for people to become politically active, to join the movement, to do something actively, and to help the movement with its struggle in a variety of ways, but they are also understood to create a sense of belonging (Snow et al. 1986; Snow and Benford 1988; Benford and Snow 2000).

The construction of a collective identity, of a 'we', arguably, is one of the most important aspects of movement framing in the CF approach. This is treated as a process of producing 'an interactive and shared definition … concerned with the orientations of action and the field of opportunities' of a movement that is dynamic, and the result of a struggle between competing movement aims and how to reach them (Melucci 1996: 44). As such, the construction of a 'we' is regarded as an open-ended and multilayered process implicating emotions and the affective dimension (Goodwin et al. 2001). However, many scholars working with this approach argue that as a result of more complex personalized and fragmented political identities that are less and less tied to strong ideological identifications, It has in recent decades become more difficult to construct such a shared definition (McDonald 2002; Saunders 2008; Bennett and Segerberg 2013). Social media are expected, from the CF perspective, to promote this fragmentation, which, in turn, is expected to impede the capacity to sustain a collective identity or, alternatively, to render it obsolete. However, others argue that collective identity remains a useful concept, and that new forms of cohesion can emerge from more diverse and heterogenous identities; this is apparent, for example, particularly in the case of the Indignados/anti-austerity movements (see Flesher Fominaya 2010; Gerbaudo and Treré 2015; Kavada 2015).

The final, but often neglected, actor in the CF approach is the 'ordinary', non-activist citizen, whose views of the movement and its aims are regarded as being crucially important for achieving social and political change. Media discourses, which rely heavily on elite discourses and, to a lesser extent, mediate activist discourses, constitute and shape a broader public discourse, which is seen as an important resource for citizens to form their political opinions. This is by no means their only resource, however, since personal experiences and peer attitudes matter, as does public wisdom, which can be designated as hegemonies or as common sense (Gamson 1992).

Some of those working with this approach argue that the cultural meaning-making process, framing practices and interactions between the discursive strategies of political elites, media elites, activists, and citizens amount to a discursive opportunity structure which channels and organizes discourse, and thereby affects the prominence and salience of particular discourses and frames (Ferree et al. 2002; McCammon et al. 2007). In relation to the UK anti-austerity movement and in response to the 2008 financial crisis, issues related to unfair taxation, increasing inequality within Western societies, and perceived democratic deficits would be expected to constitute the discursive opportunities at the core of their struggle within the framework of this perspective.

The CF approach is also problematic in several respects. Some suggest that it does not take structural impediments faced by activists as seriously as it should. Following this line of argument, culture cannot be separated from societal and political structures. It is an inextricable part of these structures because culture co-shapes these structures and plays a pivotal role in how they are justified and maintained as well as contested (Laclau and Mouffe 1985). The cognitive antecedents to the framing approach position meaning-making too much at the level of the individual and represent it as a relatively stable process. The meaning-making process is, however, inherently dynamic and conflictual, and is enabled yet simultaneously constrained by discourse. In line with the post-structuralism perspective, it is also profoundly relational and embedded in subject positions and networks of social interaction among elites, movements and publics, each impacting on the other (see Steinberg 1999).

2.1.4 *Network Approach*

A network approach to understanding social movements has been proposed to make sense of a range of movements that do not conform to the characteristics of earlier movements such as the workers' movement pre-1960s. These so-called 'new social movements' exhibited very different, more informal, and less hierarchical organizational structures, and they also had more non-materialistic demands (Melucci 1980). The network metaphor seemed relevant to social movement scholars, since it precisely emphasized the relational links and inter-connections between the various nodes in a movement, that is, among the often disparate and diverse organizations, groups and individuals that make up a social movement.

The network approach to understanding social movements emphasizes the networked nature of social movements; that is, the formal as well as the informal relational features linked to collective action. These relational connections are also regarded as being relevant in the context of the conflictual nature of a social, cultural and political struggle, and the construction of a shared collective identity (della Porta and Diani 2006: 20). In this approach the strength and extent of activist networks are expected to be expressions of social and activist capital, understood here in Bourdieusian terms (Diani 1997). This activists' capital is relevant both internally to the movement and externally with regard to other actors. A network approach to understanding social movements argues that the constitution of movement networks is not always rational, and it also departs from an emphasis on 'causal attribution' in its search for the determinants of the success or failure of a social movement (Diani 1997: 132). Rather, the impact of a movement on the fabric of society can be detected in this approach in many aspects of network relationships, including the bonds and affective relations that are established through collective action, and which are likely to have long-term consequences (Diani and McAdam 2003).

Recognition of the relevance of media and communication in the analysis of contemporary social movements served, initially, as a critique of claims made by proponents of the network approach that the relational should be central to the analysis. Critics of this claim pointed out that studies of mediation suggest that the use of the media and communicative relations can enable weaker or latent network links (Jasper and Poulsen

1993). Analysis of the proliferating use of communication technologies by activists has provided contradictory evidence of the ability of these technologies to disseminate ideas and motivational frames beyond close-knit social networks without the need for strong ties and face-to-face contact (Bennett and Segerberg 2013). In this sense, it has been suggested that media and communication defy traditional time/space relationships. Within social movement theory, the phenomenon of movement spillover (Meyer and Whittier 1994) is sometimes seen as being stimulated by mediated relationships as a result of the circulation of movement ideas, protest tactics, slogans, and symbols among activists and their movements, and this is not always associated with the strength of personal contacts (Haythornthwaite 2002).

It is the internet, above all, that has been the focus of much attention by those developing the network approach as a framework for making sense of social movements. This is not surprising, given the networked nature of the internet which connects a multiplicity of nodes, and which has arguably transformed resistance movements considerably (Castells 1997). The internet as a convergent technology facilitates both private and public forms of communication, but also enables asynchronicity and immediacy in communicative practices. It is seen as facilitating the horizontal, less hierarchical movements to which Melucci (1980) referred, and which could also be found in the cases of the Anti-Globalization or Global Justice Movement. This movement has been described as a meta-movement, a 'movement of movements' (McDonald 2002; Mertes 2004). Initially, the internet has enabled what Juris (2012: 266) calls a 'logic of networking', fostering the construction of 'horizontal ties and connections among diverse, autonomous elements'. Later, with the emergence of social media platforms, it has been found to enable a 'logic of aggregation', denoting 'the viral flow of information and subsequent aggregations of large numbers of individuals in concrete physical spaces' (ibid.). Bennett and Segerberg (2013) describe this logic of aggregation as connective action; that is, more horizontal and decentralized structures, which at times are leaderless, networked and bottom-up, implicating and connecting a wide variety of people, tied together by personal links and a respect for diversity rather than by ideological congruence or formal membership.

At the same time, it is argued that the internet has not diminished the need for, and the importance of, strong ties in the offline world as well as mutual trust in the context of collective action. This applies especially in cases of anti-systemic resistance and contention, where the cost of participation is high (Calhoun 1998; Diani 2001). The critique of an over-emphasis on internet-mediated weak ties suggests the need to take a nuanced view of the hyperbolic claims of the 1990s and early 2000s regarding the revolutionary, and so-called game-changing potentials of the internet as a means of mobilizing for and constituting collective action. The anti-austerity movement illustrates the dynamic interplay between strong and weak relational ties that underpin collective action.

Another aspect the network approach foregrounds as a result of its emphasis on activists' capital, understood in a Bourdieusian sense (Diani 1997), is the importance of skills. When media and communication are considered, the required skills that are sought within a social movement network are expected to include knowledge and expertise in art and design, connections with journalists, internet and social media skills, and other related capabilities. In this regard, lay knowledge and 'background knowledge' (Reckwitz 2002: 249) of how media, journalism and technology operate have become more commonplace amongst political activists (McCurdy 2012). Once activists have an awareness of how media production works, and which content is likely to be catchy and visually appealing, they can play with journalists' expectations, feed the media and engage in counter-spin. These media skills can lead to a 'playful awareness' (Liebes and Katz 1990) among activists such that 'mediated visibility' becomes 'a weapon in the struggles they wage' (Thompson 2005: 31). Thus one critique of the network approach is that it pays insufficient attention to the symbolic, and over-privileges the relational and organizational.

All four of the approaches discussed here highlight aspects of the study of media and communication that are relevant to understanding social movements, and the role played by the media and communication in protest and social change. I argue that they can be used in a complementary way to build a more comprehensive analytical framework for the empirical analysis of social movement which will be developed in Sect. 2.3 of this chapter. Before presenting the framework it is important to consider how the study of social movements has developed as a subfield within the media and communication field of scholarship.

2.2 Positioning Social Movements in Media and Communication Studies

The study of social movements, of resistance, and of social change is a growing subfield within the field of media and communication studies. One of the first manifestations of this was the analysis of mainstream media representations of protest and social movements. Alongside the rise of the alternative/radical media studies as a subfield, social movement self-mediation practices have become an important object of study (Downing et al. 2001; Atton 2002). Also informing the study of social movements within media and communication studies are studies which examine the relations and tensions between the material and the symbolic in the communication process (Silverstone 2002). The materiality of the media and communication technologies, their affordances, and the way they are appropriated and shaped by activists and audiences, as well as the symbolic meaning-making process, and the ability or inability of political and media elites in addition to movement actors to influence and potentially shape that process, are the focus of research in this subfield. Also explored is the complex relationship between the production of discourse and media content by political and media elites as well as by social movement actors, and the reception or consumption of these discourses by non-activist citizens.

2.2.1 *Mainstream and Alternative*

'The media'—which generally refers to liberal mainstream media and/or to journalism as a discipline—are one of the most important actors when it comes to the meaning-making process. This is acknowledged in various political and democratic theories (Christians et al. 2009). Within normative models, journalists are expected to be on the side of the citizen, defending democratic values and protecting citizens' interests. They are required to be watchdogs to protect citizens against abuses of power by economic and political elites, to create platforms for debate within society, and to be responsive to civil society (Curran 2005: 138).

However, gaining access to the mainstream media, influencing the public sphere, articulating alternative views, and receiving positive exposure in the media is, as briefly touched on earlier, less straightforward for activists and protest movements than it is for political elites and the government. While journalists fulfil a crucial mediating role in the public sphere, they also have to cope with a set of internal as well as external pressures that shape the media content they produce (Carpentier 2005). When producing news, journalists often walk a thin line between these internal pressures related to the processes involved in news selection and its newsworthiness, editorial cultures and expectations of professionalism, and external pressures from political and/or market actors.

Few journalists are able to resist these pressures at all times, and many do not meet the normative expectations that society has of them. As a result, the mainstream media producers are seen by activists, as well as by many critical media scholars, to be more on the side of the economically and politically powerful than on the side of ordinary people. Furthermore, they tend to be biased against social change and against those who attempt to disrupt the status quo. This has been confirmed by empirical studies that highlight a so-called *protest paradigm* in relation to mainstream media representations of contention, dissent and protesters (Halloran et al. 1970; Gitlin 1980; Herman and Chomsky 1988; Eldridge 1995; McLeod and Hertog 1999). This paradigm is said to be characterized by excessive critique, the demonization and delegitimization of protesters, and an emphasis on violence and the spectacular. More recent studies question the rigidity of this protest paradigm: while still relevant at times, it is understood that the media are not monolithical actors and do not always conform to an elite consensus (Cottle 2008; Cammaerts 2013). Others add detail and nuance to the protest paradigm framework by proposing a public nuisance paradigm which points to the tendency of (in particular, the conservative) media to 'paint protest as irritating and worthless, and something most would prefer to ignore—a nuisance' (Di Cicco 2010: 137).

In addition to the production of mainstream media representations, processes of mediation in relation to social change also involve and include modes of self-mediation through (semi-)independent means of communication. It is argued that activists and social movements have always sought to develop their own alternative and independent means of communication to bypass mainstream media. This is reflected in the media and communication research field by the attention given to the phenomenon of alternative or radical media (Downing et al. 2001; Atton 2002; Bailey et al. 2008).

Alternative media practices by activists and social movements include theatre, print cultures, radio and video, and the internet offers activists ample opportunities to communicate independently, to debate internally, to organize themselves, and to connect directly with those who are interested in their causes (Downey and Fenton 2003; Kahn and Kellner 2004; Cammaerts 2005). Recognition of the role of alternative media in social and political struggles has a long history, and has developed hand-in-hand with technological innovation (Darnton 1982; Negt and Kluge 1993; Sreberny-Mohammadi and Mohammadi 1994). Research shows that activists exploit all the means of communication available to them at a given time, while the state tends to limit, control or close down activists' use of both alternative media and available communication technologies.

2.2.2 *Symbolic and Material*

Power in the context of research in the media and communication field is often conceived as symbolic power (Thompson 1995). This implicates not only the power of representation but also the technical skills and resources necessary to produce media content and to distribute information. Symbolic power is frequently understood as being closely related to the management of visibility that is essential to and feeds the struggle for legitimacy. This management of visibility is linked to the requirement for social movement frames to have a strong presence in the public space so as to visibilize themselves and to develop what Dayan (2013) calls strategies of 'monstration'. This can be achieved either through the representations of mainstream media and journalists, or through self-mediation practices using a range of independent or semi-independent media and communication technologies—from printing presses, radios, and telephones to audio cassettes and the internet.

Symbolically, activists and social movements are engaged in what Gramsci (1971: LXVI) called a *war of position*. A war of position, such as was fought during the First World War, is a trench-war conducted against hegemonic common sense. It is mainly cultural and ideational, and operates in such a way that the educational system, the media, and civil society become productive spheres through which to develop and further a counter-hegemony.[1] Today, the war of position is arguably first and foremost a symbolically mediated war with material consequences. The symbolic has the power of constitution, and discourse is understood to 'produce' subject positions, relations of power, what is considered to be legitimate knowledge, and common sense; it produces a horizon of the imaginable and what is deemed (im)possible (Foucault 1981).

In terms of protest movements and social change, the communicative practices of activists are relevant in this context not merely on a discursive level or to the symbolic struggles over meaning between social movements and their adversaries. Communicative practices have an important material side. This manifests itself through media and communication technologies, and the affordances for as well as the limitations on contention embedded in these technologies, and in the ways these affordances are mobilized through a set of self-mediation practices (Couldry 2004). When communicative practices are understood in this way, it takes us away from the analysis of the textual and encourages a focus on the materiality of media production, and on what various technological innovations offer activists in support of their struggles. This perspective also encourages analysis of the way states and markets are implicated in limiting or thwarting opportunities for resistance that are offered by innovations in communication technologies. Silverstone (1994) emphasized the 'double articulation' of mediation referring to the production of symbolic meaning and media texts and to the appropriation and shaping of the media and communication technologies in tune with their material affordances.

This interplay between the symbolic and the material is illustrated by the UK's anti-austerity movement's waging of both a symbolic and a material struggle—for example, by discursively connecting austerity politics with companies that were not paying what was regarded as a fair share of taxes, and by occupying physical spaces and organizing offline direct action mediated by a wide range of media and the use of communication technologies.

2.2.3 Production and Reception

A final feature that is of central concern in the media and communication studies field, and which is also relevant in the analysis of protest movements, is the tension between the production of meaning and its reception. A wide variety of actors produce meaning in a polity. Social movement activists are one of these, but, arguably, not the most powerful one. To paraphrase George Orwell, some voices are more equal than others. Economic, political and media elites hold powerful positions in societies, which enables them to shape political agendas and the terms of debate, to control access to mainstream public spheres, and, as Herman and Chomsky (1988) argue forcefully, to 'manufacture consent'. Media elites are seen as indexing the views and debates which prevail among the political elites (Bennett 1990). While media elites are understood in this research framework to have gatekeeping and agenda-setting powers, these powers are expected to be used in a way that aligns largely with dominant views in society. This gives rise to a mediated environment that is unfavourable to social movements' attempts to introduce their messages into the mainstream media, which, in turn, encourages the social movements to develop a set of independent self-mediation practices.

What is often missing, however, from these perspectives on the power of actors in the political and media spheres, and on social movements' self-mediation practices, is a nuanced examination of those who consume the messages produced by hegemonic and counter-hegemonic actors. This is surprising as political decisions are made and protests organised in the name of the people, publics or audiences. As such, it is argued here that when studying protest and contentious politics, it is crucially important to examine the resonance of the movement's frames among non-activist audiences/citizens in order to understand the precise nature of social and political change. Reception processes and the role of the media's audiences are contested in the field of media and communication studies. While many scholars are attracted by the apparent simplicity of a transmission model of mediated communication, others adopt a ritual or symbolic model (see Carey 1989).

A common approach to the relationship between political communication and the reception of mediated content focuses on election campaigns (Graber 2005). Evidence of the political influence of the media is mixed, with some arguing that media campaigns matter, and others that election campaigning has limited or minimal effects on voter behaviour (see Semetko 2004 for an overview). The latter position seems to be supported most consistently by the empirical evidence, as it remains very difficult, if not impossible, to isolate the factors expected to contribute to any effects of communication strategies of political actors, and of the media and journalists who report on the political actors. As McQuail (2010: 527) asserts, 'it is hard to separate out the effects of media change from broad changes in society working both on the media and on political institutions'.

Even if agreement about the influence of the media is lacking in research in the field of media and communications, it is undeniably the case that citizens are increasingly dependent on a variety of media, both mainstream and alternative, for gathering (political) information. However, the role of media in opinion formation varies, because citizens are understood to form political opinions based on a wide range of influences, including experiential knowledge, peer opinion, and societal norms as well as information and news shaped by and disseminated via the traditional and alternative media (see, among others: Gamson 1992; Brewer 2001; Livingstone 2006).

The internet and social media are having a profound impact on the way media audiences are theorized, since the ways in which citizens access consumer information have changed dramatically. This is not to suggest that mainstream media are no longer important, on the contrary, but we can no longer assume that everybody receives the same information (Livingstone and Das 2013). A segmented media offer, catering to a highly fragmented audience, with individuals making very personalized choices about which news sources to access is increasingly common, and this has informed theoretical frameworks used for the analysis of the audience.

Having positioned social movements and contestation within research in the field of media and communication studies, I will now present my conceptual framework encompassing the production of discourses and framings, their circulation in society, and their reception. This framework will facilitate the analysis of the mediation opportunity structure and the circulation of anti-austerity protests, which I shall examine empirically in later chapters.

2.3 A Conceptual Framework for the Circulation of Anti-Austerity Protest

Martín-Barbero (1993) positioned popular and mediated culture in a positive light (compared, for example, to the cultural pessimism of the Frankfurt School). He imbued popular and mediated culture with the possibility of disrupting and contesting the prevailing culture; mass culture, he wrote, enables 'communication between the different levels of society'. In addition to this, he also highlights the importance of '*circulation* between the different levels' within society (ibid.: 35, emphasis added). This clearly suggests the centrality of the circulation of meaning in any analysis of protest movements.

I propose that the mediation process which connects the production of movement discourses, the framing efforts of movements, and their circulation and reception, can be deconstructed analytically by taking inspiration from the circuit of culture construct as developed in the cultural studies tradition (see Johnson 1986; Du Gay et al. 1997). The circuit of culture is a conceptual model which enables the empirical study of social and cultural phenomena in a holistic manner without over-privileging structural features or cultural production at the expense of the analysis of agency and audience reception. I shall discuss the circuit of culture and some of its strengths and weaknesses, and then set out the framework for the *Circuit of Protest*, which I employ in my study of mediation and its relevance to understanding the success and failure of social movements as well as some of the processes of social and political change in democracy.

2.3.1 The Circuit of Culture

In his seminal paper, 'Encoding/Decoding', Hall (1980 [1973]) identified four components of cultural production and reception, which he used to explain how dominant culture and meanings circulate and are decoded: 'Production', 'Circulation', 'Use', and 'Reproduction'. Hall contended that dominant meanings are not reproduced passively and uncritically, but can potentially be resisted or, to use his expression, 'decoded differently'.

In response to critiques that the encoding/decoding model over-privileges agency to the detriment of structural constraints, and treats the four components as too discrete, the model was revised to render it more dynamic and much more integrated (see Du Gay et al. 1997). The circuit and the circulation metaphor, which originates from Karl Marx's circuit of capital, was appropriated and revised to denote the circulation of meaning. The authors subsequently identified five interconnected moments that make up the Circuit of Culture, namely: (1) Production; (2) Identity; (3) Representation; (4) Consumption; and (5) Regulation. This circuit of culture was represented in such a way that each of the five dimensions influenced the others.

The Circuit of Culture stresses the importance not merely of studying the processes of production, but also of considering them in conjunction with the processes of media consumption or the reception of meaning. Proponents of the culturalist approach stress the polysemic nature of media production and reception, while at the same time emphasizing the importance of differences in the social status and contexts of those encoding and decoding meaning (Hall 1997a). This opened a space for the negotiation or rejection of meaning.

This culturalist approach goes beyond the production/consumption binary, and affords greater agency to audiences. In conjunction with cognitive social psychology approaches, this gave rise to notions such as the active audience or technology user, both implying less passive actors (Livingstone 2015).

2.3.2 *The Circuit of Protest*

I take inspiration from the Circuit of Culture model discussed above to develop a conceptual framework which theorizes the role of mediation in the context of political struggles waged by social movements and activists. The Circuit of Protest diverges from the Circuit of Culture in being less text-based, less cultural industry focused, and more related to collective than to individual actors and identities. Figure 2.1 depicts this articulation of the Circuit of Protest as comprising the following core moments: Production, Self-Mediation, Representation, and Reception. Furthermore, I also articulate a mediation opportunity structure which operates at each

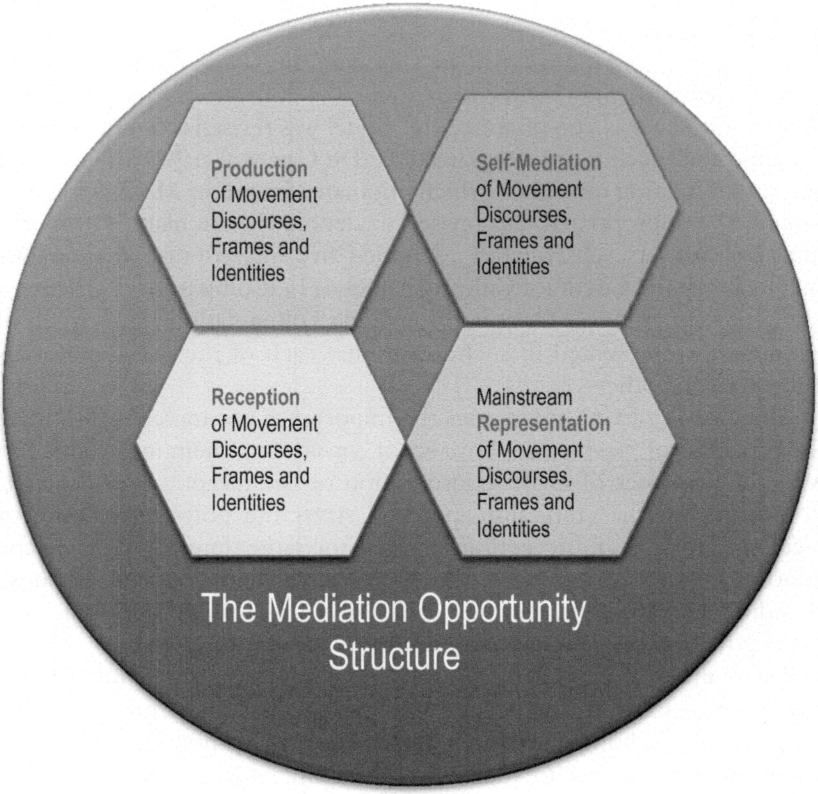

Fig. 2.1 The Circuit of Protest

of the four moments and represents the interplay between agentic opportunities and structural constraints (see Cammaerts 2012).

At the level of *production*, social movement actors produce or encode meaning through discourses and frames, whereby the former represents inherent contingency, and the latter, strategic attempts to fix meaning, to establish ideological boundaries and to construct a 'we' that is juxtaposed to a 'them'. At this level of analysis, collective identities and ideological enemies are constructed, solutions to the problems the movement wants to tackle are imagined, and a call to action is articulated.

These movement discourses and frames, and the collective identities that emerge from them, are subsequently *self-mediated* through a variety of mediation practices using textual, audio and visual formats, distributed offline and online, locally, nationally and even transnationally. Inevitably, this moves us away from the symbolic and brings in a material aspect. Different media and communication technologies have different affordances that are more or less useful to certain mediation logics relevant to activists. In addition, some self-mediation practices are more outwardly focused, while others are more inward-looking. There is also a temporal and historical dimension to self-mediation practices, potentially influencing similar or different movements elsewhere.

Besides self-mediation, social movement actors, the actions they organize and the various discourses and frames they disclose, are *represented* by mainstream media actors and journalists situated outside the movement. The cause defended, the political opportunity structure, certain journalistic routines, ideological biases, editorial lines, all have some kind of impact on the nature and tone of those mainstream media representations. At the same time, this prompts social movements to develop strategies either to cope with, adapt to or resist media routines and news values in the effort to manage their public visibility.

Another potential influencer of mainstream media representations and political actors in a democracy is public opinion, and the way that non-activist citizens react (positively or negatively) to the mobilizations and ideas of social movements. Hence the *reception* or decoding of movement discourses and frames from the perspective of extending collective identities and enlarging the scope of conflict is arguably crucially important when studying strategies of social change and their mediations. This reveals the process of opinion formation. Non-activist citizens or audiences forming their political opinions are deemed to be influenced by mainstream media content and representations, but not exclusively so.

Social media also are important, as are their personal experiences, and what is considered to be common sense at a given moment in time and in a specific context.

Finally, the *mediation opportunity structure* refers to the power dimension at the level of the production, circulation and reception of meaning. Here, power is understood as being productive in a Foucauldian sense, at the same time enabling as well as constraining. The mediation opportunity structure thus relates to the dynamic and complex relationships between agency and structure, between generative and repressive forms of power, between domination and resistance, between the power to (empowerment), the power over (domination), and the power in (discourse, subject-positions). The mediation opportunity structure balances a potential over-emphasis on the agentic, which often characterizes the culturalist tradition, but, at the same time, it does not close down the possibility of agency and change, as some domination theories tend to do. It also implicates power, which is also pivotal in the context of the circulation of meaning:

> the question of the circulation of meaning almost immediately involves the question of power. Who has the power, in what channels, to circulate which meanings to whom? (Hall 1997b: 14)

By appropriating the metaphor of the circuit and applying it to social movement struggles to achieve social and political change, I am aligning myself also with the Glasgow Media Group, who stressed the importance of analysing 'processes of production, content, reception and *circulation* of social meaning simultaneously' (Philo 2007: 175; emphasis added). However, empirical study of the different moments in conjunction with each other is not straightforward, and has important methodological implications which are discussed in the next section.

2.4 Studying the Circuit of Protest: Methodological Reflections

In the last section of this chapter, the focus shifts from the conceptual to the empirical. As scholars, we make numerous explicit and implicit choices when conducting research and, in my view, it is important to be self-reflexive about these choices.

The different moments in the circuit require different research methods in order to study and analyse them. This, I would argue, is at once the strength and the weakness of this study. The research presented in this book is rich and thick, and aimed at studying the production of discourses and frames by a social movement in conjunction with investigating their various self-mediation practices, their mainstream media representations, and the way in which these discourses and frames are received and decoded by non-activist citizens. Inevitably, because of the ambitious scope of this study and the diversity of data sets, some parts are stronger and more developed than others.

First, I justify my choice to focus on the UK anti-austerity movement. Second, I describe the data collection methods and types of analysis employed for the different moments of the Circuit of Protest, and the sometimes difficult choices made at each point in time.

2.4.1 Case Study Choice

In order to research all the moments of the Circuit of Protest in one study, I decided to focus on one national context and one specific movement. While it might have been an excellent idea to build in a comparative perspective—that is, to determine how the circuit operates differently in different contexts and within different types of movements and mobilizations, I chose to focus on the UK and the anti-austerity movement. This choice was guided in part by the urgent need for more contemporary studies on media, communication, and anti-systemic contentious politics in Western democratic contexts rather than in (semi-)authoritarian regimes. Furthermore, the UK, in particular, is a highly relevant context in which to study dissent against austerity politics, precisely because neo-liberalism has such a long-standing history in the UK, going back to Thatcherism, that the neo-liberal ideology has arguably managed to position itself as post-hegemonic; that is, without a 'valid constitutive outside' (Cammaerts 2015: 527). Despite this, the UK's anti-austerity movement precisely represents the most important contemporary *constitutive outside* of and challenge to neo-liberalism in the UK.

The rationale for choosing the anti-austerity movement can also be found in the re-emergence of a politics of redistribution in the wake of the near-systemic collapse, in 2008, of the capitalist financial system. After decades of identity politics and an emphasis on the recognition of difference (Fraser 1996), a stringent critique of capitalism, its modes of exploitation, and its profound inequalities has reasserted itself in recent years. This book is an expression of this reassertion.

Finally, I chose to focus on three specific anti-austerity 'organizations': namely, the fair taxation organization UK Uncut; a student protest organization called the National Campaign Against Fees and Cuts (NCAFC); and Occupy London Stock Exchange (LSX). UK Uncut can be credited with kick-starting the UK's anti-austerity movement. The NCAFC is relevant, given that militant student organizations played a major role in the protests against the tripling of tuition fees, which politicized of a whole generation of young people. Occupy LSX is more a mobilization than an organization, bringing together a wide variety of actors and organizations, but also individuals, to protest against the financial system, against inequality, and to lament the broken democratic system.

2.4.2 *Methodological Choices*

Table 2.1 provides an overview of the various methods of data collection and analysis used for different moments. This mixed methods design conforms to the category of ***development***, whereby the results of one method are 'used to help inform the development' of subsequent ones (Greene et al. 1989: 260). As such, the temporality of when certain methods were used is important to explain how the different methods fed into one another. Table 2.1 thus follows a timeline, which reflects when particular methods were deployed in the course of this study.

The first moment addressed methodologically is the production of UK anti-austerity movement discourses and frames. The two main discourses identified in relation to the anti-austerity movement are: (1) a renewed politics of redistribution; and (2) the need for real democracy.

Table 2.1 Overview of data collection and analysis methods

Moments	*Data collection*	*Data analysis*
Production	• Desk research	• Frame analysis
Representation	• Content analysis	• Statistics
Reception	• Survey	• Statistics
	• Focus groups	• Thematic analysis
Practices	• Desk research	• Thematic analysis
	• Semi-structured interviews	

Both discourses have a rich and productive legacy and are linked to a range of frames. Laclau and Mouffe's (1985) political discourse theory and frame analysis, relying mainly on Snow and Benford's (1988) model of diagnostic, prognostic and motivational frames, served to expose the movements' discourses and frames. A range of documents pertaining to the three organizations, and expressing these movements' aims and demands, were analysed discursively to identify the main anti-austerity frames. Frame analysis in the context of social movements is foremost:

> preoccupied with how ideas, culture, and ideology are used, interpreted, and spliced together with certain situations or phenomena in order to construct particular ideative patterns through which the world is understood by audiences. (Lindekilde 2014: 199)

The movement discourses and frames identified subsequently fed into the coding frame used to conduct the media content analysis, and into the survey questionnaire design. For the content analysis of mainstream media coverage, newspapers were preferred to television coverage and blogs, though many UK newspapers have a considerable online readership. Two separate content analyses were conducted: (1) of the mainstream media representation of the 2010 student protests, in which NCAFC was a central actor; and (2) covering a longer period, focusing on articles mentioning UK Uncut and Occupy LSX.

For the first content analysis, four newspapers were selected on the basis of their ideological leanings, with two newspapers situated broadly on the right of the political spectrum (*Daily Mail* and *Daily Telegraph*) and two centre-left (*Guardian* and *Independent*). A thorough search on *Lexis,* using keywords such as 'protest(s)', 'students', 'student protest', 'tuition', and 'fees', for the period 11 November—23 December 2010, resulted in a sample of 334 articles.[2] A pilot was conducted on 33 articles, after which new codes and variables were added.

The second content analysis focused on media representations of UK Uncut and Occupy LSX, and sampled articles from six newspapers, which were selected based on a combination of ideological leaning and type of newspaper, including the broadsheet market (*Guardian* and *Daily Telegraph*), mid-market (*Evening Standard* and *Daily Mail*) and tabloid (*Daily Mirror* and *The Sun*). Using keywords on Lexis, such as UK Uncut, Occupy LSX, and Occupy London, led to a total sample of 1505 articles, 532 of which related predominantly to UK Uncut and

1062 to Occupy LSX. The period of analysis ran from 1 January 2011 to 31 August 2012.[3]

As mentioned above, the discursive and frame analysis also fed into the design of the survey questionnaire, probing the extent to which the anti-austerity movement was supported by the UK population.[4] As well as a set of socio-demographic questions, respondents were asked to give their opinion on a set of statements that aligned with or contradicted the movement frames. Second, their knowledge of the three cases was gauged. Third, the main aims of the cases were explained and the degree of sympathy was measured. Finally, respondents' media consumption patterns were surveyed. The survey was conducted via an online panel, creating a relative degree of representativity. I say 'relative', because respondents self-select themselves for online panels and as a result such panels can never be fully statistically representative. In order to mitigate this somewhat, quotas were used so that the sample reflected gender, and generational and geographical distributions in the UK. A total of 1651 respondents (*n*) drawn from an online panel were surveyed in the period 12 December 2014 to 5 January 2015. This survey's results have a credibility interval of plus or minus 2.41 percentage points.[5]

Three focus groups were held, with the objective of obtaining a better understanding of some of the survey results, especially the relatively high levels of support for the movement frames. Since I was interested in understanding better those people who are not particularly politically active, but align themselves broadly with the movement's frames, recruitment of participants for the focus groups was geared towards this subcategory.[6] In the UK context, it is advisable to separate gender and class when conducting focus groups (Morley 1980). While the focus groups were diverse in terms of ethnicity and political persuasion, they were comprised of participants from the lower middle class (C1) and skilled working class (C2) categories. The first group interview was held on 1 June 2015 in London, with female participants in the age category 18–29 years. The second group interview was held in London on the same day, with female participants in the age category 29–49 years. The third group interview was held in Birmingham on 2 June 2015, with male participants aged between 50 and 65 years. The topic guides for the focus groups were developed on the basis of the results of the content analysis and the survey. A thematic analysis was conducted on the transcripts of the focus group interviews.

The final method employed in this study was in-depth, semi-structured interviews with anti-austerity activists. The reason I chose to interview activists last was because I wanted to share the data from the content analysis and the reception study with the activists, to elicit their reactions and responses. The interviews also served, in part, as validation of the frame analysis and desk research. As such, the interviews were also aimed at gaining a more in-depth understanding of the movement discourses and the activists' self-mediation practices beyond what could be gleaned from desk research. I conducted four interviews with key actors active in the media teams of UK Uncut (1), the NCFC (1), and Occupy LSX (2). To protect their identities I anonymized my interviewees by changing their names, and sometimes even their gender. The transcripts of these semi-structured interviews were subjected to thematic analysis, using themes that emerged from the other methods and conceptual work relating to self-mediation (see Chap. 4).

2.5 Conclusion

This introductory chapter positioned media and communication theoretically within social movement studies, and social movements, resistance and contentious politics, within media and communication studies. I introduced the idea of a Circuit of Protest as a conceptual framework to connect and integrate: the *production* of movement discourses and frames, and linked to this the construction of a 'we' as well as a 'they'; a set of *self-mediation practices* enacted by social movements and activists to communicate internally as well as externally; mainstream media *representations* of the movement; and the *reception* of movement and competing discourses and frames by non-activist citizens.

The Circuit of Protest thus represents an encompassing model that positions each moment in the circuit as equally important and relevant, and implies that each individual moment impacts on the other moments (cf. Fig. 2.1). This means that the moments need to be studied in conjunction so as to analyse the interplay between agentic opportunities and structural constraints present at each of these moments. Bringing these together, I argue that this interplay constitutes a *mediation opportunity structure*.

From a social movement studies perspective, the Circuit of Protest enables us to highlight and bridge tensions between resources, agentic opportunities, and structural constraints. It exposes the mediation processes, both internal and external, to social movements, and combines attention to the symbolic aspects of protest and contestation with material considerations and a practice-oriented approach.

From a media and communications studies perspective, the circuit emphasises the pivotal role of media and communication in contentious politics, but at the same time it avoids being overly media- or discourse-centric. As Martín-Barbero (1993: 187) pointed out, in relation to the mediation process and circulation, while 'communication has become a strategic arena for the analysis of the obstacles and contradictions that move [societies]', we have 'to lose sight of the "proper object" [i.e. media] in order to find the way to the movement of the social in communication, to communication in process' (ibid.: 203).

As such, it is argued here that by studying a social movement through the prism of the circuit, and by implicating mediation as the conceptual glue collating the different moments of the circuit, I can present a holistic picture of a specific struggle, since the circuit allows me to highlight and include in a single study an analysis of:

- the aims, goals and messaging of a movement;
- the collective identity of the movement;
- the nature of the connections between different actors;
- the internal organizational structures (or lack thereof);
- the type of (direct) actions and protest events the movement enacts;
- the resonance of the movement in the public/media space;
- the resonance of the movement among ordinary, non-activist citizens; and
- the degree of resistance it encounters from the powers that be.

This enables a more nuanced perspective on, and complex picture of, the degree and nature of the success of a movement which can be situated at various levels, not necessarily only at the level of policy or political change in the here and now.

The Circuit of Protest can be applied to numerous movements, but in this book it is used to analyse the UK's anti-austerity movement. Subsequent chapters will theorize the different moments outlined above in more detail, and present the analysis of the data that were gathered. The concluding chapter will reflect on the dialectic between opportunities and constraints, between generative and repressive forms of power with regard to the different moments of the Circuit of Protest, and assess the failures and successes of the UK's anti-austerity movement.

Notes

1. Gramsci did not use the term counter-hegemony, but he implied it by referring to the need for 'intellectual and moral reform' (Gramsci 1971: 132).
2. The coding was done by the author and the results of this content analysis of the media representation of the student protests was discussed in Cammaerts (2013).
3. For the second content analysis, research assistants were recruited and trained to help with the coding of the articles: Ariel Shangguan, Yuanyuan Liu and Kullanit Nitiwarangkul. Coordination was by Brooks DeCillia.
4. The survey was conducted by Toluna: see https://uk.toluna.com/.
5. When polling an online panel it is not possible to calculate the probability of participation of everyone in the population (N). As a result of this, Bayesian credibility intervals are preferred over and above the classic margin of error (Simpson 2012).
6. The focus groups were conducted by Britain Thinks: see http://britainthinks.com/.

CHAPTER 3

The Production of Anti-Austerity Discourses and Frames

In this chapter, the moment of ***production*** in the Circuit of Protest is addressed in more detail. It is in this moment that the movement discourses are shaped, and frames are articulated with a view to building collective identities and mobilizing for action, and where the actions themselves constitute a way to further reinforce and perform the movement discourses and their framings.

The anti-austerity movement has, in my view, two core discourses: (1) a renewed politics of redistribution; and (2) a real democracy. These discourses are interlinked; that is, a broken democracy impedes a renewed politics of redistribution. Like most discourses, redistribution and democracy have long historical legacies. These discursive histories and their polysemic nature are the reasons why they are discourses and not frames; redistribution and democracy are in many ways excellent examples of what Laclau (1996) called empty signifiers: open to negotiation and (re-)appropriation, potentially leading to innovative renewal and purposeful retooling, but also to contestation.

Within the discourse of redistribution and democracy, the anti-austerity movement has constructed a broad set of frames that aim to: (1) identify problems (diagnostic frames); (2) articulate solutions (prognostic frames); and (3) call for action (motivational frames). This follows the triad of collective action frames foregrounded in Wilson (1973) and Snow and Benford (1988). This set of movement frames subsequently feeds the articulation of a 'we', of a collective identity, which, inevitably, implies the

B. Cammaerts, *The Circulation of Anti-Austerity Protest*,
https://doi.org/10.1007/978-3-319-70123-3_3

construction of a 'they', the so-called constitutive outside or ideological enemy (Laclau and Mouffe 1985). The success and scope of constructing this collective 'we' is largely dependent on what Snow and Benford described as the process of *frame alignment*. This relates to the efforts of social movements to gain traction or momentum, to build networks and broaden the scope of conflict, to achieve higher resonance and to bring more people on board in pursuit of their goals and aims and in the struggle in question. This process of frame alignment, consisting of frame bridging, amplification, extension and transformation, was very prevalent in the anti-austerity movement.

Before addressing the anti-austerity discourses and frames, it is necessary and useful to address the complexity of the relationship between discourse and framing within social movement studies, but also conceptually.

3.1 The Interplay Between Movement Discourses and the Various Framings of a Socio-political Struggle

At the intersection of political science with media and communication studies, we can observe two distinct epistemologies and conceptual toolboxes that explain how the way in which political and media actors describe, analyse and make sense of the world impacts upon that world and, arguably, even shapes it. In one corner is framing theory, which has antecedents in anthropology, social psychology and sociology. In the other corner is discourse theory, which grew out of a sociolinguistic and, in particular, a post-structuralist paradigm. The appropriation of both framing and discourse theory in social movement studies should be considered the result of a cultural turn in social movement theory; that is, the increased recognition that culture, ideology, language, and communication play central roles in processes of political contestation and social change (see Johnston 2009).

Given the close links between the discipline of sociology and the field of social movement studies, framing theory as developed by Bateson (1955) and, especially, Goffman (1974), was adopted into social movement studies before discourse theory was incorporated. According to Goffman (1974: 21), frames are 'schemata of interpretation' or 'primary frameworks' that serve to 'locate, perceive, identify and label' phenomena. A frame thus organizes and structures information and knowledge in a very particular way according to a series of schemes which subsequently impact on how the information and knowledge is being perceived, positioned and understood.

Framing theory served to explain the importance of ideations in a social movement's efforts to communicate its aims, to build collective identities, and to mobilize (Snow and Benford 1988; Klandermans 1988). Social movement frames—understood broadly as schemata of interpretation—provide justifications and rationales for struggles, and for the ways in which these struggles need to be conducted. They constitute a prism through which to make sense of the world according to the movement—they 'assign meaning to and mobilize potential adherents and constituents, to garner bystander support, and to demobilize antagonists' (Snow and Benford 1988: 198).

The strategic framing approach in social movement studies proposes three meta-frames, which tend to be present in social movement mobilizations:

1. *diagnostic frames,* which identify the problem that needs fixing and aim to weaken the frames of opponents;
2. *prognostic frames,* which aim to convince recruits of the goals, provide possible solutions or remedies to the problem articulated by the diagnostic frames, and propose a particular strategy and set of tactics to achieve the identified goals; and
3. *motivational frames,* which are aimed at mobilizing recruits for action; they are the agency component of social movement frames.

In line with the other social movement scholars mentioned above, Gamson (1992) appropriated Goffman's notion of frames and linked it to social movements and collective action by invoking injustice and moral indignation frames to articulate the reasons for the social movements' combativeness. Furthermore, he identified an agentic component of collective action frames; this component suggests not just that 'something can be done, but that *we* can do something' (Gamson 1995: 90; emphasis in original), which aligns with motivational frames. The construction of this 'we', of a collective identity, is the final component of collective action frames. However, Gamson (1992: 27) refers also to the discursive when he speaks of media as a 'good reflection' of the broader notion of 'public discourse'. Public discourse, he argues, is an important conversational tool when people talk about politics. However, Steinberg (1998: 846) laments the lack of engagement with:

> discourse as a collective and contested process of meaning production [which] slights key problems both within the internal logic of frame analysis and more generally its capacity to analyze the contentious process of meaning production.

When discussing discourse and the role of the discursive in relation to social movements, a relevant theoretical resource would be the Derridean notion of deconstruction, which invites us to expose the hidden and unspoken facets of the dominant reading of a text. An important insight was the recognition that the dominant reading is dependent on, and even constituted through, what it is not, or by what is excluded, by 'the constitutive outside' (Derrida 1978: 39–44). Another related concept is *différance* or the 'freeplay' of signifiers, which determine meaning and which dominant readings deny us.

Foucault (1981) was also hugely influential on our understanding of discourse, or rather, what discourse does. Discourse or 'orders of discourse', Foucault (1972: 49) wrote, are 'practices that systematically form the objects of which we speak', but they also shape subjects and subject positions. Ultimately, discourse is a space of struggle and contention, it is 'the power which is to be seized' (Foucault 1981: 52–53). As such, Foucault promoted an anti-essentialist position in his approach to discourse, emphasizing contingency and fluidity, while at the same time being interested in the workings of order. Much of his work is geared towards making us understand how difficult it is to operate or position ourselves outside of the *épistémè*, outside 'the conditions of possibility of all knowledge, whether expressed in a theory or silently invested in a practice' (Foucault 2002: 183).

The influence of the post-structuralist canon on social movement studies is arguably more recent than the adoption of framing. Post-structuralist notions of discourse, in relation to social movements and their struggles, are relevant on two levels. First, as Carpentier (2010: 252) points out, '[t]he articulation of discursive elements plays a vital role in the construction of the identity of objects as well as of individual or collective agents'. Discourse plays a constitutive role in the construction of collective identities through the establishment of chains of equivalence built in juxtaposition to common ideological enemies (Laclau and Mouffe 1985). Second, discourse also plays a constitutive role through the ways that social movements contest 'old' ways of seeing and/or doing things—that is, the *épistémè*—and how they propose new ways to imagine another world, in doing so they construct an alter-reality.

Melucci (1996) made an important contribution to the development of a more discourse-oriented perspective on social movements and social change. He articulated a less class-based definition of the political, and argued strongly for the view that social and political conflicts are not only expressed through political action but are also concerned with posing 'cultural challenges to the dominant language, to the codes that organize information and shape social practices' (ibid.: 8). Crucial in this regard is the constitutive and simultaneously contingent role of the symbolic, which ultimately was seen to represent an important field of action for activists and movements. As Melucci (ibid.: 92) rightly argued:

> in order for highly differentiated systems to be able to guarantee their internal integration, it becomes necessary to extend the system's control over the symbolic levels of action, so as to include in its scope the spheres where the meanings and motives of behaviour are constituted.

In linking the social construction of meanings to motives, actions and practices, discourse and the role of the discursive was recognized as an important and proper 'medium of social conflict and symbolic struggle'—a field of contention in its own right (Koopmans and Statham 1999: 205). As mentioned in Chap. 2, this led some scholars to refer to the existence of a 'discursive opportunity structure', which is deemed to be semi-independent of the more traditional political opportunity structure (Ferree et al. 2002; McCammon et al. 2007). It explains:

> why certain actors and frames are more prominent in public discourse than others. The mass media are clearly central to this meaning-making process, but they are only a part of the institutional and cultural structures that channel and organize discourse. (Ferree et al. 2002: 62)

However, the precise relationship between movement discourses and movement frames remains relatively underdeveloped. Elsewhere, I address this debate in more detail (Cammaerts forthcoming), but it suffices here to point out that frames are the strategic attempts of various political actors to fix or, as discourse theory would put it, to sediment meaning. Steinberg (1998: 848) critiques frame analysts for articulating 'frames … as relatively stable systems of meaning', because from a discourse perspective this is an ontological impossibility. Discourse theory, by emphasizing the contingent rather than fixity, highlights an inherent and, above all, unavoidable chaos in the meaning-making process—to put it in Derridean terms, 'there is no final meaning, the text remains a field of possibilities' (Bertens 2014: 115). In other words, hegemony can never be total or absolute. However, totally unfixity is also ontologically impossible (Laclau and Mouffe 1985: 112).

This positioning of the two traditions considers discourse and framing theory, not as commensurable or interchangeable, but as related and in conversation with each other. From this perspective, the framing process becomes inherently discursive, as also argued by Pan and Kosicki (1993). Thus frames can be approached as articulations of discourse, rather than as producing discourse. They invoke and relate to the complex and ever-changing interplay between hegemony and its ideological others. Framing should thus be understood as the variety of strategic attempts enacted by a variety of political subjects (politicians, journalists, activists) to stabilize meaning. However, this can never be total, as discourse refers to the open, contingent and ultimately conflictual horizon of possible meanings.

Returning to Melucci (1996: 67), we can relate this interplay between discourse and frames to the notion of collective identity, defined as an 'interactive process'. The construction and development of a collective identity, like discourse, is an open, dynamic and contested process. Frames and framing efforts solidify or 'crystallize', Melucci wrote, the precise nature of the collective identity by establishing boundaries and providing clarity about what needs to be fixed, and how and why we need to act. While the processes of meaning-making are pivotal to the production of movement discourses, frames and the constitution of a collective identity, the 'we', the process of collective identity formation also confronts productively the dualism between 'behaviour and meaning, between *objective* conditions and *subjective* motives, between *structure* and *agency*' (ibid.: 69; emphasis in original).

This way of defining the dynamic interplay between discourse and framing, with a focus on social movements and social change, also emphasizes that both framing and discourse are collective processes that are an expression of the constitutive role of 'ideology in social movement mobilization and action' (Steinberg 1998: 863). This also positions frame analysis as a 'causal-oriented and focused version of discourse analysis' (Lindekilde 2014: 222).

Before presenting our analysis of the UK anti-austerity movements' discourse and frames, we need to provide a sense of what constitutes the context and discourse of austerity against which the anti-austerity movement positioned itself.

3.2 The Context and Discourse of Austerity

The trigger for the financial crisis of 2008 was the result of a combination of an inflated real estate market in the USA, relaxation of the regulatory regime imposed on the banking and financial sectors, the ever more complex and intertwined financial products they developed to reduce risks, and a breakdown in corporate ethics and governance. Without going into the precise details of all these causes of the financial crisis, it is clear that the near-collapse of the financial, and by extension the capitalist, system in 2008 was a major economic and political event with worldwide consequences. As a US inquiry concluded, the financial crisis 'was a fundamental disruption—a financial upheaval, if you will—that wreaked havoc in communities and neighborhoods' (National Commission on the Causes of the Financial and Economic Crisis in the United States 2011: xv). Europe proved to be very vulnerable too, especially since many European banks (and their unsuspecting customers) had underwritten what turned out to be toxic US mortgage debt. This led to several leading banks in the UK and across continental Europe defaulting.

To avoid a systemic crash of the global financial system, the US and European governments poured massive amounts of public money into the global banking system and the wider economy. In 2008 alone, the US Federal Reserve, the European Central Bank and other Central Banks injected a staggering US$2.5 trillion into the financial system, paradoxically to stimulate lending again, and committed another US$1.5 trillion to direct equity investment (Altman 2009). The UK government nationalized several banks that otherwise would have defaulted, including Northern Rock (the healthy bits were sold off to Virgin Money in 2012, while at the time of writing the toxic assets are still owned by the state); Bradford & Bingley (its mortgage assets are still owned by the state); the once largest bank in Europe, the Royal Bank of Scotland (majority stake); and HBOS and Lloyds TSB (which were merged and the UK sold its stake in March 2017). A total of some £101 billion of public money was pumped into the British banking sector (BBC 2008; Treanor 2012).

These huge expenditures combined with the economic crisis that followed the financial emergency, led unavoidably to a ballooning of public debt. In the UK, public debt as a proportion of gross domestic product (GDP) more than doubled, from 43.6% in 2007 to 89.4% in 2014.

Figure 3.1 shows that many other European countries saw similar increases in public debt levels as a result of bailing out their banks, on the one hand, and the economic downturn that was the result of this near-fatal crash, on the other.

In Europe, similar dysfunctions to those in the USA were identified. In other words, not just the banks and the private sector were implicated, but the political system and the ideology of deregulation were also deemed to be part of the problem. A report by the UK Parliament concluded that:

> Bankers have made an astonishing mess of the financial system. However, this was a failure not only within individual banks but also of the supervisory system designed to protect the public from systemic risk. (House of Commons 2009: 110–11)

However, instead of addressing these political deficiencies and strengthening the regulatory regime, the pressures on public finances (and currencies) prompted many European political parties, on the right as well as the left, to advocate a politics of austerity and emphasize the need for cuts in public spending in order to reduce public debt. By doing so, they rejected more Keynesian solutions, which called on the state to stimulate the economy through investment (Krugman 2012).

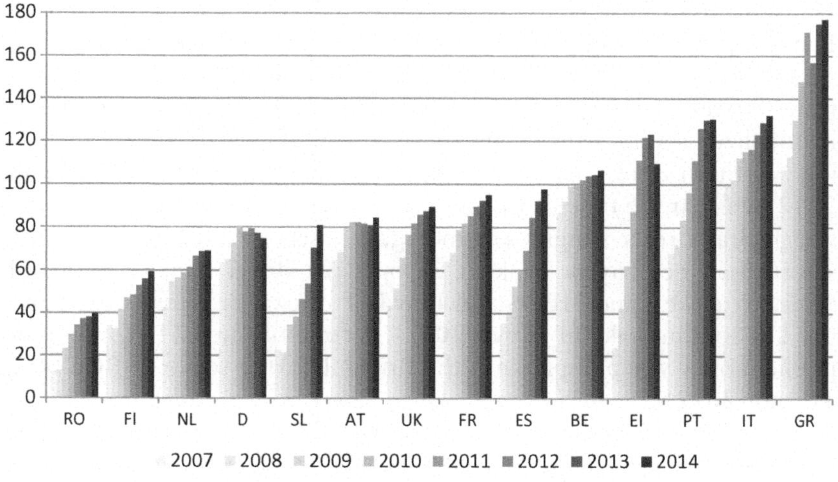

Fig. 3.1 Public debt as a percentage of GDP for a selection of EU countries (2007–2014). Source: http://www.eurostat.eu

It is also clear that some right-wing parties in Europe, and particularly in the UK, saw the financial and economic crisis and the increased public debt as a golden political opportunity to push through radical neoliberal policies geared towards reducing the state and attacking the welfare system (Seymour 2014). In the UK, since 2010, the discourse of austerity has been extremely prominent in the output of political think tanks, and was used as justification to reduce state spending to alleviate the rising public debt incurred in the aftermath of the 2008 financial crisis (Anstead 2017). It should be noted also that the discourse of austerity is not entirely new in the UK context, but can be traced back to a post-Second World War political discourse. At that time, the austerity discourse was mainly Labour-inspired, and expressed the need to get Britain 'back on track' after the war.

The financial and subsequent economic crisis hit the UK particularly hard, given the over-reliance of the UK economy on its financial sector (in 2009, almost 10% of GDP came from the banking sector),[1] but also because of the reluctance of the ruling political elites to stimulate the economy and create jobs, which led to a considerable increase in unemployment rates (from 5% in 2008 to almost 8.5% in 2011)[2] and a substantial decline in overall living standards. Regarding the latter, whereas the median income adjusted for inflation (retail price index—RPI) was £480 per week in 2008, this dropped to £455 in 2011. In particular, those not receiving a pension—that is, people on low and average salaries, the unemployed, the sick and the disabled, etc.—have suffered the most from austerity politics (Belfield et al. 2015). Furthermore, the insistence of Chancellor of the Exchequer George Osborne, on reducing the top rate of taxation for high-income earners, from 50% to 45%, exacerbated the indebtedness of the public finances and provided further justification for more cuts.

This is the economic, social, and ideological context from which the anti-austerity movement emerged. The following is a deeper analysis of what constitutes the anti-austerity discourse, and the frames that correspond to that discourse.

3.3 The Discourse and Frames of the Anti-Austerity Movement

Like most social movements, the anti-austerity movement encompasses a variety of actors, groups, organizations, and orientations. It had forerunners, including the Global Justice Movement and other anti-neoliberal mobilizations (see Gill 2000; Smith 2001; Mertes 2004; della Porta 2015;

Gerbaudo 2017). The anti-austerity movement we know today gained momentum after the near-systemic collapse, in 2008, of the financial systems in the USA and Europe, and the ensuing economic recession. It represents the most contemporary expression of contestation against the persisting influence of neoliberalism (Seymour 2014), highlighting the fundamental 'crisis of neoliberalism' (della Porta 2015: 3).

As touched on in the introduction to this chapter, in my view, the anti-austerity movement relies on two interrelated and long-standing *orders of discourse* to which its frames speak. The first relates to the redistribution of wealth with a view to ensuring social justice and fostering equality; and the second refers to the way this is achieved—through democratic rather than revolutionary means. Both discourses, redistribution and democracy, have a complex genealogy and, as a result, are open to negotiation and contestation.

Redistribution is a long-standing discourse, established to pacify the contentious issues and societal tensions regarding inequality and property rights. De Sade's *Juliette* (1768 [1799]: 118), provides an early articulation of this entrenched conflict:

> Tracing the right of property back to its source, one infallibly arrives at usurpation. However, theft is only punished because it violates the right of property; but this right is itself nothing in origin but theft.

Rather than abolishing private property, as also advocated by Karl Marx and Friedrich Engels in *The Communist Manifesto* (1848), a politics of redistribution through taxation presented itself as a reformist alternative, led by socialists and social democrats, but also right-wing political forces. Taxation was first introduced to fund wars and the expanding state apparatus, but later it also served to buy social peace and enable the consumption of mass-produced goods by the working classes. It was accompanied by a general sense of the necessity and fairness of redistributive measures to tackle market failures, alleviate poverty, and reduce overall inequality.

This redistributive consensus broke down in the 1980s and 1990s, when a neoliberal discourse of a minimal state, low taxes, and individual choice challenged the politics of redistribution and managed, slowly but surely, to dislocate the welfare state paradigm and, with it, redistribution. Thus the focus of the anti-austerity movement on taxation, on inequality and on the need for more regulation should be seen in the context of a rejection of neoliberal ideology, and a reassertion of the politics of redistribution. In this regard, some argue that we are witnessing a new materialist turn in current manifestations of contentious politics (Bailey 2014; Peterson et al. 2015).

The struggle for universal suffrage and for democracy ran largely in parallel with the struggle to force through a redistribution of wealth. For many, democracy represented the most legitimate means by which the nature and extent of redistribution could be decided, organized and enforced. However, as we know, democracy is the ultimate 'essentially contested concept' (Gallie 1956), something 'to which any and all can attach their dreams and hopes' (Brown 2010: np).

Some approach democracy as a legitimate means of electing the right kind of political elites, who then decide wisely in our name and protect us from the populist sentiments trying to erode liberal rights (Schumpeter 1973 [1942]: 242). Others are keen to maximize democratic practices throughout the whole of society, taking at face value rule for the people by the people, seeing democracy as highly participatory and embedded in a democratic culture that is inclusive and fosters dissent (Pateman 1970; MacPherson 1977; Bobbio 1987: 42–44). As well as the tension between the centralization and decentralization of decision-making, there is also another tension that divides democratic theory, namely between conflict and consensus. Some approach democracy as inherently conflictual, as a way to (temporarily) pacify the many competing and clashing interests inherent to each society (Mouffe 2005). Others see democracy precisely as a means to foster and harness harmony, social cohesion and societal consensus (Habermas 1996). These differences aside, democracy came to be seen as a legitimate form of decision making, but also as an ever-expanding horizon, what Derrida (1997: 5) called *democracy to come*, where 'the endless process of improvement and perfectibility, is inscribed in the concept'.

However, in recent years, this notion of a continually receding horizon of the possible, of which Derrida spoke, has arguably broken down. Democracy has failed massively on its promises; it has not perfected itself. On the contrary, as the authors of a recent audit of the UK's democracy put it, democracy is 'in long-term, terminal decline' (Wilks-Heeks et al. 2012: 16–17). Part of the problem, according to Wilks-Heeks and his co-authors is that 'the power which large corporations and wealthy individuals now wield on the UK political system is unprecedented' (ibid.). This also explains why some argue that we are living in a post-democratic or even a post-political age whereby democracy serves as an empty shell to protect the interests of the few over and above those of the many (Crouch 2004; Mouffe 2005; Brown 2015).

Democracy, as it functions today, is viewed more and more as a broken system, controlled by an unrepresentative and 'distant' elite with 'little in common with the ordinary citizens they are supposed to represent', and not acting 'in accordance with the views of the citizens' (Prentoulisa and Thomassen 2013: 174). From this perspective, it is not entirely surprising that one of the main slogans of the Spanish Indignados was: '¡No Nos Representan!' [They Don't Represent Us!]. However, contrary to revolutionary and anarchist movements, the Indignados in Spain and the anti-austerity movement in the UK, do not give up on democracy as a system of governance; rather, they want to reclaim it, calling for '¡Democracia Real Ya!' or 'Real Democracy Now!'.

As will become apparent, in relation to the complexity and contingency of the redistribution and democracy discourse, the frames act very much as simplifying devices and as tools to sediment a collective identity and identify a constitutive outside, a common ideological enemy. The articulation of the diagnostic, prognostic and motivational frames is addressed first to subsequently analyse the process of frame alignment, which relates to attempts to increase the resonance of the movement frames and generate support for them.

3.3.1 Diagnostic Frames

Diagnostic frames are important discursive devices. They identify what the movement is about and define with what it takes issue with, and as such they make apparent the societal problems that need fixing. The diagnostic frames of the UK anti-austerity movement refer to the discourses of redistribution and democracy and include: (1) an injustice and indignation frame; (2) an unnecessary cuts frame; and (3) a broken democracy frame.

3.3.1.1 Injustice and Indignation Frame

One of the core-messages of the anti-austerity movement regarding what happened in the post-2008 period expresses a profound sense of injustice concerning austerity politics. It argued that ordinary citizens were not to blame for the financial and economic crisis, which was caused by the greed of bankers and other wealthy elites. From this perspective, the idea that ordinary citizens should pay and suffer for the consequences of an elite-induced crisis, mainly through an onslaught on public services and the welfare state, was considered deeply unfair, as some quotes from publications and websites illustrate:

> The government cuts are *not 'fair'*, we're not 'all in it together'.[3] (UK Uncut 2010; emphasis added)

> We refuse to pay for *the banks' crisis*. (Occupy LSX 2011a; emphasis added)

> We oppose the *unfair cuts and regressive taxes*, currently inflicted on those vulnerable groups least able to bear the burden. (Occupy LSX 2011d; emphasis added)

These quotes also demonstrate a deep-seated sense of moral indignation, which is a long-standing feature of many social movement frames, including those of the anti-austerity movement (Gamson 1992; Jasper 1997; della Porta 2015). This feeling of moral indignation was rendered poignant by the juxtaposition of the victims of the cuts—ordinary people and the weak in society—with the perpetrators—the rich ruling elites and the banks:

> *A cabinet of millionaires* have decided that libraries, healthcare, education funding, voluntary services, sports, the environment, the disabled, the poor and the elderly must pay the price for the recklessness of the rich. The public are being made to pay for a financial *crisis caused by the banks*. (UK Uncut 2015a; emphasis added)

> Since 2008 hundreds of thousands of people have lost their jobs and millions have experienced pain and hardship because of *reckless financial practices*. (Occupy LSX 2011d; emphasis added)

An important component of the injustice frame is the degree of inequality, both within Western democracies and globally, which, according to the movement, has reached unsustainable, even dangerous, levels. In addition, it is argued that the degree of inequality is being exacerbated by the politics of austerity:

> The cuts are dismantling the welfare state, sending *inequality sky-rocketing and hitting the poorest hardest*. (UK Uncut 2015a; emphasis added)

> The economic system we live in increasingly *benefits the few over the many*. We believe it is fundamental to the future health of society to reduce economic inequality and its grave social consequences …It cannot continue. (Occupy LSX 2011d; emphasis added)

The linking of injustice to inequality, and the argument that the degree of inequality has reached unacceptable levels, was strengthened considerably by Piketty (2014), providing additional empirical ammunition for the movement. Central to this injustice frame is the inherent immorality of capitalism and of neoliberalism, which is reflected in 'resonant visions of the crisis as produced by elites' greed, contrasted with the sufferance of the people' (della Porta 2015: 109). These tensions, and the resulting sense of indignation, feed into the motivational frames and an urgent need to act (see Sect. 3.3.3).

3.3.1.2 Unnecessary Cuts Frame

The cuts in public spending are not only positioned as unfair; they are also deemed to be undesirable and, above all, avoidable. By positioning the cuts as unnecessary, the anti-austerity movement ideologizes them. As such, austerity is positioned as being a part of a broader neoliberal agenda and ideology (see also Brown 2010; Crouch 2012; Seymour 2014). Austerity politics is not inevitable, but rather fits with a long-standing ideological strategy to reduce the role of the state in society, to weaken workers' rights, and to punish and marginalize the poor:

> We do not accept the cuts as either *necessary or inevitable*. (Occupy LSX 2011a; emphasis added)

> The brutal cuts to our public services being inflicted by the current Government are unnecessary, unfair and *ideologically motivated*. (UK Uncut 2015a; emphasis added)

The movement argues, further, that the cuts to the funding of public libraries, health care provision, non-governmental organizations (NGOs), voluntary organizations, etc., amount to a frontal attack on the social, cultural and democratic fabric of UK society:

> The UK government's approach is *damaging its own citizens* now and the future of generations to come. Cuts to public services are having a disastrous impact on education, employment, business, health, social care and law and order. (Occupy LSX 2011d; emphasis added)

As briefly mentioned earlier, university tuition fees, which tripled in 2010,[4] became a highly symbolic and contentious issue around which in particular students and young people—that is, those affected most directly—rallied and protested vigorously (Walker et al. 2010; Cammaerts 2013). Thus it is not entirely surprising that, as well as taxation, the lack of free education provision also received much attention from the UK anti-austerity movement:

> We reject the idea that *private profit, exploitation and marketization* can bring the education system any benefit (NCAFC 2012/2014; emphasis added)

> we unite to *resist the neoliberal assault* on education and research. (NCAFC 2012/2014; emphasis added)

In its framing efforts, the anti-austerity movement aimed to shift the emphasis from cuts in public spending towards taxation. In so doing, they highlighted that rich individuals and large companies were not paying their fair share to the societies in which they were operating. Tax dodgers, as the anti-austerity movement denotes them, use loopholes and all sorts of complex mechanisms to avoid having to pay taxes on their profits and created wealth, while 'ordinary' working people must pay their fair share.

3.3.1.3 Broken Democracy Frame

The anti-austerity movement in general, but Occupy LSX in particular, is highly critical of the UK's parliamentary democratic system, which, to paraphrase Jürgen Habermas, is seen as democratic in name only. There seems to be a broad alignment with Crouch's (2004) and Brown's (2010) assessments that we live in a post-democratic age. Representative democracy is fundamentally broken, it is argued. Democracy represents the interests of the few—of the wealthy elites, of corporations— and not those of the many, of ordinary citizens (see also Prentoulisa and Thomassen 2013). These views are reflected in the anti-austerity movements' diagnostic framing efforts:

> The current system is unsustainable. It is *undemocratic and unjust.* (Occupy LSX 2011a; emphasis added)

> The way corporations and governments are intertwined fundamentally *undermines democracy.* (Occupy LSX 2011c; emphasis added)

One manifestation of this, according to the anti-austerity movement, is the inadequate or non-existent democratic control over corporations, as a result of the successful lobbying power of corporate actors and a decades-long discourse of deregulation and privatization. This is manifest in the phenomenon of regulatory agencies, which exist to protect citizens' interests, being captured by the very interests they should keep in check. As a result, these agencies lack credibility and legitimacy. This issue of co-optation is a long-standing critique in political economy (Jessop 1990) that is reproduced by contemporary anti-austerity movements attacking corporate lobbying efforts and challenging the independence of state regulators:

> Corporate lobbying *subverts our democracy*. Last year corporations spent £2 billion influencing the British government. We believe exploitative corporate lobbying has no place in a democratic society. (Occupy LSX 2011c; emphasis added)

> We want regulators to be *genuinely independent* of the industries they regulate. (Occupy LSX 2011a; emphasis added)

Another manifestation of representative democracy failing its citizens, according to the anti-austerity movement, is the deliberate underfunding of the tax authorities and the unethical 'sweetheart deals' they make with powerful corporate actors:

> [the Government is] *cutting funding* to HM Revenue and Customs by a quarter, making them *toothless* in the face of the corporate tax evaders. (UK Uncut 2010; emphasis added)

This high level of distrust and delegitimization of formal democratic institutions also has an impact on the way the anti-austerity movement organizes and structures itself; on its internal democratic processes. As will become clear in the discussion about prognostic frames, the movement does not necessarily aim to 'save' liberal democracy, but rather points towards innovative associational forms, prefigurative politics, high degrees of self-reflexivity, and inclusive decision-making processes with which to replace it (see also della Porta 2015: 157).

3.3.2 Prognostic Frames

Prognostic frames are related to Lenin's famous question: *what is to be done?* They envisage how the ills and problems diagnosed by the social movement can or, rather ought, to be cured or fixed. In other words, prognostic frames articulate an alternative vision and advocate an agenda of agency to overcome the problems identified by the diagnostic frames. They counter the inevitability or 'there is no alternative' frame of the political elites:

> We need *alternatives*; this is where we work towards them. (Occupy LSX 2011a; emphasis added)

> *There are alternatives*! (UK Uncut 2010; emphasis added)

The prognostic frames of the UK anti-austerity movement include: (1) a strong public services frame; (2) a fair taxation frame; and (3) a real democracy frame.

3.3.2.1 Strong Public Services Frame

This frame expresses the view that, rather than a contraction, what is needed is an expansion and strengthening of public services. This goes against the common neoliberal mantra limiting the extent of the choices to either rationalizing or privatizing public services, a well-known neoliberal strategy.

The public services frame foregrounds the need to invest more in the social and cultural fabric of society, rather than cutting its public funding. This is deemed to be of crucial importance to redress the inequalities and enact a politics of genuine redistribution:

> The world's resources must go towards *caring for people and the planet*, not the military, corporate profits or the rich. (Occupy LSX 2011a; emphasis added)

> we shouldn't be losing these *public services*. (UK Uncut 2015a; emphasis added)

What this pro-public services frame also indicates is that other political choices can and should be made. We can choose to protect public services and the welfare state, for example, by cutting the many subsidies to business or military expenditure, by raising taxes or by enforcing the existing tax regime (cf. fair taxation frame, Sect. 3.3.2.2. below).

When it comes to (higher) education as a specific public service, tuition fees must be abolished, according to the anti-austerity movement, and existing student debts dealt with. Young people should not have to start their adult lives with several tens of thousands pounds of debt:

> We seek the *abolition of all fees* in higher and further education and the *abolition of all student debt owed.* (NCAFC 2012/2015; emphasis added)

> [We] defend the concepts of education and research as *social goods.* (NCAFC 2012/2014; emphasis added)

Furthermore, as is apparent from these quotes, the current tendency towards the marketization of education and research is juxtaposed with a view of education and research as a social good that should be free at the point of delivery and accessible to all.

3.3.2.2 Fair Taxation Frame

Funding free education for all and better public services is not as 'unrealistic' as the proponents of austerity would have us believe. According to the anti-austerity movement, reducing inequality, better social services and increasing welfare can be achieved by ensuring that corporations, high-income earners and wealthy individuals pay their fair share of tax, which currently they do not:

> [We must] *force the big companies to pay the tax* that they owe us … Reclaiming that money would make over half of the government's planned spending cuts unnecessary' (UK Uncut 2010; emphasis added)

> [Abolishing tuition fees and student debt is] to be funded using the wealth of those who can afford it: we demand *progressive and fully enforced taxation of business and the rich.* (NCAFC 2012/2014; emphasis added)

This is a strong frame within the anti-austerity movement, and links in with the politics of redistribution and the injustice frame. A fair and just tax system would ensure that companies and rich individuals pay much more taxes than they currently do, which would enable increased public investment rather than cuts:

> We must *abolish tax havens and complex tax avoidance schemes*, and ensure corporations pay tax that accurately reflects their real profits. (Occupy LSX 2011c; emphasis added)

> We want *structural change* towards authentic global equality. (Occupy LSX 2011a; emphasis added)

As the last quote here also highlights, this solution does not merely affect and implicates the national level; it also has repercussions at the international level, where certain states encourage tax evasion and avoidance.

3.3.2.3 Real Democracy Frame

Juxtaposed with the broken democracy frame is a real democracy frame. A real democracy is needed, according to the anti-austerity movement; a democracy that represents the real interests of the people rather than corporate interests and the interests of the wealthy elites that seem to run our broken democracy. It is argued that we need a more participatory, more open, and more transparent democracy:

> united in our diversity, united for global change, we demand global democracy: global governance by the people, for the people ... Like the Spanish Tomalaplaza we say "Democracia Real Ya": *True global democracy now!* (Occupy LSX 2011b; emphasis added)

One way that the anti-austerity movement throughout Europe performs its alternative vision of democracy is via its general assembly model, which is horizontal in structure, autonomous in its decision-making and anti-representative in spirit, and aims to 'create a social space facilitating equal voice' (Prentoulisa and Thomassen 2013: 177). As occurred in the Spanish Indignados movement meetings (Nez 2012; Romanos 2013), these public assemblies were held in a deliberative spirit; a certain etiquette developed including the appropriation of a set of codes and hand signals to govern discussion, to signal agreement/disagreement or add a point, amounting to what some described as 'the democracy of direct action' (Razsa and Kurnik 2012: 241).

Anti-austerity movements across Europe combine 'pre-figurative practices of radical democracy within social movement spaces with a highly organized attack on the illegitimacy of representative democratic institutions' (Flesher Fominaya 2015: 154). This maps onto movement frames of horizontalism and consensus decision-making:

> We will organize through *democratic assemblies* at the lowest possible levels. (NCAFC 2012/2014; emphasis added)

> *Open discussion* is at the heart of our Occupation and our decision-making process. The more people we can involve in our debates, the stronger and more representative the results will be. (Occupy LSX 2011e; emphasis added)

In line with New Left visions of participatory democracy (Pateman 1970), the anti-austerity movement has an agenda of extending democratic values and equal participation beyond Parliament and voting, for example, in schools, universities and the workplace. In addition, solidarity with global democratic struggles is part of the real democracy frame:

> We want schools, colleges, universities and research institutions and the work they do to be *public, democratic, open and accessible to all*, and to be oriented towards free enquiry, the needs and interests of society, and liberation from existing hierarchies and oppressions. (NCAFC 2012/2014; emphasis added)

> The citizens of the world must get *control over the decisions that influence them* in all levels—from global to local. (Occupy LSX 2011b; emphasis added)

Weak regulatory regimes need to be strengthened and made more accountable. To achieve this, proper sanctions need to be in put in place for those that transgress and act unethically, according to the anti-austerity movement:

> Regulators must be *totally independent, transparent, publicly accountable* and provided with proper *enforcement powers*. (Occupy LSX 2011d; emphasis added)

> Those directly involved in the decision-making process must be held *personally liable* for their role in the misdeeds of their corporations and duly charged for all criminal behaviour. (Occupy LSX 2011c; emphasis added)

This speaks also to an agenda of retribution, *vis-à-vis* the 2008 financial crisis, and a call for genuine accountability of economic and financial elites. These elites are (white-collar) criminals, according to the anti-austerity movement, and should be treated as such.

3.3.3 Motivational Frames

Motivational frames point to action and political agency; they are essential in view of the efforts of social movements to mobilize, to increase support for the movement, and to activate people. Thus motivational frames call upon us to act urgently, taking the symbolic to the material, increasing the visibility of the struggle, and confronting the ideological enemy. Motivational frames 'suggest not merely that something can be done but that *we* can do something' (Gamson 1992: 7; emphasis in original). As such, part of the motivational frames is the construction of a collective identity, of a 'we'; it denotes the 'processes through which a collective becomes a collective' (Melucci 1996: 70). Besides collective identity frames, we can delimit contentious action frames as a part of motivational frames.

3.3.3.1 Collective Identity Frames

The construction of a collective identity is an essential aspect of the ontology of a social movement. Social movements distinguish 'the Self'—that is, what 'we' stand for—from 'the Others'—that is, what 'they' stand for. The notion of *Unterscheidung* between ideological enemies and friends is very relevant in this regard (Schmitt 1996 [1927]; Mouffe 2005). As such, on the one hand, collective identity is an assertion of a collective, a 'we', but on the other hand it simultaneously constructs and identifies the constitutive outsides, to refer to Derrida. Political identities are thus formed through antagonisms and 'by their common reference to something external' (Laclau and Mouffe 1985: 127).

In articulating a *we*, the UK anti-austerity movement adopts very broad terms and positions itself as an inter-sectional movement, aiming to maximize its reach:

> *We are you.* We are mums and pensioners, students and trade unionists, the disabled and school children, private sector employees, small business owners and the unemployed. We are ordinary people standing up (or sitting-in) for what we believe, and for the change we want to see. It's your movement. (UK Uncut 2015a; emphasis added)

> *We* are of all ethnicities, backgrounds, genders, generations, sexualities dis/abilities and faiths. (Occupy LSX 2011a; emphasis added)

In line with this, we can refer to the Occupy slogan '*We* are the 99%'. This slogan, in a way, is the embodiment of what Laclau (2005: 171) called a populist reason, whereby unavoidable heterogeneities are masked by the establishment of 'some form of unity …through equivalential political articulation'. The idea of the 99% implicates and includes (almost) everybody; it appeals to the 'virtual totality of the political community of a given country', as Gerbaudo (2017: 90) asserts. The slogan points also to efforts 'to blur the boundaries between the inside and the outside of the movement' and to 'the reluctance to openly exclude people from the movement' (Kavada 2015: 883–84). This ties in with the broader strategies of frame alignment, which are discussed below in Sect. 3.3.4.

The way this collective identity is sedimented is by juxtaposing the 'we'—the 99%, with a 'they'—the ideological enemy, *the 1%*, which again is articulated as a set of different actors:

> We use acts of creative civil disobedience to show our opposition to the *Government's* cuts to our public services. (UK Uncut 2015a; emphasis added)

> We have shut down *tax dodgers* from Vodafone (again and again) to Fortnum & Mason. If the Government won't make them pay, we will. (UK Uncut 2015a; emphasis added)

> Corporations are rarely transparent or accountable to the people. This *corporate system* is broken. (Occupy LSX 2011c; emphasis added)

> *Financial institutions* have increased in size to dominate our economy but have not become socially accountable in line with their increased power. (Occupy LSX 2011d; emphasis added)

> There has been a widening of the chasm between *rich* and poor in the last 30 years (Occupy LSX 2011d; emphasis added)

From these quotes we can derive that the ideological enemy of the anti-austerity movement comprises wealthy individuals and corporations who pay no (or very little) tax, financial institutions (and bankers in particular), neoliberal universities, and the UK government, which allows tax dodging, lowers taxes for the rich, and cuts public services.

On the other hand, the *we*, in a way, is all of *us*, 'a common unity' (Melucci 1996: 71), implicating, both cognitively and emotionally, a wide variety of groups and constituencies, and mobilizing them against the privileged elites, against the establishment; a typical populist meme (Laclau 2005).

3.3.3.2 Contentious Action Frames

Other motivational frames do not necessarily construct a sense of belonging, but they are frames of contentious action, stressing the urgency to act now. In this regard, the UK anti-austerity movement, from its inception, has stressed the utmost importance of direct action, of what Kluge (1982: 212) described as the 'immediate on-the-spot struggle'. The movement's main direct action repertoire consists of the physical occupation of public as well as private spaces that symbolize the injustice they resist. In its motivational framings, it insists on the urgency to act and to confront and distress its ideological enemies in a mildly forceful manner:

> Austerity-economics ... cannot be stopped by asking nicely. If we want to win the fight against these cuts (and we can win) then we must *make it impossible to ignore* our arguments and impossible to resist our demands. (UK Uncut 2015a; emphasis added)

> Now is the time to *get angry, get organized, get creative*, and to build a resistance to austerity. See you on the streets! (UK Uncut 2015a; emphasis added)

> We will demonstrate, we will lobby, and we will take *direct action and industrial action*. (NCAFC 2012/2014; emphasis added)

However, it is not enough, in this regard, to stress the importance of getting organized or to be creative in organizing direct action. It is important also to show your supporters that the struggle at hand is not a hopeless one, but rather a battle that is winnable, as expressed by this quote from a UK Uncut activist:

> The fight against the cuts will be the fight of our generation. And it is a fight that is *winnable*, as long as we're willing to get creative tactically. (Baker 2010; emphasis added)

The collective action frames of UK Uncut also include the use of capitalism and consumption as an action frame. Through its actions on the high street, targeting brands that do not pay taxes, the movement invites the wider public to boycott these brands.

Part of the process of frame articulation (i.e. the attempts to fix or to crystallize meaning) are the various strategies that movements enact to align their frames with other and past struggles, and by doing so amplify their own, movement-specific, frames.

3.3.4 Frame Alignment

As discussed earlier, framing is also used to enlarge the scope of conflict, to build chains of equivalence among various struggles, and to ensure that the diagnostic, prognostic, and motivational frames analysed above resonate beyond those who are like-minded. Frame alignment involves four distinct processes: (1) frame bridging; (2) frame amplification; (3) frame extension; and (4) frame transformation (see Benford and Snow 2000). I address each in turn.

3.3.4.1 Frame Bridging

Frame bridging links several frames that are ideologically similar, making interconnections. This, Benford and Snow (2000: 624) consider, is one of the most prevalent framing strategies—it concerns 'the linking of two or more ideologically congruent but structurally unconnected frames regarding a particular issue or problem'. We can also refer here to the social movement phenomenon of building alliances, congruent with a relational network approach to social movements (Diani and McAdam 2003).

The calls for redistribution within the anti-austerity movement tend to be accompanied by demands for the recognition of (gender, ethnic, sexual) difference, as well as other political struggles related, for example, to climate change or animal rights. In many ways, current social movements, including the anti-austerity movement, have appropriated and, at the same time, embody Laclau and Mouffe's (1985: 182) call for 'the equivalential articulation between anti-racism, anti-sexism and anti-capitalism, for example ... equivalent symbols of a unique and indivisible struggle'.

The related, but somewhat unconnected, struggles to which the anti-austerity movement refers in its framing efforts include: feminist and LBGTQ (Lesbian, Bisexual, Gay, Transgender, Questioning) struggles; anti-racism; anti-ableism; and environmentalism. We can observe here attempts to bridge a politics of recognition and a politics of redistribution (see also Fraser 1996; Honneth 2001):

> The present economic system pollutes land, sea and air, is causing massive loss of natural species and environments, and is accelerating humanity towards irreversible *climate change*. (Occupy LSX 2011a; emphasis added)

> It is the ***disabled, the unemployed, ethnic minorities and women*** who will feel the brunt of these cuts. (UK Uncut 2010; emphasis added)

> [We strive for] an academic environment that is *feminist, pro-LBGTQ, anti-racist and anti-ableist*, and that actively works against oppression and for inclusion. (NCAFC 2012/2014; emphasis added)

Besides the construction of chains of equivalence between their own struggle and other related struggles, the UK anti-austerity movement clearly links its own frames to broader, long-standing, historical struggles.

3.3.4.2 Frame Amplification

A part of network building and extending the scope of conflict and support for change is a process of amplification, achieved through the interlinking of movement frames with existing values or beliefs (Benford and Snow 2000: 624). It refers to the need to relate transformative strategies to the primary frameworks ingrained in society. The process of amplification also involves attempts to disseminate the movement frames to gain traction and visibility as a movement.

As outlined above, the politics of redistribution and the struggle over what democracy entails, have a long history, on which the anti-austerity movement draws. The movement attempts to appeal also to a sense of social justice and moral indignation; for example, by emphasizing the tension between cuts to social services and the rich avoiding paying taxes, or democracy not representing the interests of those who do pay their taxes—that is, ordinary people, workers, the unemployed, the sick and disabled, pensioners, etc.

The process of amplification is fostered also by self-mediation practices, such as the production of flyers, posters and placards, and ensuring that the media are aware of these actions:

> Several days before an action call up your local paper and radio station: tell them what you are doing, make a good pitch and sell your action. Try and get them to come down on the day. Take photos which you can give them. (UK Uncut 2015b)

> You'll probably want to take some flyers, some posters or placards and a banner. Letters to workers explaining that they are not the target of the action can also be effective. (UK Uncut 2015b)

These self-mediation practices, geared to frame amplification, are analysed in more detail in Chap. 4.

3.3.4.3 Frame Extension

The objective of frame extension is to maximize resonance through the inclusion of 'issues and concerns that are presumed to be of importance to potential adherents and constituents' (Benford and Snow 2000: 625). However, frame extension carries some dangers; it can lead to an identitary and ideological dilution in the bid to gain traction.

Despite a primary focus on the UK context, in terms of frame extension, the UK anti-austerity movement frequently expresses solidarity with similar struggles being waged elsewhere:

> We stand together with occupations all over the world … We stand in solidarity with the global oppressed and we call for an end to the actions of our government and others in causing this oppression. (Occupy LSX 2011a)

It actively supports labour-union, student, and worker and unemployed mobilizations. In other words, the UK anti-austerity movement is a movement that makes concrete attempts to build class alliances, a common tactic of social movements:

> We support the strike on 30 November and the student action on 9 November, and actions to defend our health services, welfare, education and employment, and to stop wars and arms dealing. (Occupy LSX 2011a)

> We will build solidarity and cooperation between students, workers and the unemployed. (NCAFC 2012/2014)

The 99% slogan refers to this, comprising of 'every heterogeneous element that is oppressed and exploited and stands to lose from austerity and entrenched neoliberalism' (Seymour 2014: 197). As such, it promotes the building of alliances—or chains of equivalence—among different agendas and involving different people from various backgrounds and classes, all of whom are affected, in both different and similar ways, by austerity:

> Get in touch with as many local groups as you can: trade unions, sympathetic political party groups, anti-cuts groups, student unions, local campaigning groups ... you never [sic] who might want to get involved. (UK Uncut 2015b)

This 'big we' can also be seen as a reaction against fragmentation and a long legacy of infighting within the left (Gerbaudo 2017: 90). However, while these multiple 'associations, bonds, linkages and networks' might be the most exciting feature of the anti-austerity movement, as Chomsky (2012: 45) argued, they can also be seen as a potential weakness, since the movement risks being perceived as engaging in too many battles at once.

3.3.4.4 Frame Transformation

Frame transformation is tied to what Mouffe (1979: 191) calls the 'process of ideological transformation', which is central to neo-Gramscian discourse theory. In other words, frame transformation requires a process of *dislocation*, whereby common-sense elite frames are exposed for what they are: namely, ideological devices. Frame transformation represents the moment when the hegemonic nature of dominant discourse is revealed to be temporary, fundamentally contestable and ultimately defeatable. Goffman (1974: 347) spoke of failure in the 'applicability of the frame, a break in its governance'. To achieve frame transformation, hegemonic frames need to be discursified or, to put it differently, need to be made, once more, 'malleable and emergent' (Oliver and Johnston 2000: 40), so that they become contestable and challengeable.

From the anti-austerity movement's perspective, this would imply unsettling the dominant neoliberal ideology, which celebrates personal greed, individual responsibility and a minimal state (Crouch 2012). While prognostic frames project an alter-reality, arguing that other choices are possible, diagnostic frames contest the elite frames—for example, the view that cuts are unavoidable and distributed fairly. These elite frames are exposed as being ideologically motivated:

> The [Tory—LibDem] coalition government is ideologically committed to cutting public spending, hitting the poorest and most vulnerable in our society hardest. (UK Uncut 2010)

However, arguably, dislocating the neoliberal hegemony is not straightforward (see Cammaerts 2015), and the extent to which, and the way in which, the anti-austerity movement is able to de-territorialize the neoliberal hegemony are important questions that this book tries to address.

3.4 Conclusion

This chapter has outlined how the UK anti-austerity movement produced a set of frames, pertaining to two main orders of discourse with a long historical legacy: (1) a renewed politics of redistribution with an emphasis on taxation and public services; and (2) calls for a better, stronger and more democratic democracy. The movement frames were positioned as strategic attempts to fix meaning within the broader and contested discourse.

In the case of a renewed politics of redistribution, an injustice frame was deployed to link aggressive tax evasion by the rich and by corporations discursively with detrimental cuts to public services. Furthermore, it was argued that these cuts to public services and welfare state provisions are ideologically motivated rather than necessary and unavoidable. Instead, the movement posited, we need strong and well-funded public services and genuine solidarity among all the different groups and constituencies within society. A fair tax-regime ensuring that the wealthy and corporations contribute their fair share was proposed as providing the means to fund public services and the welfare state. In other words, redistribution should be achieved through the state, and through a fair and progressive taxation system.

The second major problem that is identified discursively by the anti-austerity movement is the broken and defunct democratic system, which fails to take into account the real interests of the people it claims to represent and in whose name decisions are made. The liberal representative model of democracy and the party-political system is seen to protect the interests of the few ('the 1%') at the expense of the many ('the 99%'). This is juxtaposed with a prefigurative horizontal model of decision making as practiced by the movement itself, as well as calls for a *real* or genuine democracy that is more participatory, more encompassing of people's interests, and thus more able to contest and reverse the austerity agenda. It would also enable the establishment of more stringent and equitable regulatory frameworks to make the markets and capitalism subservient to society rather than the reverse.

As well as denoting the problems that need fixing, and providing a set of solutions to these problems, the framing efforts of the anti-austerity movement are also geared towards constructing a collective identity—a 'we'. This study aligns itself with Gerbaudo and Treré (2015: 866) in arguing that, '[f]ar from having disappeared from the horizon of contemporary activism, collective identity still constitutes a pivotal question for activists and scholars alike'. However, this collective identity is neither stable nor imbued with clarity, as might seem to be implied by the analysis of the frames in this chapter; on the contrary, it is contested and in flux, negotiated and contested internally.

By pitting the 99% against the 1%, a populist tactic was employed which can also be understood as an attempt to build class alliances and implicate a wide variety of subject positions; students, teachers, nurses, mothers, LGBTQ, workers, less-abled, the unemployed, etc. If anything is to change, the 99% need to act and rise up; complacency or passive endurance of austerity politics is not an option, contestation on the contrary is a must.

To assess the extent to which the movement discourse and frames has been able to displace or unsettle the neoliberal hegemony of austerity politics through its contentious actions requires an in-depth study of how these discourses and frames circulated further through the Circuit of Protest. First, by analysing a set of self-mediation practices geared at communicating movement frames independently, and at managing mainstream media attention, which is the focus of Chap. 4. Second, by analysing the representations of the movement and its frames by journalists, which will be addressed in Chap. 5; and finally, by analysing the reception of movement frames by non-activist citizens, which is discussed in Chap. 6.

Notes

1. See Burgess (2011).
2. See Eurostat (2015).
3. This is a reaction against some 2010 statements from leading figures in the UK Conservative Party, claiming that the cuts to public services were 'necessary' and 'fair'. George Osborne, Chancellor of the Exchequer, also launched the catchphrase: 'We're all in this together', implying that everyone will need to make sacrifices.
4. In 2010, the cost of tuition fees for a three-year BA degree rose from £9000 (€11,000 or US$12,000) to a staggering £27,000 (€32,500 or US$36,000). This huge sum is financed by the state initially, but has to begin to be repaid once the graduate's earnings exceed a certain threshold (in 2017, this was set at a pre-tax yearly income of £21,000/€25,000/US$28,000). In addition, the government decided also to scrap the Education Maintenance Allowance (EMA), a weekly grant that college students from low-income families had received to incentivize them to continue studying.

CHAPTER 4

The Self-Mediation Practices of the Anti-Austerity Movement

In this chapter, the *self-mediation* moment of the Circuit of Protest is assessed. The self-mediation moment addresses a set of mediation practices of activists. This emphasis on media and communication practices shifts the focus away from the textual and the symbolic towards the material aspects of a mediated struggle, and implicates a mediation repertoire of contentious action.

This repertoire is shaped and influenced by the affordances provided by a variety of media and communication technologies. Different media and communication technologies have distinct embedded affordances that are relevant to activism; these can be visible and apparent, but can also be hidden and may yet be undiscovered. This opens up the potential for activists to shape these technologies to their needs. The relevant mediation possibilities include public and private forms of communication, taking place in real time or asynchronously, but also the ability to conceal identity and encrypt content. As discussed in more detail below, these core affordances play out differently with regard to print, telecommunication, broadcasting, and various internet protocols.

Social movements and their activist members tend to use all the media and communication technologies available, and to combine their technological affordances to fit with their various activist strategies. However, it is not enough, in this context, to consider the use of media and communication technologies to push or disseminate the movement's discourses and frames. Arguably, this is important, but it is just one possible

B. Cammaerts, *The Circulation of Anti-Austerity Protest*,
https://doi.org/10.1007/978-3-319-70123-3_4

mediation practice. For instance, the affordances offered by media and communication technologies are exploited intensively to mobilize for (direct) action. Also, media and communication technologies are used increasingly to coordinate protest actions and connect people within the movement. Internal organization is increasingly mediated. Finally, mediation is relevant also for recording protests, producing protest artefacts and documenting police violence (cf. sousveillance practices), while the archiving and circulation of protest artefacts are also mediated.

I propose to use Foucault's notion of Technologies of the Self as a useful way to theorize the interplay between the mediation affordances and practices. Foucault (1988) spoke of Technologies of the Self in relation to the way in which individuals internalize rules and constraints, and how they construct their personal identity, but I apply this here to the constitution of collective actors and identities. Foucault identified four technologies of the self—disclosure, examination, remembrance, and the interpretation of dreams. While the interpretation of dreams can be linked to imagining another and better future, the three other (Stoic) Technologies of the Self represent three distinct mediation logics that map on to the mediation repertoires of activists.

First, I introduce affordance theory and identify the core affordances of a variety of traditional and new(er) media and communication technologies, which enable a repertoire of activist mediation practices. Foucault's Technologies of the Self serves, subsequently, as a useful theoretical framework to structure these self-mediation practices.

4.1 Mediation Affordances and Practices

Affordance theory provides insights into what it is that media and communication technologies can afford activists. Gibson (1977), an ecological psychologist, coined the notion of affordances to explain how an animal's environment constitutes a given set of affordances, which are both objective and subjective, recognized and hidden. Affordances, Gibson (1977: 75) explained, are a 'unique combination of qualities that specifies what the object affords us', and they represent opportunities or, rather, potentialities for a set of actions, which we perceive or not. Also, as we use these objects, they become an extension of ourselves, disrupting the subject-object dichotomy; think of how people use and engage with their mobile phones today. Gibson (1979/1986: 41) argued that:

> the capacity to attach something to the body suggests that the boundary between the animal and the environment is not fixed at the surface of the

skin but can shift. More generally it suggests that the absolute duality of 'objective' and 'subjective' is false.

The concept of affordances became popular in technology and innovation studies, to make sense of our relationship with and our shaping of technologies, especially media and communication technologies (Hutchby 2001). Thus print media, telecommunication, broadcasting, the internet, mobile technologies, etc. all carry an inherent set of affordances, which the users (in this case, the activists) need to recognize. Different media and communication technologies have different affordances, and taken together they constitute a sort of mediation repertoire—a communication toolbox—from which activists and movements choose, depending on their specific needs. Hutchby (2001: 44) explains it excellently in writing that affordances are:

> functional and relational aspects which frame, while not determining, the possibilities for agentic action in relation to an object. In this way, technologies can be understood as artefacts which may be both shaped by and shaping of the practices humans use in interaction with, around and through them.

From this perspective, the appropriation of media and communication technologies by activists is situated at the 'intersection between social context, political purpose and technological possibility' (Gillan et al. 2008: 151). However, what is technologically possible may not have been intended when the technology was designed, which opens up a space for user resistance and for innovation (Williams 1997: 328).

Relevant recent examples of this are the use of text messaging or Facebook by activists to mobilize for direct action, to garner support or to recruit members (Colonel 2001; Hermanns 2008; Harlow 2011). Neither SMS (Short Messaging Service) nor Facebook was designed to mobilize for or coordinate direct actions, but the affordance to do so had always been there. It took some innovative activists to recognize these affordances (often in the face of other constraints) and to start using the technologies in ways not anticipated by their designers and, in doing so, to advance the movement's aims.

Table 4.1 juxtaposes two sets of mediation affordances to provide a matrix of self-mediation affordances and corresponding media and communication technologies: (1) the affordance to communicate in real time

Table 4.1 Matrix of self-mediation affordances, and media and communication technologies

	Real time/fleeting	*Asynchronous/permanency*
Public/outward	• Broadcasting • Streaming • Social media	• Print (essays/manifestos, posters, stickers, flyers) • Film, video and photographs • Social media and website
Private/inward	• Telephone • Internet relay chat • Voice over internet protocol (VOIP)	• Letters • Email • Text messaging and private messages on social networking sites

or asynchronously; and (2) the affordance to communicate privately or publicly.

Regarding the first tension—real-time versus asynchronous communication—activists will assess the intentionality of their communication strategy when choosing with which media to communicate. For example, organizing or coordinating direct action will require different communicative practices and technologies compared to activists wanting to disseminate their movement frames through independent channels, or to coordinate internally. This brings us to the second tension: between private and public forms of communication. Some communication technologies (such as letters, telephone or email) allow for more private forms of communication, while others (such as radio, Twitter or a website) enable public communication.

We should also take into account the potential reach of communication technologies. Some communication tools enable activists to reach mass audiences (broadcasting), while others (social media) are more attuned to narrowcasting. Finally, another important aspect often considered by activists in other than Western contexts, is the extent to which literacy matters; some ways of communicating require the recipients of the communication to be literate (essays, text), while others do not (visuals, radio).

A final mediation affordance of relevance to activists is that of surveillance, but also of anonymity and concealment. Networked technologies enable the state, but increasingly also corporate actors, to surveil citizens/consumers in minute detail. At the same time, various technologies enable activists to encrypt their internal communication or to anonymize communication flows. These two affordances—of surveillance and of concealment—became especially pressing and apparent in the wake of the Snowden revelations, exposing so-called dragnet surveillance practices by the US and UK governments.

Mediation affordances enable a set of activist mediation practices. Martín-Barbero (1993: 188) defined 'mediations' as constructions of cultural meaning made up of 'the articulations between *communication practices* and social movements and the articulation of different tempos of development and practice' (emphasis added). Hence the notion of media practices, or what Couldry (2004: 118) calls, 'things that people do with the media' in their situated everyday lives, is deemed to be of prime importance here. A focus on practices, enabled by affordances, shifts attention away from media and journalism as powerful institutions, and from the analysis of text and discourse. Instead, the way in which media and communication technologies are used and embedded in everyday life is foregrounded, as are the dominant and resistance practices they enable. This ties in with a shift from a preoccupation with media effects towards questions probing what people do with media, and the gratifications they get from using them (Blumler and Katz 1974).

Practice theory emerged from the paradigmatic confrontation between those emphasizing individual agency when explaining social phenomena, and those stressing the determinism of social structures. Practice theory, as articulated initially by writers such as Bourdieu (1977), Foucault (1979) and Giddens (1979), proposes ways of rescuing agency without falling prey to an over-determination of either agency or structure. Habitus, the field, doxa, épistèmé, governmentality, bio-power, resistance, contention, structuration, and the dialectic between generative and restrictive power, all relate to the complex interplay between the two ends of this core dichotomy in social theory. In doing so, they address the ways in which society, social life and socialization shape the way we act, live our lives and do the things we do or do not do; by putting in place constraints, but also by creating opportunities for agency, change and constant renewal. Overall:

> [practice theory] takes the human body to be the nexus of arrays of activities, or practices, that agents perform with greater or lesser commitment, dexterity and grace. Whilst some of these practices are widely diffused across social space and time, others are found clustered in configurations that change over time through the socially (re)productive agency of practitioners. (Postill 2010: 11–12)

Practice theory was introduced into media and communication studies via an anthropological approach to studying audiences, and the gradual acknowledgement that what is commonly known as *the audience* of media was a highly complex and far from unified actor; this is discussed further in Chap. 6. Couldry (2004: 129) drew our attention to the potentially complex interrelationships or orderings between media-related practices and other social and cultural practices:

> we need the perspective of practice to help us address how media are embedded in the interlocking fabric of social and cultural life ... how practices (possibilities of action) are differentially ordered for those with ready access to media resources (whether as media producers or as privileged media sources) and for those without.

Adopting a mediation practices approach is a fruitful way to analyse and systematize the self-mediation practices of activists and social movements, which concurs with Mattoni and Treré (2014). In what follows, I introduce a conceptual framework to study the self-mediation practices of social movement actors, relying on the three Stoic Technologies of the Self, as outlined by Foucault (1988).

4.2 Technologies of Self-Mediation

Foucault's notion of Technologies of the Self is a useful way to theorize the interplay between the affordances and constraints of social media for protest movements and activists. Bakardjieva and Gaden (2012) also mobilized this Foucauldian concept, in order to make sense of the internet's role in terms of self-constitution, but also to link the Technologies of the Self to other technologies such as the production of signs and, ultimately, power. By applying the notion of the Technologies of the Self not to individuals, but to collective actors, I take this experiment further. By doing this, I argue that there is a need for a more complex understanding of what Honneth (2012) recently called 'the I in We', or the way in which we all negotiate and navigate the relationship between our own complex individual identities and a panoply of collective identities.

I use technologies of self-mediation here as a metaphor, pointing to the way in which self-mediation practices are constitutive of the construction of collective identities, and have become highly relevant in view of disseminating, communicating, recording, and archiving a variety of movement discourses and deeds. Technologies of self-mediation, and their associated self-mediation practices, should thus be seen as the tools through which a social movement becomes self-conscious as a movement, and imagines a better, more just future. Furthermore, just as the Stoics conceived life as an ongoing work in progress, social movements can also be approached as a dynamic, ever-changing phenomenon.

The Technologies of the Self, as theorized by Foucault, relate to how individuals internalize rules and constraints. Through Technologies of the Self, we ultimately discipline ourselves, but at the same time they are those devices, methods or 'tools' that enable the social construction of our personal identities; they:

> permit individuals to effect by their own means or with the help of others a certain number of operations on their own bodies and souls, thoughts, conduct, and way of being, so as to transform themselves in order to attain a certain state of happiness, purity, wisdom, perfection, or immortality. (Foucault 1988: 18)

Technologies of the Self and the construction of personal identities are, however, not merely about processes of self-compliance with the structures of coercion; they are also the space where resistance resides and is practised. Commenting on Foucault's work, Burkitt (2002: 224) contends that Technologies of the Self are:

> a form of practical action accompanied by practical reason, which aims to instil in the body certain habitual actions—either moral virtues (that is, right ways of acting in a situation) or technical skills—and, later, to give people the reflexive powers to reason about their virtues or skills, providing them with the capacity to refine, modify or change them.

Foucault identified three Stoic Technologies of the Self: (1) *disclosure*; (2) *examination*; and (3) *remembrance*. Disclosure relates to what Foucault (1988: 29) calls 'cultivation of the self'—expression of self by which we reveal ourselves. Here, the notion of confession plays an important role. The second Stoic Technology of the Self, examination, is concerned with the self-reflexive powers that Burkitt mentions; it amounts to what Foucault (1988) called 'taking stock' (p.33) or conducting 'a review of what was done, of what should have been done, and comparison of the two' (p.35). This is suggestive of the idea of perfecting one's 'self', the ability to be reflexive and change course, to acknowledge one's mistakes. The third Stoic Technology of the Self is remembrance, which refers to capturing and recording, or the 'memorization of deeds' (ibid.: 45).

The fourth Technology of the Self that Foucault identified was not Stoic, but originated with Artemidorus (2nd century AD). It referred to the *interpretation of dreams,* which is part of a strategy of self-care rather than self-knowledge. The interpretation of dreams serves as 'an announcement of a future event', and the ability to be a 'self-interpreter' (ibid.: 39). It implies the ability to imagine and prepare for the future:

> the interpretation of dreams was a highly popular technique of self-care in antiquity, for dreams were believed to be portents of the future for which it was important to prepare. (Hutton 1988: 134)

In the context of social movements, the interpretation of dreams can be related to the ways in which activists and movements imagine and prepare for another, and ultimately a better, world. The interpretation of dreams, in our context, is about articulating and interpreting an alter-reality. This was addressed in Chap. 3 in terms of the prognostic and motivational frames, which articulate a specific vision of the future and how to reach this better future through action. In the present chapter, the focus is on the Stoic technologies of the self, namely disclosure, examination and remembrance, which can in turn be mapped on to the contentious mediation practices identified above:

1. *Disclosure*: communication and dissemination of movement discourses and frames, the mobilization efforts for direct action and the performance of protest;
2. *Examination*: on-the-spot coordination of direct action, internal organization, and decision making or permanent revision of strategies and tactics; and
3. *Remembrance*: production of protest artefacts, documenting of police violence, and archiving of the movement's self-representations.

In terms of mediation affordances, it would be fair to say that the outwardly-oriented and public forms of communication have more salience for disclosure and remembrance, while the inwardly-oriented forms are often, but not exclusively, relevant to strategies of examination. In addition, the tension between communication situated in the here and now, and asynchronous and delayed communication, prioritizes the distinction between fleeting communication and communication patterns that can be archived for posterity. The latter form part of the long-term collective memory of dissent and contentious politics, while the former are more ephemeral, or mediations in the moment. In terms of the technologies of self-mediation, it could be argued that the fleeting is more redolent of practices centred on self-reflexivity within the movement, and thus related to the examination of self, while permanency is more aligned to remembrance of self.

In what follows, the logics of disclosure, of examination and of remembrance are discussed in relation to the self-mediation practices of the anti-austerity movement and the mediation affordances outlined above.

4.3 The Logic of Disclosure and the Anti-Austerity Movement

The logic of disclosure, which, according to Foucault, has both a confessional and an expressive aspect, relates to the widest possible dissemination of the movement discourses and frames, through a variety of channels of communication as well as to communication practices geared to mobilizing for direct action. Direct actions are obviously also in themselves communicative acts through the performance of protest. At the same time, the logic of disclosure is also aimed at clearly identifying and negatively representing the movement's ideological enemies.

The logic of disclosure is predominantly outwardly oriented, relying on both asynchronous and real-time self-mediation practices, but on the former more than the latter. Self-mediation practices following the logic of disclosure are geared towards: (1) independent dissemination of movement discourses and frames; (2) mobilization for direct action, both online and, in particular, offline; and (3) performing protest. In what follows, each of these three dimensions is addressed in more detail.

4.3.1 Independent Dissemination

Media and communication technologies enable activists not only to produce media but also to communicate their self-produced media independently, mobilizing public and asynchronous affordances. Although the internet is increasingly important as an enabling medium, we need to acknowledge that older media technologies, such as print, photocopy, photography and video, also play a role in push-practices. George, a student occupier active within the NCFAC, explained that:

> Besides the internet and social media there was definitely also a role for print. One of our student activists was very manic about this, he loved propaganda and postering and flyering. He used to plaster the campus with all kinds of mad stuff every day. So, there was definitely a very vibrant pamphleteering culture that came out of the movement. (personal interview, 23/02/2017)

As already touched on briefly in the Introduction, UK Uncut published a range of 'ready to print' material on its website, which started out as a blog. Activists were asked to download the flyers and posters and print at home with a view to distributing them to the general public or to fellow activists.

Figure 4.1 is a good example of this. It depicts a pamphlet published in October 2010 on UK Uncut's blog. Sympathisers were encouraged to download, print and distribute it during the direct actions against Vodafone. The pamphlet was addressed to Vodafone employees and gave the reasons for UK Uncut's actions. In particular, it made clear that the actions organized by UK Uncut were not directed at the employees, but at the problematic practices of their employer (UK Uncut 2010a). The document also attempted to articulate a collective identity and common interests between the workers and the protesters.

Like UK Uncut, Occupy LSX produced 'offline' media. One example is *The Occupied Times of London,* a weekly print newspaper, first published one week after the occupation began. See Fig. 4.2 for an illustration of the front page of the first issue. The *Occupied Times* had an editorial team of 14, some of whom were active in Indymedia UK, plus volunteers from within the occupied spaces. Its 'newsroom' was a tent inside the St Paul's Cathedral camp, and the newspaper was started explicitely to contest mainstream media narrative about Occupy, and to be an independent voice for the Occupy movement (Vale 2011). Initially, the newspaper had a print run of around 2000 copies, distributed free to protesters, city employees and the general public. The paper aimed to reflect 'the movement, bringing together the wide range of voices of supporters as well as challenging the issues behind why we are all here' (co-editor Mircea Barbu quoted in press release: Occupy LSX 2011f). The content produced was serious in nature, which, according to Dave, a member of the media team, gave Occupy LSX:

> a certain degree of credibility as it allowed for really serious deep-digging journalism of the sort you do not even get in the Guardian. It was difficult to assess what impact it had, but it carried a quite high-level narrative. (personal interview, 10 October 2016)

[Logo: Vodafone]

Hello Vodafone employees! You're probably wondering why we're here, right?

Vodafone has been engaging in dodgy tax deals involving the acquisition of German company Mannesmann. They avoided paying a very large amount of tax to the British government. The taxman has eventually given in trying to force them to pay up. Big corporations are very good at avoiding tax - in fact they avoid about £12bn of it every year!

At the same time, the government tells the public that the only way to save money in the recession is by cutting things like education and welfare. Cutting public spending hits the poorest and most vulnerable in our society hardest. Reclaiming unpaid tax money from Vodafone and others like them would make over half of the government's planned spending cuts unnecessary.

We are not "all in it together": most taxpayers including both yourselves and those protesting here today are being punished, while the very wealthy get even richer. Like others protesting against Vodafone in cities across the country, our problem is with not with the workers. We are protesting solely against the company and the government, and do not aim to intimidate you in any way.

Fig. 4.1 UK Uncut 'ready to print' pamphlet directed at Vodaphone employees

To generate sufficient funds to cover the printing costs (about £600 per issue), the movement initially exploited the crowdfunding platform, Sponsume.com. Later, it solicited donations via *The Occupied Times of London* website. The paper continued to be published after the occupations at St Paul's Cathedral and Finsbury Square ended, though eventually it only appeared monthly. The most recent issue at the time of writing (August 2017) was dated March 2016 (OT26), but contributions have continued to be published on the *Occupied Times* website.

The Occupied Times
-OF LONDON-

#01 26OCT2011

HERE TO STAY

Stacey Knott

Anti-cuts activists in the heart of London remained defiant this week as Occupy London Stock Exchange nears its first fortnight in action - infrastructure and all.

An estimated 5000 people have passed through the sprawling camp on the steps of St Paul's Cathedral, with a resident population around 300.

The camp is part of a global movement against corporate greed and unregulated banking systems, subverting hierarchies and creating a space where people are encouraged to join - with a second, growing occupation established at Finsbury Square on Saturday.

It has been nearly two weeks since the initial chaotic scenes on October 15 when police kettled protesters, arresting eight on suspicion of police assault and public order offences.

Since then the camp has turned into a solid, peaceful working community - complete with kitchen, university, prayer room, waste management and power generation - and speakers at the camp's daily general assemblies have frequently voiced plans to stay "until Christmas."

German student Nikita Haag told the Occupied Times he planned to stay as long as the camp remained. "I'm going to stay here as long as it exists, the thing is going to exist until we reach some change," he said.

All work done at the camp is voluntary, with occupiers lending their support when needed.

Meanwhile food, clothing, equipment and monetary donations have flooded in; mostly gifted to the occupiers from people passing by.

One camper, Sean, told the Occupied Times he had put his experience as a civil servant to use in the information tent, a first point of call for many visitors - along with stints in the kitchen, tech tent and setting up Finsbury Square.

Since his arrival on the 15th he had seen the camp become more and more organised, he said: "We spent the first week getting the structure together - the working groups - and getting people used to our direct democracy."

The camp is founded on direct >>

Fig. 4.2 Front page of first edition of *The Occupied Times of London*, 26 October 2011

As these two print media examples make clear, in the activist world, print media can no longer be separated from the use of online platforms and websites. Alongside their print media, UK Uncut and Occupy LSX were active online, using websites and social media to push and disseminate their movement frames and discourses. As an Occupy activist of the social media team put it: 'new media are democratizing communication in a way that we have never seen before' (Maggie, personal interview, 17 October 2016). The three cases have their own web spaces, which enable them to communicate independently with sympathisers and anyone else interested in their aims, struggles and actions (see Table 4.2). All three websites offer the facility of donating money to the organization.

Clearly, social media has in recent years become more and more important in the dissemination strategies of activists; the UK Anti-Austerity movement has a relatively strong presence on Facebook and Twitter, the two social media platforms used most widely by activists.

During periods marked by a low intensity of direct action, social media continue to be used extensively to spread the word, to share information, to prepare for future direct action, to connect to other struggles, and to keep the contestatory fire burning among sympathisers and followers. In line with this activity, social media, such as Facebook and Twitter, are used extensively by the three organizations to express solidarity with other organizations and mobilizations, both locally and abroad. This is enabled by affordances of re-tweeting, hashtags or posting of individual tweets expressing solidarity.

Table 4.2 Overview of online presence

Case	*URL website*	*Facebook*	*Twitter*	*YouTube*
UK Uncut	http://www.ukuncut.org.uk/	158,400 likes	@UKuncut 96,000 followers 16,500 tweets	24 videos 69,000 views
Occupy LSX	http://occupylondon.org.uk/	137,800 likes	@OccupyLondon 65,000 followers 43,000 tweets	241 videos 134,000 views
NCAFC	http://anticuts.com/	10,600 likes	@NCAFC_UK 7400 followers 8700 tweets	No Official YouTube Page

Source: Facebook, Twitter and YouTube (Data gathered in August 2016)

For example, the NCAFC supporting the strikes in higher education for fair pay, and Occupy London supporting the UK branch of Black Lives Matter:

- Solidarity with the @UCU strike today! See you on the picket lines. #fairpayinHE (@NCAFC_UK, 25 May 2016)
- Black Woman Locked In Psych Ward For 8 Days Because Cops Couldn't Believe She's A Businesswoman #BlackLivesMatter (@ OccupyLSX, 22 July 2015)
- #BlackLivesMatter needs more Legal Observers, get involved attend this London @GBCLegal training, this Saturday (OccupyLSX re-tweeted, 16 April 2015)

Finally, it is important to understand that the use of social media from the perspective of disclosure, according to the activists, enables relatively small organizations effectively to punch above their weight. George, who was active in the NCAFC, pointed out that:

> Social media allows a small independent organisation to achieve great things without the support of strong formal structures, in our case the NUS [National Union of Students]. With the benefit of social media, the NCAFC could punch above its weight and it enabled it to become the lightning rod for people to join and to become engaged. (personal interview, 23 February 2017)

4.3.2 Mobilizing for Direct Action

As already discussed in Chap. 3, in the analysis of movement frames, the motivational/action frames of the anti-austerity movement are strong and very compelling. Direct action and the enactment of a set of semi-confrontational tactics were seen as being pivotal to a strategy of genuine social and political change needed to contest the status quo. It is argued that, in the absence of direct action and confrontation with the powers that be, nothing will change.

The websites of all three organizations are also used to recruit sympathisers and spur them to become active within the movement. The websites are used to mobilize for upcoming actions through the provision of detailed information. In the case, especially, of UK Uncut and Occupy LSX, resources were made available to sympathisers to allow them to organize their own, semi-independent direct actions. This included flyers, logos, posters, banners, suggestions and guidelines for the activists' use. On UK Uncut's website, prospective activists can watch a YouTube video explaining how to organize direct action.

The video describes the following six steps:

1. Choose a target (health service, libraries, education, etc.);
2. List the action on the UK Uncut website;
3. Spread the word both offline and online, call the local press with an email address to ask for advice on who to contact;
4. Get props like 'flyers, some posters or placards and a banner. Letters to workers explaining that they are not the target of the action can also be effective';
5. Know your rights with contact details of the legal team;
6. Turn up!; and
7. Report back to UN Uncut.

(http://www.ukuncut.org.uk/organising-an-action/)

Social media platforms such as Facebook and Twitter, have become instrumental in facilitating mobilization and are widely used to organize dispersed and unconnected activists for direct action. For example, UK Uncut uses Twitter extensively for this purpose. The flashmob or smart-mob tactic requires an online platform that directs often unconnected activists to very specific targets, or towards a particular offline space, after which time further details are communicated face-to-face.

Tina, a leading UK Uncut activist, denotes the creation of the hashtag '#ukuncut' as the start of UK Uncut, exposing the extent to which communication and mediation is positioned at the centre of the organization and its mobilization efforts (personal interview, 4 November 2015).

Also, for Occupy, there was a direct connection between their appropriation of new media tools and offline mobilization and, in particular, in the case of social media platforms such as Facebook and Twitter:

> Facebook played a crucial role in terms of events, talks, and information that needed to be circulated. (Dave, personal interview, 10 October 2016)
>
> There was also an inevitable link between our social media use and more conventional tactics such as direct action. We were Occupy, so we had to go occupy something out there, take on a bank, etc. Social media was instrumental in this (Maggie, personal interview, 17 October 2016)

The use of social media for mobilizing for direct action enables the activists engaged in direct action to connect with those that are not, and with sympathisers, which gives the more involved activists a boost. It makes those on the barricades feel they are supported by a large community, as student activist George makes apparent:

> The other thing about social media, is that even though there might only be as few as 100 people actively occupying a university room, you get the feeling of a much larger community being engaged through messaging, sharing and liking, so social media has this amplification effect as well, and through that you feel more powerful than you actually are. (personal interview, 23 February 2017)

This contradicts pessimistic accounts of online engagement as being inconsequential and a form of lazy participation which does not have any consequences in the so-called real world; we think here of the often mentioned notion of slacktivism (Morozov 2009).

4.3.3 The Performativity of Protest

It is not unreasonable to acknowledge that, in our screen and media obsessed societies, the importance of visibility and mediated resonance often induces a repertoire shift towards a set of protest tactics that activists deem will generate high media resonance while at the same time being an expression of the movement's frames. Direct actions represent a form of communication, a staged performance imbued with meaning. As such, the direct action tactics themselves become part of the self-mediation practices of the movement.

The performative protest tactics of the anti-austerity movement were varied and can be situated at each of the action logics identified by della Porta and Diani (2006)—numbers, damage and bearing witness to injustice. Despite being normalized and becoming increasingly 'less noticeable and newsworthy' (Dalton 1996: 71), mass demonstrations can still be spectacular and attract high levels of media attention today—for example, through mobilizing large numbers of people (logic of numbers). In particular, students enacted this repertoire of mass demonstrations against government plans to triple tuition fees.

Before the vote, which was held on 9 December 2010, several demonstrations took place, for which various student organizations mobilized.

The first major demonstration against the plans of the UK government took place on 10 November 2010 and was organized by the National Union of Students (NUS) using the slogan 'Fund Our Future: Stop Education Cuts'. It attracted some 50,000 students. The second demonstration, on 24 November 2010, and the third on 30 November 2010 were much smaller in size and were organized by the National Campaign Against Fees and Cuts (NCAFC), a more militant organization than the NUS.

The final demonstration took place on the day of the vote in Parliament—9 December 2010. There were actually two separate protest events taking place that day. While the NUS organized a serene candlelit vigil on Victoria Embankment close to Parliament, the University of London Union (ULU) and the NCAFC organized a rally that converged on Parliament Square. This 30,000-strong demonstration was very erratic, and police tactics heavy-handed and aggressive, using mounted horses at some point to charge into crowds, kettling protesters and thereby dispersing the protesters throughout central London.[1]

The second logic that della Porta and Diani (2006) identify—the logic of damage—was also very prevalent in the student protests, and to a lesser extent within UK Uncut, amounting mainly to the damage of symbolic property, clashes with police or the forceful occupation of shops, which adds up to a radical performance, or what Scalmer (2002: 60) called dissent events—'playing at revolution'.

During the first student demonstration on 10 November 2010, some 1500 to 2000 student protesters left the main demonstration and converged on the Conservative Party headquarters. They smashed windows and some 200 of them occupied the building, while many more held a peaceful vigil outside. At some point, Edward Woollard, a college student, threw a fire extinguisher from the roof of the building, almost striking a police officer. Woollard was later sentenced to two years and eight months imprisonment in a youth offender institution. During the subsequent student protests, damage was also part of the student protest repertoire; examples of this were the destruction of a police van, the spraying of slogans on monuments (see Fig. 4.3), the burning of a Christmas tree donated by Norway in Trafalgar Square, smashing of the windows of the Treasury (the ministry responsible for the budget), and vandalizing the Rolls-Royce of Prince Charles and Duchess Camilla on Regent Street while shouting slogans such as 'Off with their heads!'. As will be discussed

Fig. 4.3 Situationist May '68 Slogan in Parliament Square, London, 9 December 2010

in Chap. 5, the violence and these tactics of damage led to very negative mainstream media representations of the student protests, and ultimately to a split in the student movement between the NUS and more militant student organizations. It also elicited a high degree of police violence.

UK Uncut's smart mob tactics, targeting high street shops and banks, as discussed in the Introduction to this book, could also be positioned within a logic of damage, not necessarily through the destruction of property, but rather as disruptive actions preventing customers from entering business premises by occupying them. One such action that was deemed to be especially disruptive, and a watershed moment in terms of the media attention for UK Uncut, was the occupation of the luxury store Fortnum & Mason on 26 March 2011, during a massive anti-austerity protest organized by the Trade Union Congress (TUC). Almost 140 UK Uncut activists were arrested, and the store claimed it suffered more than £54,000 in lost sales (BBC 2012).

The final action logic identified by della Porta and Diani (2006) is the use of political gimmicks, dressing up, doing something out of the ordinary, which amounts to a logic of bearing witness to injustice. This was arguably the most prevalent protest logic within the anti-austerity movement. We could refer here to DeLuca's (1999: 3) notion of image politics or the staging of 'tactical image events'. Both UK Uncut and Occupy mobilized this direct action logic extensively.

The smart-mob tactics of UK Uncut targeted high street branches of mobile phone companies, retail brands and banks to visibilize their protest against the aggressive tax evasion strategies these companies deploy. In doing so, a protest spectacle was organized to raise awareness of these strategies, and cause reputational damage to these brands. As this repertoire developed further, it also became more performative. One example of this was the 'Emergency Operation', a direct action targeted at the UK government's cuts to, and its plans to reform—i.e. privatize, the National Health Service (NHS) (Quinn 2011). In 40 places across the country, protesters dressed as doctors and nurses enacted mock operations using fake blood outside as well as inside branches of popular banks. Around 100 activists also held a mock trial of the health secretary, Andrew Lansley, in Camden. This was clearly part of their mediation practices, as Tina from UK Uncut (personal interview, 4 November 2015) made clear:

> our actions are performative and media-oriented geared towards getting something across … Another important aspect in terms of a media strategy is to make sure that you continue to rejuvenate yourself in terms of the actions you organise, the media loves that. First we were occupying shops and then we moved on to the banks, then we were blocking things and then glueing ourselves to shop windows.

For Occupy London Stock Exchange (LSX), the initial plan was to converge on and occupy Paternoster Square, where the LSX is located, but a pre-emptive High Court injunction was put in place to prevent anybody from accessing the square. Instead, the protesters camped outside St Paul's Cathedral, near the LSX, and on Finsbury Square, north of 'The City', London's financial district. A month later, the activists also squatted an empty office building owned by the Swiss bank UBS, renaming it The Bank of Ideas (Walker and Owen 2011). All this was highly symbolic and performative, taking contestation to the spaces where injustice resides. As Maggie of Occupy pointed out:

> The actions of Occupy were tailored to visibilize injustice in the spaces where injustice is taking place and so just by being in the vicinity of the financial heart of London we created a media event. (personal interview, 17 October 2016)

4.4 The Logic of Examination and the Anti-Austerity Movement

The logic of examination relates to self-reflexivity and to the ability to adapt to changing circumstances. The logic of examination is an important aspect of self-mediation, which is often ignored. The dynamic context of the political, the various ways in which elites and citizens react to the actions of social movements and those active within them, requires reflexivity on the part of the activists, and a continuous comparison between 'what was done' and 'what should have been done'. In other words, the activists need to be introspective and agile in the face of ever-changing circumstances. As McAdam et al. (2001: 56) observe:

> participants in contentious politics constantly manipulate, strategize, modify and reinterpret the identities of parties to their contention, including themselves.

The logic of examination is clearly more inwardly oriented, relying on both asynchronous and real-time self-mediation practices. Nevertheless, although the logic of examination is mediated, it can and often does take place face-to-face rather than being mediated. At the same time, communication tools also play an increasingly central role in enabling internal communication, coordinating direct actions, and in the decision making processes within a movement.

4.4.1 Internal Communication

The smartphone has become almost a necessity for internal communication, via text messages and phone calls to discuss issues and resolve problems. Maggie from Occupy pointed out that 'mobile phones played a very important role in terms of internal communication between ourselves' (personal interview, 17 October 2016). The mediation of internal communication through mobile technologies was essential, because not everyone could be in the camp at all times. In addition to the camp at St Paul's Cathedral, there were other contentious sites, such as The Bank of Ideas in Hackney, and the Finsbury Square camp. Mobile communication was essential to coordinate between and bridge these different sites, as Dave pointed out:

> on the ground and in the camp telephone numbers were exchanged a lot and there was a lot of use of smartphones to coordinate and talk amongst

> ourselves, especially because not everybody was in the camp 24/7; for example, many people had jobs to go to during the day or were active in other places such as The Bank of Ideas. (personal interview, 10 October 2016)

However, activists were acutely aware of the dangers inherent to the use of mobile communication: 'We were also aware that police might be monitoring us,' Maggie told me (personal interview, 17 October 2016). This emphasized the need to secure internal communication, as highlighted by Tina from UK Uncut:

> When we were having an online discussion as a group we used a secure site, we used ToR software, so that the police could not hack that, which is cool. (personal interview, 4 November 2015)

The knowledge that communication technologies were not completely secure had led to more face-to-face meetings, where issues could be discussed with mobiles switched off and SIM cards removed. Maggie from Occupy LSX recalled that:

> We were also very cautious when it came to mobile phones. There were many times that we met face-to-face and everybody had to switch off all phones; we were especially suspicious of the Apple iPhone in terms of surveillance. (personal interview, 17 October 2016)

There was certainly an awareness among the activists that surveillance was in place, to which George alluded: 'There was definitely a consciousness of the fact that electronic communication could be monitored' (personal interview, 23 February 2017), and steps were taken to secure internal communication and the movement's website. At the same time, they did not let this awareness impede their direct action, as Dave from Occupy LSX illustrates:

> while being mindful [of police surveillance] is sensible when you do activism, this cannot be a barrier to act or impede you to do things. So despite this context of surveillance you just get on with things. (personal interview, 10 October 2016)

4.4.2 Coordinating Direct Action

Mediation enabled not just mobilization, but also on-the-spot coordination of direct action. Use of certain platforms that enable instant real-time communication among protesters or between an organization's leaders and sympathisers has increased. Twitter, as a platform enabling real-time communication, is a useful tool in this respect; UK Uncut exploits Twitter heavily to coordinate its direct action and inform protesters. The role of Twitter was so pivotal that it was even used to provide protest training aimed to 'showcase [tactics and strategies] best-suited to our urban environment' (UK Uncut Brighton 2011: np).

An example here is the protest action with the hashtag #ResignCameron that occurred in the wake of publication of the Panama Papers, exposing massive tax dodging by rich individuals, including the father of Prime Minister David Cameron. During the protest, UK Uncut sent out several tweets telling protesters the location of successive waves of the protest, to allow the activist twitterati to join the protest at a convenient point:

- Hundreds of people already at Downing St demanding that @David_Cameron resign because of his links to tax dodging
- Panama protest at Downing St. Come on down. #ResignCameron #closetaxloopholes
- If you're late to the #resigncameron #closetaxloopholes protest we're coming up to Trafalgar Square so join there!
- The #ResignDavidCameron #closetaxloopholes protest now moving east down the Strand!
- The #ResignDavidCameron #closetaxloopholes protest now outside Conservative spring forum on Great Queen Street!
- People heading back to Downing St #ResignDavidCameron
- #ResignCameron demonstration still going strong. If you're in London, get on down to Downing St.

(@UKuncut, 9 April 2016)

In addition to Twitter, text messaging on mobile phones is a well-used means of coordinating direct action and facilitating quick internal communication. It is used in particular if activists do not want information about an upcoming action to be in the public domain prior to it actual happening:

> We had a phone tree through which we could reach people fast and in a direct way, which was especially useful in terms of internal communication. When we were worried about security or police being nearby, you could send out a message to everyone. (George, personal interview, 23 February 2017)

I had a text-list of everyone who was either a supporter of direct action or who was part of the direct action working group. We would contact them prior to an action, to alert them or to ask them to get in touch with others. (Maggie, personal interview, 17 October 2016)

During direct action, online platforms were used for on-the-spot and real-time coordination. During the student protests, Google Maps was used to counter the police tactic of kettling, which was used to isolate and contain groups of protesters (see Fig. 4.4). Exploiting the power of the crowd, protesters uploaded and permanently updated police positions on a Google Maps page, which was accessible to other protesters with smartphones, enabling them to change tactics and avoid being kettled by the police. This allowed 'roving' protests, involving relatively small groups of protesters, to move through the streets of central London in an agile and flexible manner (BBC 2010).

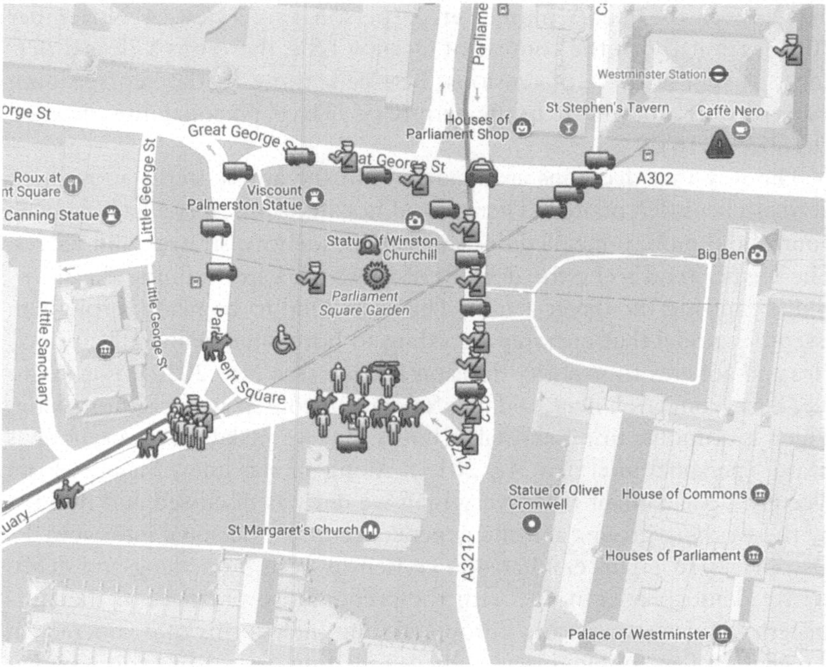

Fig. 4.4 The use of Google Maps by student protesters to avoid being kettled by the police (November 2011)

Nevertheless, George questioned whether this use of Google Maps was really extensive or rather a gimmick to show what was possible technologically:

> This worked to a variable extent, it was very much in its infancy and a prototype. It was a cool thing, but also somewhat gimmicky; I don't know if it had that much practical use on the ground at the time. (personal interview, 23 February 2017)

4.4.3 Internal Decision Making

Whereas there is certainly an ethos of horizontality and democratic decision making attached to all the cases in this study, the popular idea of a 'leaderless' organization is fallacious. Tina, from UK Uncut, clarified that 'a leaderless movement does not exist, there are always people that are organizing, that answer the emails, that do the twitter and the Gmail, that answer the media phone, etc.' (personal interview, 4 November 2015). Similarly, in the context of Occupy LSX, there was a clear difference, as well as a set of tensions, between 'those in the centre doing loads of stuff' and those 'in the periphery' (Dave, personal interview, 10 October 2016).

The way that decisions are made within the anti-austerity movement needs to be differentiated. There are ad hoc decisions, made daily or even hourly, and more principled decisions about identity, strategy and tactics. The former tend to be the domain of those who are 'running the show' and organizing the direct action. The latter tend to be made through an assembly model that operates according to horizontal deliberative principles and adheres to majority decision making (see Nez 2012). For example, Tina, from UK Uncut, said they 'operate by consensus decision-making, which is arduous, tiring and takes hours, but we make sure everybody is heard' (personal interview, 4 /2015). Along similar lines, Maggie, from Occupy, was adamant that 'everything we did was discussed and decided by the working groups and the general assembly' (personal interview, 17 October 2016). This emphasis on consensus decision making and deliberative democracy is in line with the prefigurative practices of the anti-austerity movements across Europe, placing 'new forms of democracy in the centre of the public space' and even inviting passers-by to join in and to participate (Romanos 2013: 211).

However, this form of decision-making is not problem-free. According to Dave, from Occupy LSX, decision-making by consensus 'tends to lead to conservative decisions', and this, he argued, 'compromised [Occupy's] flexibility' (personal interview, 10 October 2016). Similarly, George, from NCAFC, pointed to the massive effort that was put into face-to-face decision making by consensus, but said that 'there were, of course, also tensions with that' (personal interview, 23 February 2017). The discourse of horizontalism and non-hierarchical structures runs counter, also, to practical issues related to organization, exclusion and the emergence of informal systems of authority, as acknowledged by an Occupy LSX activist (quoted in Deel and Murray-Leach 2015: 187–88):

> Anyone that pretends Occupy is a completely leaderless movement is just denying reality. There's a core group of maybe 20 people, maybe 30 people that are basically coordinating the work that's happening: facilitating amongst working groups outside of the open forum process—background work.

While general assemblies took place offline, mediation was required to satisfy the need for transparency of the process and to communicate the consensus decisions being made by the assembly, to those unable to be present in person. In the case of Occupy, online spaces were used to complement the offline decision making. The general assemblies were broadcast live, and, at times, those watching the stream would be 'given the opportunity to participate remotely by asking questions or making comments' (Kavada 2015: 880). Often transparency was achieved by decisions being reported on movement websites. However, decisions made during the NCAFC general assembly, held on 12 June 2016 in Edinburgh, were tweeted, albeit in a succinct way:

- Motion 2 passed. Now discussing motion 3: NSS [National Student Survey] sabotage. #NCAFCconf
- Debating amendments to motion 3. #NCAFCconf
- Motion 3 passes as amended. #NCAFCconf

…

- A minute of silence for the victims of the attack in Orlando. #NCAFCconf

- Closing remarks from @Deborah_Malina: 'go back to your campuses, build activist groups. I'm excited to continue the fight!' #NCAFCconf (@NCAFC_UK, 12 June 2016)

Occupy LSX had a policy of transparency for general assemblies and had begun to stream them live; for example, their Radical General Assembly, called the Brick Lane Debates, held on 14 May 2015 after the general election which gave David Cameron an overall majority ushering in an all-Tory government, were streamed and the video recordings of these debates were also made accessible by the Occupy News Network,[2] through bambuser.[3] Thus it was not only a real-time communication but it could also be viewed asynchronically. Inevitably, this implicates a logic of remembrance, which is the focus of the next section.

4.5 The Logic of Remembrance and the Anti-Austerity Movement

The logic of remembrance is of particular importance in a consideration of social movements and contentious politics. Social movements do not reinvent the wheel continuously; they build on and learn from ideas and tactics developed by other movements, and from activists who join the movement bringing experience from other movements. Dave referred frequently during his interview to this bringing of experience : 'from experiences prior to Occupy, I knew that' (personal interview, 10 October /2016) and George, who was active in the NCAFC, spoke repeatedly of the 'activist milieu' of which he was a part (personal interview, 23 February 2107). Thus activists are frequently involved in inventive imitation or in a 'fruitful interference of repetitions', as Tarde (1903: 382) put it.

Communication and mediation in terms of remembrance are significant for what is called movement spill-over, describing the process involving the transfer of ideas, symbols and tactics of contention from one movement to another (Meyer and Whittier 1994). The material and potentially permanent nature of protest artefacts enables their embedded symbols and discourses to circulate and be transmitted culturally on a long-term basis, feeding future struggles and effectively building what can be called epistemic communities (Lipschutz 2005; Johnston 2009). Referring to the work of Halbwachs (1980 [1950]) on collective memory,

Daphi (2013: 160) argues that '[m]emory provides ways for group members to understand the world, particularly in the sense of defining the group as an entity'. She also states that 'a collective memory determines which experiences are shared, and it places these experiences in a meaningful order' (ibid.).

The logic of remembrance requires outwardly-oriented self-mediation practices, which need to be asynchronous and thus enable the produced and archived protest artefacts to travel across space and time. In terms of self-mediation practices, the logic of remembrance refers to: (1) the production of protest artefacts (increasingly facilitated by mobile technologies); (2) the long-term archiving of these protest artefacts; and remembrance also has relevance for (3) the documenting of police violence.

4.5.1 *Producing Protest Artefacts*

An important aspect of any struggle is the production of protest artefacts that symbolize the movement's frames, are reproducible, and can subsequently circulate through time and space. An example is the role of protest songs in the Labour and anti-war movements, the iconic image of Che Guevara, and the more recent ubiquity of Guy Fawkes masks in protests across the world. Protest artefacts play an important role in the mobilization efforts of social movements, especially those with diffuse goals and complex identities. These artefacts tend to 'represent the ideologies and injustices that animate their production, and the collective action frames that develop' (Johnston 2014: 75).

Important protest artefacts are the logos produced to represent the organization or mobilization. Figure 4.5 depicts the logos of the three cases analysed in this book. The UK Uncut logo is simple and direct; it

Fig. 4.5 Logos of the three cases

resembles a traffic sign showing a pair of scissors, representing the cuts, which the organization contests. The NCAFC logo is imaginative and symbolic in using a reversed pound sign to replace the F in NCAFC.

Occupy's logo looks the most professional, because it is the work of professional designers sympathetic to the Occupy movement. It was the work of the group that created the design for *The Occupied Times*. In an interview, one of the designers stated that:

> Protest collectives are often limited in terms of their communications ... graphic design is a way to ...present the cause in a better way and make it more approachable to different people. (Rallis, quoted in Sinclair 2012)

In addition to logos, the visual self-representations of protest and direct action play a crucial role for protest movements. The embedding of high quality photo cameras in mobile phones has facilitated the production of photographic self-representations by activists:

> You have got to think Instagram, think image, think how you are going to communicate, and experiment with the medium. (Maggie, 17 October 2016)

The production of slogans that encapsulate the movement frames are significant in this regard. According to Maggie, 'the key thing that Occupy did was set the paradigm of the 99% versus the 1%, that was the most important thing it did' (personal interview, 17 October 2016). Dave agreed, but was less convinced that the idea of the 99% was a viable one:

> Details fade, but the idea of the 1% has persisted. People framing themselves as part of the 99% works less well. It is very difficult to achieve in an 'aspirational' context. The metaphor of the 99% aggregates too many different people with too many disparate interests. (personal interview, 10 October 2016)

4.5.2 *Archiving Protest Artefacts*

Among the most important protest artefacts are photographic self-representations of the movement by individuals in the movement. Dave discussed this in the context of Occupy:

> The ability of positive self-representation is massive. These new communication tools enable activists to provide evidence of what is really taking place, which constitute an empowerment of activists. (personal interview, 10 October 2016)

For some of the cases, their organizational websites serve as repositories of protest artefacts (see Table 4.3). Occupy LSX has several photos and videos stored on its website; similarly, UK Uncut has a gallery with photographic self-representation. The NCAFC does not have a specific section on its website for photographs and videos, but it makes extensive use of social media (mainly Facebook and Twitter) to disseminate visual self-representations. UK Uncut and Occupy LSX also have a large number of photos on their social media pages.

Wikimedia contains about 70 photos of Occupy LSX, but UK Uncut and the NCAFC are much less visible there, with only a couple of photos archived. However, Wikimedia has many photos of the student and anti-austerity protests that are not linked or tagged to UK Uncut or NCAFC.

In addition, ordinary citizens and activists in their personal capacities, and media organizations, post myriad images and videos online. Keying 'UK Uncut', 'Occupy London'/ 'Occupy LSX' or 'NCAFC' into a search engine results in huge numbers of visual representations of the movements. For example, for UK Uncut, Google finds almost 16,000 videos, and 22,500 for Occupy LSX. Again, NCAFC is the least visible, with 2100 videos.

Mediated self-representations by activists are relevant not only to inspire future movements but also to serve as reminders that injustices persist, according to Dave:

> The digital footprint of Occupy not only potentially inspires future movements, but it is also a mirror and reminds people that the injustices which we see today were already flagged up and discussed five years ago. (personal interview, 10 October 2016)

Table 4.3 Number of photos and videos stored online

Case	*Website*	*Facebook*	*Twitter*	*Wikimedia*
UK Uncut	56	1190	1401	5
Occupy LSX	321	5791	5663	70
NCAFC	0	809	672	3

Source: Websites, Facebook, Twitter and Wikimedia (data gathered in August 2016)

4.5.3 *Documenting Police Violence*

There is a particular form of mediated remembrance worthy of being highlighted here. It does not concern activists' self-representations, but focuses the camera on the state—and more specifically on the police. It is a very focused mediated tactic, which has been termed sousveillance, or reverse surveillance. The pervasiveness of protesters with handheld cameras has led to what Mathiesen (1997) called a synoptic viewer society—the many watching the few. This is used by activists as a counter-tactic to expose police violence. YouTube carried the postings of numerous protesters and bystanders showing their visual narratives of police brutality witnessed during the student protests. George told me that:

> Having mobile phones around that can film was in some cases quite useful in terms of documenting things that were done by the police. This was especially the case in the context of trials against protesters for violent disorder, having that kind of counter-media in view of mounting a defence was important. (personal interview, 23 February 2017)

The video on You Tube of a student protester, Jodie McIntyre, being pulled out of his wheelchair and dragged across the road was viewed over 133,000 times.[4] This was one of many videos documenting police violence during the student protests. A YouTube clip of protesters being charged by mounted police armed with truncheons was viewed over 611,000 times.[5] About a year after the vote to triple tuition fees, another video exposed police use of *agents provocateurs* during a march organized by the NCAFC to contest and commemorate the government decision; the video received just short of 17,000 viewings.[6] Similarly, a video clip showing police violence against Occupy protesters who converged on Parliament Square after a trade-union-organized protest, had become the most popular clip on the YouTube page of Occupy London, with 18,000 views (audience data in this paragraph gathered in February 2017).[7]

This documenting of police violence through the tactic of sousveillance is important because it is also picked up by the mainstream media, which sources the videos, embeds them in their news websites and reports on the incidents (cf. Chap. 5). However, as Dave from Occupy LSX stressed, while the internet 'creates new opportunities for dissident forces', we should never forget that it 'is also a very potent propaganda tool for the powerful and that they will always be better positioned to manipulate and limit the impact of these technologies' (personal interview, 10 October 2016).

4.6 Conclusions

In this chapter, the self-mediation practices of the anti-austerity movement were analysed, using as a framework Foucault's Stoic Technologies of the Self—disclosure, examination, and remembrance. At the level of disclosure, more public and asynchronous self-mediation practices can be observed. Activists used print media as well as the internet to communicate their movement frames independently, and to mobilize sympathisers for their direct action. Furthermore, activists also carried out protests with the intention of attracting media resonance. This was done through the spectacle of numbers, through inflicting damage and disruption, or through the tactic of bearing witness to injustice.

The logic of examination invokes more private and real-time self-mediation practices, geared towards communication within the movement and coordination of direct action. At this level, social media were important, in particular mobile phones and text messaging along with applications such as Google Maps. While decision making took place largely offline during general assemblies, characterized by consensus building, some degree of mediation could be observed, particularly for ad hoc decisions by the core activists, and to achieve transparency for those unable to attend meetings in person.

In relation to the logic of remembrance, asynchronicity is important, and public forms of communication are more relevant than private ones. Anti-austerity protesters produced a wide range of what could be called protest artefacts, such as logos and positive self-representations of protest, which subsequently were stored and archived on various online platforms, allowing them to be accessible publicly in the future. In addition, mobile phones in the hands of activists proved to be potent in documenting police violence.

The concept of the technologies of self-mediation also invokes a reflection on the relation between agency and structure, about the productive nature of power and the need to see self-mediation practices as both shaping and constraining action and imagination. They are implicated as much in the production of practices and empowerment as in the practices of domination and restrictive power. This interplay is particularly salient in the context of social movements and contestation, where structural limitations and the drive for agency are overly prevalent.

In this chapter, the awareness of surveillance practices and the need to protect activist identities has been mentioned, but the dialectic between mediation practices aimed at self-mediation and structural domination will be addressed in more detail in the final chapter of the book, Chap. 7,which focuses, among other things, on the nature of the mediation opportunity structure in the Circuit of Protest.

Notes

1. Kettling is a tactic used by police forces to control crowds by containing or corralling them in an enclosed space and preventing anyone from leaving the corral.
2. See URL: http://occupylondon.org.uk/brick-lane-debates-radical-general-assembly/.
3. bambuser.com is a Swedish live-streaming platform popular among activists because it enables the live streaming, from a laptop or mobile phone, of direct action and meetings. The broadcasts are also recorded and archived for viewing after the event.
4. https://www.youtube.com/watch?v=OUHzSQgayXY, 9 December 2010.
5. https://www.youtube.com/watch?v=jz0Z5_h_CtY, 25 December 2010.
6. https://www.youtube.com/watch?v=OUHzSQgayXY, 9 November 2011.
7. https://www.youtube.com/watch?v=3Nb1J8JsR3w, 19 October 2014.

CHAPTER 5

The Media Representation of the Anti-Austerity Movement

In this chapter, the moment of *representation* in the Circuit of Protest is addressed in more detail. Representation, unlike self-mediation, is practised by political actors outside of the movement. While undoubtedly the self-mediation practices of activists and movements play an important role, and arguably have become easier and more widespread thanks to the internet, mobile technologies and social media, it would be wrong to downplay the importance of representation by others. More than two decades ago, Gamson and Wolfsfeld (1993) described social movements and mainstream media as 'interacting systems', and, more recently, Rucht (2013: 262) argued that, despite the emergence and increased importance of the internet, '[t]o reach the public at large, the key channel was and is getting access to and coverage by the established media'. Their importance is also acknowledged, by activists themselves through their various attempts to manage journalists and influence their own media representations positively.

This is, however, not easy to achieve, as media production is shaped by a set of routines and news values. These are dependent in part on the structural and technological attributes of the medium and the media genre (print, radio, TV), but there are also a set of journalistic practices that transcend the medium and shape the ways that political agents are represented, and journalists select news and construct a news narrative (see Galtung and Ruge 1965; Ryan 1991). For example, journalists have a tendency to focus more on spectacular events, on novelty, or to give

B. Cammaerts, *The Circulation of Anti-Austerity Protest*,
https://doi.org/10.1007/978-3-319-70123-3_5

experts and elite spokespersons more voice than is given to ordinary citizens or, indeed, protesters.

In addition, there is ample evidence of ideological bias against protest and activism in the mainstream media (Halloran et al. 1970; Gitlin 1980; Smith et al. 2001). Journalistic routines, the attribution of news values, and ideological biases have given rise to what is commonly called a *protest paradigm*, governing and shaping the reporting of direct action and political contention (McLeod and Hertog 1999), and this is complemented by another paradigm that puts great emphasis on the public nuisance caused by protests (Di Cicco 2010).

I first present an overview of the literature on the relationship between media and protest. I also address the ways in which activists try to manage journalists. This is followed by the results of two content analyses—one focused on the media representations of the 2010 student protests against the tripling of higher education tuition fees, in which NCAFC played a pivotal role,[1] and the other on the ways in which UK Uncut and Occupy LSX were represented.

5.1 Mainstream Media Representations of Protest

In liberal theories of the press, mainstream media and journalists are required not only to be an independent power in a democratic society but also to act as the *fourth estate,* as the watchdog over powerful interests in society (Siebert et al. 1956). As such, early journalistic mores were oriented to critiquing, controlling, and scrutinizing the ruling elites, and protecting the public from potential—or rather, inevitable—abuses of power (Boyce 1978). Thus journalists were seen as the guardians of democracy and defenders of the public interest—the good guys. Famous investigative stories, such as Watergate and the Pentagon papers, exemplify this benign view. Such examples feed our expectations that the media and journalists, above all, should be socially responsible actors in a democratic society, not only critical of the powers that be, but also responsive to dissensus and contestation in democracy (Curran 2005: 138).

5.1.1 The Media as a Guard Dog

Despite many examples of good journalism, fulfilling these normative roles and expectations has been somewhat problematic and rife with tensions. A 'free' media is mainly a commercial—some would say, a capitalist—media, owned by a powerful oligarchy, which is part of and partial to the economic and political elites of the demos. In this regard, Keane (1991: 97; emphasis in original) observed that:

> *communications markets restrict freedom of communication* by generating barriers to entry, monopoly and restrictions upon choice, and by shifting the prevailing definition of information from that of a public good to that of a privately appropriable commodity.

This is not a new phenomenon; from the outset, the liberal media catered mainly to the interests of a very specific class, the growing bourgeoisie, and served to protect the status quo (Habermas 1989; Conboy 2004). This led some to claim that journalists are not watchdogs that control the powers that be, but rather lapdogs subservient to those powers they should be controlling (Herman and Chomsky 1988). Along the same lines, Donohue et al. (1995) argued that the metaphor of a guard dog is more accurate than that of a lapdog because journalists are not invariably dependent, uncritical and obedient, as implied by the two examples of investigative journalism cited above. Donohue et al. (1995) conclude that while journalists are the sentries of the prevailing power structures in society, they are also often critical, but mainly if an individual acts against core system values (as in cases of corruption and deceit, for example).

To extend the metaphor, given that journalists tend to guard the systemic status quo, they can become attack dogs if the actors challenge the status quo and endanger their masters. Therefore protest movements—especially anti-systemic and disruptive ones—traditionally have experienced great difficulties in achieving positive media resonance. At the same time, the overall negative portrayal of protest is the result not only of an ideological bias against protest movements but also, in part, caused by the journalistic routines and conventions guiding and shaping mainstream media representations of ‘the day’s events’, as argued in Halloran et al. (1970).

In this early study of the representation of protest by UK media, Halloran and his colleagues noticed that news routines and the criteria regulating news values and newsworthiness, as outlined in Galtung and Ruge (1965), influenced heavily the coverage of protesters and protest events. Galtung and Ruge found that proximity, scale of the event, clarity, elite opinion, personification, negativity, exceptionality, amplitude, etc. had a huge impact on the nature of the news coverage. They concluded that mainstream media tend to focus on events, not processes, emphasize effects more than causes, and thrive on conflict rather than on consensus; in other words, good news is no news. Furthermore, and highly relevant for activism and contestation:

> News routines are micro-structures which, when woven together, create media opportunities for government and corporate insiders. Simultaneously, news routines profoundly limit challenger access to the media. (Ryan 1991: 141)

To a large extent, Galtung and Ruge's work still holds in the current, and, arguably, much more complex and highly saturated, media environment.

5.1.2 The Protest and Nuisance Paradigms

The reporting of protest is often shaped by a dynamic combination of ideological animosity, journalistic routines and the attribution of news values. As mentioned briefly above, some argue in this regard that we can discern a *protest paradigm* in the reporting of dissensus. McLeod and Hertog (1999: 310) speak of a 'routinised pattern or implicit template for the coverage of social protest'. This template consists of the following main characteristics:

- highlighting the spectacular, the drama, and violence;
- emphasizing the deviance of the protesters;
- focusing on the confrontations between protesters and police;
- favouring official sources and police over and above the voice of protesters; and
- using a language that delegitimates, marginalizes and demonizes protest and protesters.

Common to the representation of protesters and protest events are both description and selection biases, which tend to operate in conjunction with one another. In the case of selection bias, the media and journalists fulfil a gatekeeping function, they decide whether and to what extent visibility and voice are given to protesters, which is related somewhat to the earlier discussions regarding media access and news values (Gamson and Meyer 1996; Koopmans 2004: 373). Regarding description bias, the way in which the protesters are given a voice matters. So, even if a social movement manages to attract media attention, which is not easy to achieve, 'this attention tends not to serve the interests of the movement in promoting public awareness and understanding of the issues about which they are protesting' (Smith et al. 2001: 1417).

This, in turn, can be related to the ideological animosity that usually prevails in the context of anti-systemic resistance. It could be claimed that, often, social movements and media are engaged in a framing war. Gitlin (1980: 27), for example, found that protesters and their aims tended to be 'trivialized, polarized, marginalized and disparaged' by the mainstream media. Along the same lines, Murdock (1981: 210) concluded that mainstream media are set on depicting protesters as criminals so as to rob the protest of its 'radical political content', thereby making it possible to neglect the 'underlying causes' of the protest completely.

The media also tends to invoke moral panics by demonizing protesters and presenting them as folk devils (Cohen 1972). The depiction of anti-systemic protesters as the new folk devils serves to silence oppositional voices, as well as de-individualize them by symbolizing them as thugs, as a mob. This in turn prevents large sections of the population from identifying with them. As Donson et al. (2004: 26) point out in their study of anti-capitalist protests in the UK:

> By removing the identity of the individuals and focussing on the group as 'anarchists' and 'thugs' they become associated with the violence that the media chooses to focus upon, not the message their activism seeks to advance.

In recent years, we can also observe that journalists are increasingly depicting protests as being irrelevant and as an annoying nuisance. Di Cicco (2010: 136) describes this as the public nuisance paradigm whereby journalists highlight 'the annoyances and inconveniences perceived to be caused by protests'. The protest paradigm and the public nuisance paradigm overlap to a degree, but the latter indicates 'a more negative view of protest in general through an emphasis on perceived bothersome effects that, to some extent, inhere in protest as a tactic' (ibid.). An example in a UK context is the consistently negative way that strikes and unions are reported (Philo 1995).

As Shoemaker (1984) and Boyle et al. (2012) point out, the nature of the protesters' aims influences the media representation of protests. The more radical the demands and the more anti-systemic the movement, the more negative the media representation tends to be. Similarly, the degree to which certain protest tactics are considered deviant and disruptive has a huge impact on whether the protest and the public nuisance paradigm are triggered.

Indeed, we also need to acknowledge instances of consonance between social movements and mainstream media; there are many cases to which the protest paradigm is not applicable or breaks down over time (Hallin 1986; van Zoonen 1992; Cottle 2008; Cammaerts and Carpentier 2009). First, 'the media' is not a monolithic actor; media, and in particular newspapers, tend to have distinct ideological positions and editorial lines. Second, Hallin (1986) makes us aware of the role of elite opinion concerning the issue a movement wants to raise or address. Hallin observes that it was only when the consensus within the political and economic elites regarding the Vietnam war began to break down that the media started to adopt a more critical stance towards the war, and to take a more conciliatory tone towards the anti-war movement. This demonstrates the important part played by elite dynamics and temporality on the way that the media report on social movements and their frames (Bennett 1990). Finally, the nature of the issue also matters. There are issues that generate more or less controversy; some mobilizations challenge the status quo more directly than others. All of these aspects affect the extent of, or potential for, media consonance or dissonance.

5.1.3 Managing Visibility

In reaction to the protest and public nuisance paradigms, activists developed a range of strategies to deal with mainstream media and as part of their 'struggle for public visibility', in order to increase their media resonance (Rucht 2004: 27). Rucht spoke in this regard of the Quadruple A—Abstention, Attack, Adaptation, and Alternatives—as main strategies to deal with this negative and biased media attention. The strategy of developing alternatives to bypass mainstream media was discussed in the previous chapter. In view of today's hyper-mediated environment, however, it appears that total abstention is no longer a viable strategy for activists. Back in the 1990s Ryan (1991: 217) wrote that 'challengers pay a high price for their invisibility in mainstream media', and this price has only increased since. An attack strategy would refer to the voicing of both implicit and explicit critiques towards the mainstream media and the interests they protect, which frequently still occurs; many activists will, for example, refer to the work of

Chomsky and the propaganda model, using words such as 'flak'. Adaptation, finally, relates to strategies of activists that cater to the media routines and values, and provide journalists with what they want and need to write their stories; this is a strategy that has been fully embraced by many contemporary activists, including those under consideration in this book.

Activists are increasingly aware and knowledgeable about the production process of media content expressed through 'the complexity of the linkages between source activity, public attitudes, media agenda and the political domain' (Anderson 1993: 55), which requires prior knowledge and expertise in journalistic routines and news values (Ryan 1991). We can observe, in this regard, an increased media awareness and lay knowledge among activists, but also an awareness that mainstream media matter (see, also, McCurdy 2012). As Dave from Occupy LSX explained:

> I think that the mainstream media is just as, if not more, relevant than social media. After all, the information that circulates online is predominantly produced by the mainstream media. As activists we underestimate, at our peril, the influence and dominance of the mainstream media on people's opinions and political views. (personal interview, 10 October 2016)

A focus on the relational also implicates internal debates about how to relate to and deal with 'the media', especially journalists (Anderson 2003; McCurdy 2010). In many cases, activists will position journalists as the enemy, as part of the problem (cf. the attack strategy). At the same time, we can also observe an acknowledgement among activists that not all journalists are disagreeable. Activists establish personal relationships with journalists as part of their media strategy, but they often distinguish between good and bad journalists, as Tina from UK Uncut and student activist George point out:

> We made a point of establishing a personal connection with a selected number of journalists that know us and that we can trust, we don't bother talking to someone else. Over time we established a bond with about 20 to 30 journalists that we phone when we are planning an action. We also meet up with them to have coffee and chitchat. (Tina, personal interview, 04 November 2015)

> There was also a difference between journalists who were seen to be more sympathetic towards the movement, people like Paul Mason, for example, and those who weren't. The former got a more open access, as we could trust that they would be fair and respect confidentiality. (George, personal interview, 23 February 2017)

Increasingly, radical protest coalitions are becoming aware of the need to cope with and manage the media, to have spokespersons, issue statements, concede interviews, grant access to journalists, etc. This is confirmed by Birks and Downey (2015: 175), who found that UK Uncut relied heavily on the 'experience of working with the media in NGOs and previous activism to appeal to dominant news values'. We can observe similar experience within Occupy LSX, where a media team was set up 'to deal with' media attention:

> I was very impressed with how we organized our external communication. It was a small media team, but they played the media establishment game really well. There were a few people that were really good at getting key messages across. (Dave, 10 October 2016)

One of the practices common to the management of visibility is the monitoring of mainstream media representations, linked to instant rebuttal strategies, at times leading also to activists confronting journalists about their negative framing of the movement:

> Our press team was not only running our own social media operation, but they were also monitoring and tracking impact and media references. That was then subsequently fed back to the different general meetings. Journalists that would be unfairly critical were at times confronted through Twitter. (George, personal interview, 23 February 2017)

In line with the adaptation strategies outlined by Rucht (2004), activists are becoming increasingly media-savvy in relation to crafting their actions, imagery and messages to fit media routines and news values. Dave, from Occupy LSX, stated that they received media training in the camp, and that he adopted a different kind of language when speaking to the media:

> There was also an element of learning involved as I noticed myself playing the game more further down the line, I started to use muted language that made you sound more serious and is much more in tune with the media discourse. So suddenly, I would be saying things like: 'We, as a movement, have deep concerns about' instead of shouting 'it is absolutely outrageous that this is happening'. (personal interview, 10 October 2016)

Similarly, George, who was active in the NCAFC, referred to media training sessions being given to the student protesters:

We had a few people around who had been involved in political press offices before so they gave some basic training for the people that got involved in the media relations working group. (personal interview, 23 February 2017)

Let us now examine to what extent these strategies to manage the mainstream media attention that activists crave and need were successful in the context of the UK's anti-austerity movement.

5.2 Mainstream Media's Representation of the Anti-Austerity Movement

This section presents the results of two content analyses of media representation of the anti-austerity movement in the UK media. One codes media representations of a few student protests against the rise in tuition fees announced in November/December 2010, in which the NCAFC played a pivotal role. The other codes the media representations of UK Uncut and Occupy LSX over a longer period, from January 2011 to August 2012.

The sampling for the first content analysis was exhaustive and included all the articles published on the student protests in four newspapers, between 11 November and 23 December 2010. It resulted in a total of 334 pieces, including news articles, interviews, editorials, and commentary pieces. A trained second coder coded a 10% sample of the articles; this yielded intercoder reliability of >80% for all the variables.[2] Reliability greater than 80 per cent is considered to be high, and indicates a well-defined coding scheme and a robust sampling validity that can stand the test of being replicated (Bauer 2007; Krippendorff 2013).

The second content analysis, focusing on representations of UK Uncut and Occupy LSX, spanned the respective periods January 2011 to August 2012, and September 2011 to August 2012. The justification for the longer period examined in the case of UK Uncut is that it preceded Occupy LSX, which emerged only in September 2011. An exhaustive corpus of 1505 newspaper articles for the periods of analysis was also collected (532 for UK Uncut and 1062 for Occupy LSX). For this second content analysis, five coders were trained and a 10% sample was coded twice, also resulting in an intercoder reliability of >80% for all the variables.[3]

The first aspect to emerge from scrutiny of Tables 5.1 and 5.2 is that reporting of a spectacular protest event, such as the student protests, is spread more or less evenly across the different publications analysed. However, over a longer period of analysis it becomes obvious that compared

Table 5.1 Distribution of articles across titles (CA student protests)

	%	N	*Type*	*Average weekly readership in 000s (print + online)*[a]
Guardian/Observer	35	116	Left-wing broadsheet	5432
Independent/Independent on Sunday	22	73	Left-wing broadsheet	4002
Daily Mail/Mail on Sunday	17	58	Right-wing bid-market	12,188
Daily Telegraph/Sunday Telegraph	26	87	Right-wing broadsheet	4998
	100	334		

[a]Figures for the main publication (excl. Sunday papers) for March 2013 from National Readership Survey, are combined (paper + online) figures: http://www.nrs.co.uk/nrs-data-tables/

Table 5.2 Distribution of articles across titles (CA UK Uncut and Occupy)

	% UK Uncut	*N UK Uncut*	*% Occupy*	*N Occupy*	*Type*	*Average weekly readership in 000s (print + online)*
Guardian/ Observer	65	346	70	741	Left-wing broadsheet	5432
Daily Mirror/ Sunday Mirror	7	38	2	26	Left-wing tabloid	7847
Evening Standard	6	29	9	91	Right-wing mid-market	3850
Sun	4	22	3	37	Right-wing tabloid	13,674
Daily Mail/ Mail on Sunday	8	42	5	53	Right-wing mid-market	12,188
Daily Telegraph/ Sunday Telegraph	10	55	11	114	Right-wing broadsheet	4998
	100	532	100	1062		

to the left-leaning newspaper, *The Guardian*, the right-wing and tabloid media are less keen to report protest and give voice to activist organizations, such as UK Uncut and Occupy LSX.[4]

In both content analyses, the following aspects of media representation of the UK anti-austerity movement were assessed: (1) the overall tone towards the activists and the movement; (2) the sources used for the articles and activists' voices; (3) the reproduction of the movement frames; and (4) the representation of disruptive protest tactics. In what follows, each of these aspects is addressed in more detail.

5.2.1 Overall Tone

Assessment of the overall tone of the media representation of a series of student protests in 2010 shows a quite apparent ideological bias. The tone of the right-wing press was generally fairly negative towards the students and the 2010 student protests, most pronounced in the *Daily Mail* (cf. Fig. 5.1). However, in some of the right-wing press articles, the student protesters were represented more positively, usually in conjunction with a distinction between 'good' moderate and 'bad' radical students, or interviews with union leaders praising the students for their protest action. This differentiation is unsurprising; George, a leading student organizer,

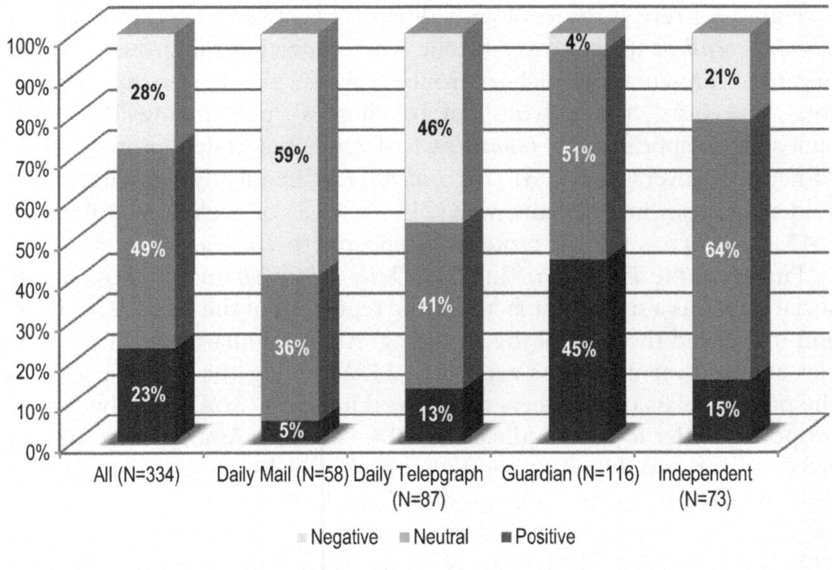

Fig. 5.1 Overall tone of the articles towards student protesters. Source: Own data ($p < 0.05$)

explained that: 'the media will always try and drive a wedge in exactly that space between different groups adopting different tactics and having a varied political approach' (personal interview, 23 February 2017).

However, it should be noted that both the *Daily Mail* and *The Daily Telegraph* were sympathetic to some extent to the protesters' cause, but very disapproving of the tactics employed by militant protesters:

> this wasn't a typical protest. For a start, these students have a legitimate grievance, as it is about to become very much more expensive for middle-class Britons to get an often poor quality university education. (*Daily Mail*, 11 November 2010)[5]

> without condoning the violence, we should be mindful of the deep sense of grievance among today's youth—the widespread feeling that they have a raw deal. This generational inequity is most starkly exemplified by the imposition of student fees by people whose own university education was lavishly subsidised. (*The Daily Telegraph*, 11 December 2010)[6]

Figure 5.1 reveals the ideological differences between *The Guardian* and *The Independent* in their overall tone when reporting the protests. While negative representations such as 'troublemakers', 'rioters', 'truants', 'agitators', 'anarchists', 'thugs', 'yobs', 'mobs', 'hordes', 'perpetrating illegal acts', almost never appear in *The Guardian* to describe the student protesters (4% of negative coverage, $n = 5$), *The Independent* frequently represented the student protests in a negative way (21%, $n = 15$) or took a neutral stance (64%, $n = 47$) towards the protesters compared to *The Guardian*.

Finally, as the *Daily Mail* and *The Daily Telegraph* quotes above show, social class was a significant factor in the reporting of the student protests, and influenced the tone of the reporting. Almost a quarter of all the articles analysed mention class explicitly (24%); among these, some refer to the political class (4%), others to the working class (36%), but the largest proportion refer to the middle class (60%—$n = 50$). Among these articles referring to the middle class, some were positively disposed (30%—$n = 15$), describing the protesters as emancipated, as claiming their legitimate right to protest, as burdened, as being hit the hardest, etc., but the majority (70%—$n = 35$) described them as spoiled, privileged and unreasonable. This negative disposition towards the middle class was most pronounced in the right-wing media. In the *Daily Mail* and *The Daily Telegraph*, more than 85% of articles mentioning the middle class did so in a negative and disparaging way.

A similar outcome for overall tone emerged from the second content analysis, focusing on the long-term media representations of UK Uncut ($N = 532$) and Occupy LSX ($N = 1062$). Overall, as Figs. 5.2 and 5.3 show, UK Uncut received more positive coverage than Occupy LSX. However, it should be noted that, in terms of media attention, the sample is dominated by *The Guardian*, with over 65% and 75%, respectively, of all articles on UK Uncut and Occupy LSX being published in this left-leaning newspaper. *The Guardian* was also predominantly positive in its reporting of UK Uncut and Occupy. The left-wing tabloid the *Daily Mirror*'s reporting of Occupy is more neutral than its representation of UK Uncut, which received enthusiastic support from it (almost 60% of its coverage of UK Uncut is positive, compared to only 20% of its coverage of Occupy).

The results in Figs. 5.2 and 5.3 show a degree of ambivalence among the right-wing press towards Occupy LSX, and in particular towards UK Uncut. Some of the right-wing newspapers' reporting was relatively positive about the movement: about 30% of the articles on UK Uncut in *The Sun*, the *Daily Mail* and *The Daily Telegraph* took a positive tone compared to some 15% in coverage of Occupy LSX. An example of this positive tone in the right-wing press is the following *Daily Mail* editorial. It

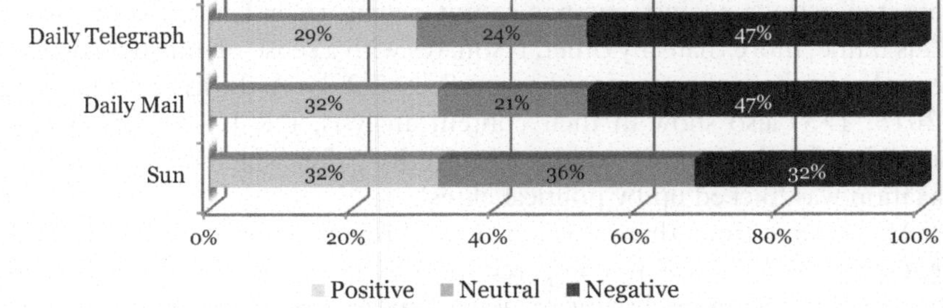

Fig. 5.2 Overall tone towards UK Uncut ($N = 532$). Source: Own data ($p < 0.05$)

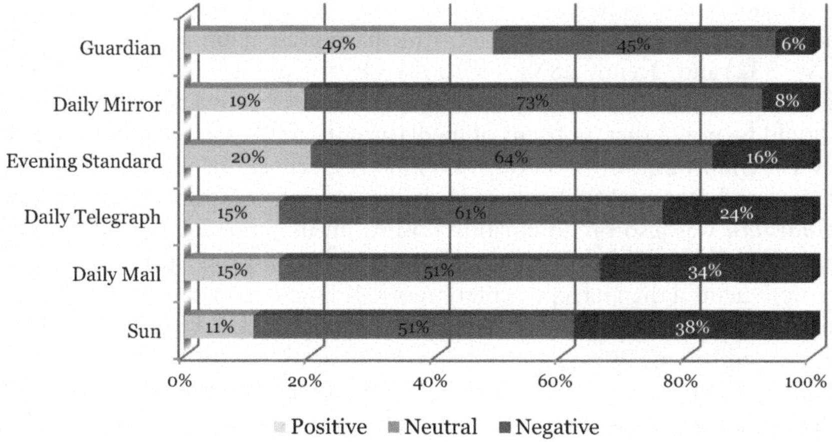

Fig. 5.3 Overall tone towards Occupy LSX ($N = 1062$). Source: Own data ($p < 0.05$)

not only refers explicitly to UK Uncut, but it seems also (almost) to endorse the movement's core message:

> Tax avoidance (organized by expensive teams of accountants) is perfectly legal. Yet it comes at the expense of millions of hard-working people who are not in a position to exploit such loopholes and have to bear the brunt of subsequent cuts in public services and increases in their own taxes. (Brummer 2010)

The more positive representation of UK Uncut *vis-à-vis* Occupy LSX might be explained by the former's more concrete demands and highly targeted actions against companies not paying their fair share of taxes. This frame, more than any other, resonates with a sense of injustice, prevalent also in the right-wing media (see Sect. 5.2.3). As Birks and Downey (2015: 173) also show in their content analysis, UK Uncut 'effectively amplified the alternative narrative to austerity', after which the issue of fair taxation was 'picked up by political elites'.

At the same time, there was less neutral reporting and more polarized reporting of UK Uncut compared to Occupy LSX, which might be explained by the more disruptive tactics deployed by UK Uncut (see Sect. 5.2.4). As UK Uncut's actions became more frequent and more disruptive, the mood swung to being more aggressive, as the following headline in the *Daily Mail* dated 26 December 2010 illustrates: 'Bodybuilding fanatic brings chaos to Britain's high streets as ringleader of anti-tax avoidance movement.' A few months later, the occupation of the luxury store Fortnum & Mason, mentioned in Chapter 4, provoked highly negative representations and demonizations, especially in the right-wing media, which invariably described the activists as:

- 'thugs' (*Sunday Express*, 27 March 2011)
- 'yobs' (*Sunday Mirror*, 27 March 2011)
- 'Mobs attacked stores' (*The Daily Telegraph*, 27 March 2011)
- 'vandals and hooligans' (*The Times*, 28 March 2011)
- '1000-strong mob' (*The Sun*, 28 March 2011)
- 'a rag-tag bunch of self-styled anarchists, far-Leftists, squatters and students' (*Daily Mail*, 28 March 2011)

In reporting on UK Uncut and Occupy LSX, there was also a high level of critique and ridicule (see Table 5.3) in the right-wing media, which was much less prevalent in the left-wing media and, in the case of the *Daily Mirror*, a left-wing tabloid, almost totally absent. *The Sun* called Occupy LSX a 'pathetic protest', and the journalist pondered:

> how many of these so-called anti-capitalists are posting pictures on their iPhones, slurping coffee from Starbucks and gorging hamburgers from McDonalds? Hypocrites. (Galloway 2011)

Nevertheless, Occupy LSX seems to have attracted somewhat less critique and ridicule from the right-wing media than UK Uncut. This can be

Table 5.3 Presence of critique and ridicule

	% Critique of		*% Ridicule of*	
	UK Uncut	*Occupy*	*UK Uncut*	*Occupy*
Guardian	9	15	10	8
Daily Telegraph	42	28	29	23
Evening Standard	45	25	17	18
Daily Mail	36	30	53	26
Daily Mirror	0	0	0	4
Sun	3	30	23	22

Source: Own data ($p < 0.05$)

explained by the latter's more disruptive and militant tactics, which the then Tory MP, Louise Mensch, described as 'intolerable bullying' (quoted in Elliott 2012). London LSX was also disruptive, but less so, and was more contained and less threatening, as shown by the data. At the same time, as mentioned earlier, this contradicts the overall more positive tone towards UK Uncut and its issues than was received by Occupy LSX. In the case of Occupy LSX, the lack of a clear set of demands and a coherent agenda was mostly to blame for the critiques in the centre-left media.

While this negative ideological bias in the reporting of the UK anti-austerity movement might not be surprising, it is important to stress that this negative bias was not total. Even within the right-wing media, there was a degree of sympathy with some of the anti-austerity movement's messages regarding tuition fees, fair taxation and the banks. Furthermore, as student activist George explained, negative bias towards some of the more confrontational segments of the movement could lead to more positive representation of the moderate wing, which, compared to militant tactics, appears reasonable and tame:

> So what you got was the *Daily Mail* and sorts denouncing the Black Bloc activists, but having more sympathy towards the more liberal UK Uncut. In a way, the depiction of the bad protester and the negative representation of very confrontational tactics can lead to other slightly less confrontational tactics being approached as much more reasonable and being given more voice. (personal interview, 23 February 2017)

5.2.2 *Sources and the Presence of Activists' Voices*

As well as the overall tone, it is important to assess the sources used by journalists, and link them to the presence in media coverage of the voices of activists or lack of them. Given that sources and quotes feature less in opinion pieces and editorials, only regular news articles were analysed for sources (n = 244 for the student protest analysis; n = 377 for the UK Uncut analysis; and n = 778 for the Occupy analysis).

In the case of the student protests, the intensity of internal conflict within the student movement regarding the legitimacy of using militant tactics imposed the need to distinguish between moderate and more militant student voices. Other voices used as sources in the various articles include: civil society sources, politicians, police and government officials, and members of the public.

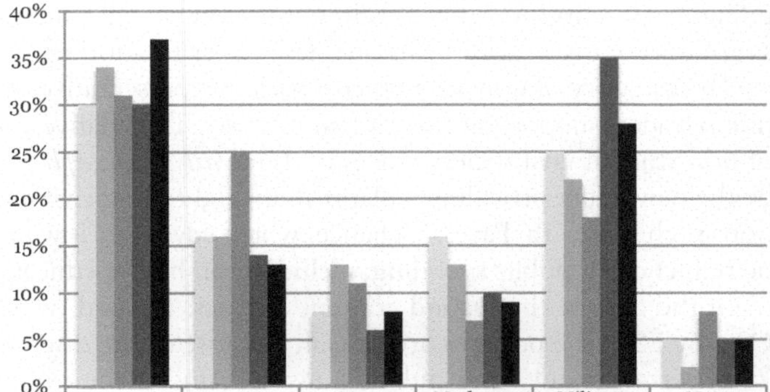

	Politicians	Police and officials	Experts and Witnesses	Moderate Student Protesters	Militant Student Protesters	Non-Student Civil Society
All (N=717)	30%	16%	8%	16%	25%	5%
Daily Mail (N=120)	34%	16%	13%	13%	22%	2%
Daily Telegraph (N=186)	31%	25%	11%	7%	18%	8%
Guardian (N=250)	30%	14%	6%	10%	35%	5%
Independent (N=161)	37%	13%	8%	9%	28%	5%

Fig. 5.4 Distribution of sources used in the reporting of the student protests (Total number of sources $N = 717$). Source: Own data

If we consider the number of sources used per newspaper, and cross-tabulate this with the type of source, we can compare the distribution across different types of sources per publication (cf. Fig. 5.4). For example, while 30% of the total sources were politicians, in *The Independent* 37% of all sources were politicians, compared to 34% in the *Daily Mail.* Nevertheless, the relatively even distribution of the different types of sources across the various newspapers analysed is striking, suggesting relative homogenization in terms of news production and use of sources.

As expected, *The Daily Telegraph* paid a disproportionate amount of attention to police and official spokespersons, compared to other newspapers. Also, the right-wing media made use of a bigger number of independent experts, and in particular more quotes from eyewitnesses to describe events. Overall, the protest paradigm would seem to be confirmed by the higher proportion of official and recognized sources used.

At the same time, it seems that militant student voices were given more prominence than those of moderate student protesters, by all the newspapers, and particularly *The Guardian*, where 35% of sources ($n = 45$) were militant students. As shown below, the context in which these militant sources were used varies from one newspaper to another.

The category of non-student civil society representatives refers mainly to union leaders supporting the student protests. The relatively higher number of non-student civil society voices in *The Daily Telegraph* can be explained by the newspaper providing a platform for right-wing civil society organizations such as the TaxPayers' Alliance, which advocates low taxes and a drastic reduction in public spending, including on higher education.

In the case of the second content analysis, focused on UK Uncut and Occupy LSX, the patterns are similar. Because of the discrepancy between *The Guardian* and other publications in terms of the extent of reporting of UK Uncut and Occupy LSX, the source analysis bundles together the left-wing (*The Guardian* and *Daily Mirror*) and the right-wing (*Evening Standard, Daily Mail, The Sun* and *The Daily Telegraph*) publications.

In the case of UK Uncut, it is clear that the activists were used much more as sources by the left-wing compared to the right-wing media (see Fig. 5.5). In the case of sources, the protest paradigm seems to apply

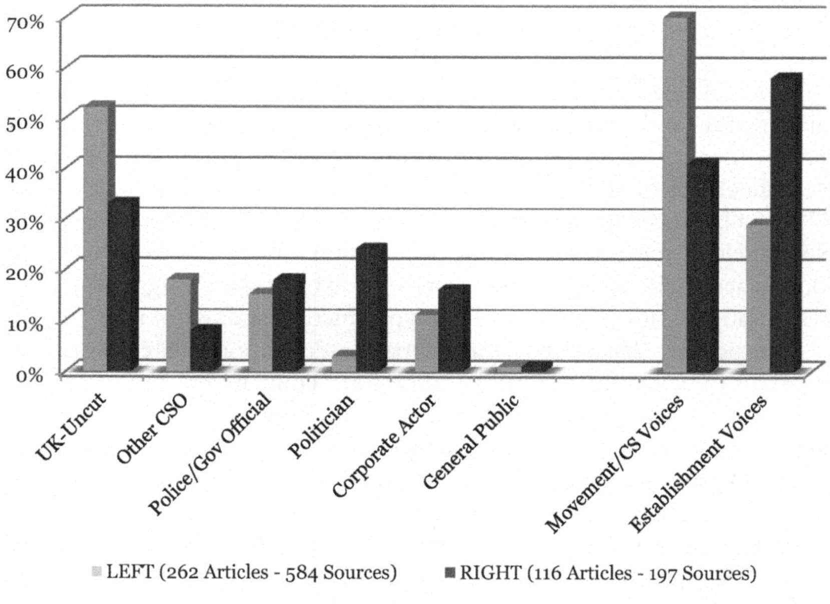

Fig. 5.5 Distribution of sources used in the reporting of UK Uncut (Total number of sources used $N = 781$). Source: Own data

strongly to the right-wing media in the context of the reporting of UK Uncut, with many more establishment voices (police, government officials, politicians and corporate actors) present than movement and civil society voices.

However, Fig. 5.6 shows that the protest paradigm is less apparent in the sources used in the reporting of Occupy LSX. Here, there seems little difference between left-wing and right-wing newspapers regarding the number of movement and civil society sources. However, the right-wing media use considerably more establishment voices than do those of the left wing in their reporting of Occupy LSX.

The number of words attributed to sources were also analysed. The amount of words attributed to sources was divided by the total number of words in the article, and an average calculated per type of source and per

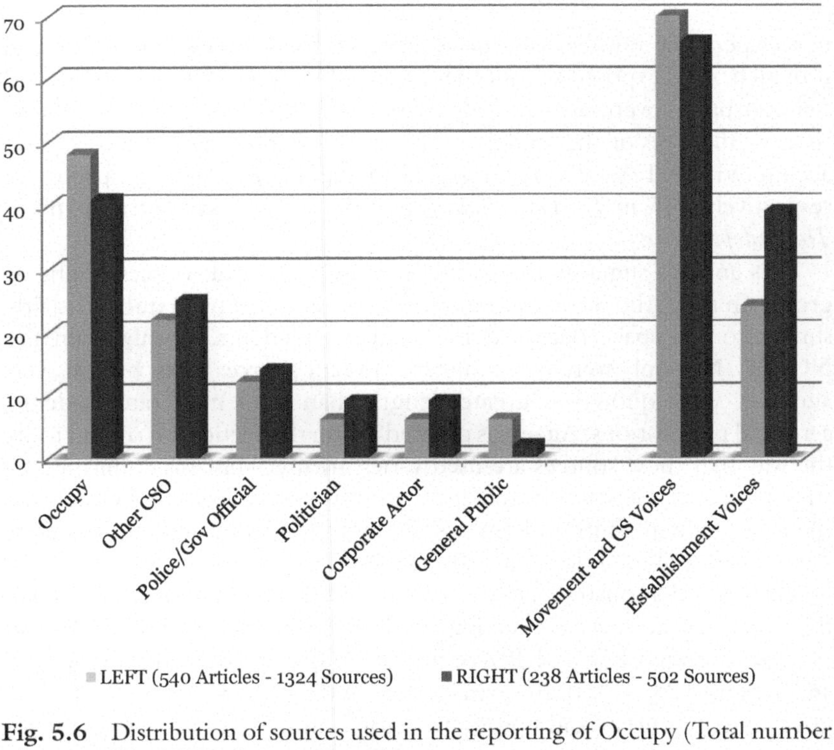

Fig. 5.6 Distribution of sources used in the reporting of Occupy (Total number of sources $N = 1788$). Source: Own data

Table 5.4 The average percentage of article space taken up by sources when quoted, and number of news articles in which sources are quoted—student protests

	Total	*n*	*Daily Mail*	*n*	*Daily Teleg.*	*n*	*Guardian*	*n*	*Indy*	*n*
Politicians	15%	113	17%	19	14%	33	16%	35	16%	26
Police	13%	75	13%	13	14%	25	12%	20	11%	17
Experts	11%	39	11%	7	11%	13	10%	11	11%	8
Moderate student protesters	11%	48	8%	9	9%	12	15%	17	11%	10
Militant student protesters	17%	87	17%	15	19%	20	17%	32	13%	20
Non-student civil society	14%	29	20%[a]	1	14%	14	18%	7	7%	7

Source: Own data

[a]This figure should be disregarded since it relates to only 1 article, an interview with a labour union leader

newspaper. The number of articles in which the sources appeared is also provided. This exposed yet another aspect of the reporting (editorials and opinion pieces were also excluded from this analysis). Table 5.4 shows that, in the case of the student protests, on average, politicians' quotes accounted for 17% of a news article in the *Daily Mail*, compared to, respectively, 14% in *The Daily Telegraph*, 16% in *The Guardian* and 16% in *The Independent*.

This analysis suggests that, while the use of official sources might be greater in total, the relative amount of space they occupy in quotes is fairly similar to the space occupied by (militant) students, mainly from the NCAFC. Not only were more militant student sources used, but on average they were quoted at greater length than were moderate students, across all publications. Again, as pointed out in the section on overall tone, the way that these sources are used varies greatly. This was confirmed by student activist George's statement that: 'it is not necessarily the case that the more militant stuff undermines the more moderate activists and messages' (personal interview, 23 February 2017).

Table 5.5 demonstrates that, in terms of UK Uncut and Occupy LSX, the voices of activists are strong, with activists' quotes taking up, on average, between 15% and 20% of the article space in the left-wing media, and around 17%–18% of the article space in the right-wing media. Police, government sources and corporate actors' quotes were given a reasonable space, but less than that given to activists.

Table 5.5 The average percentage of article space taken up by sources when quoted, and number of news articles in which sources are quoted—UK Uncut and Occupy

	UK Uncut				*Occupy LSX*			
	Left		*Right*		*Left*		*Right*	
	%	*n*	%	*n*	%	N	%	*n*
S.M. actor	21	153	17	44	15	250	18	102
C.S. actor	10	86	8	27	2	257	3	98
Gov. actor	17	61	14	28	11	117	11	55
Pol. actor	9	15	8	30	2	65	2	29
Corp. actor	12	30	15	20	16	22	17	14

Source: Own data

Table 5.6 Presence of activist voices in the news articles

	UK Uncut (n = 377)		*Occupy LSX (n = 778)*	
	Left (*n* = *261*) %	*Right* (*n* = *116*) %	*Left* (*n* = *540*) %	*Right* (*n* = *238*) %
No movement voice	36	52	66	71
Leaders of the movement	29	23	31	27
Activists of the movements	35	25	3	2

Source: Own data ($p < 0.05$)

In the articles on UK Uncut, the voice of activists was more prominent than in the reporting of Occupy LSX (see Table 5.6). In reporting of UK Uncut, only 36% of the articles in the left-wing media did not contain the voice of an activist, and this rose to over 50% for articles in the right-wing media. However, in the reporting of Occupy LSX, between 65% and 70% of the articles did not include any activists' voices.

It seems that, in the case of UK Uncut, more ordinary activists were given a voice across both the left- and right-wing media, compared to Occupy, in which spokespersons and movement leaders played a more prominent role and, again, consistently across the left and right-wing media. This is a surprising result, since Occupy prided itself on its horizontal structures and open democratic ethos.

5.2.3 *The Reproduction of Movement Frames*

Probably the most important aspect of media resonance is getting the message across, or ensuring that the media reproduce the movement's frames in their reporting. Generally, this is assumed to be difficult in the face of the protest paradigm, which directs the journalists' focus to the spectacular protest tactics rather than the issues the movement wants to put on the political agenda. Nevertheless, across the three cases, the student protests, UK Uncut and Occupy, a degree of reproduction of the anti-austerity frames can be observed, in left- as well as right-wing newspapers. However, again, it has to be recalled here that the total amount of coverage of the anti-austerity movement, especially in the cases of UK Uncut and Occupy LSX, is much higher in the left-wing compared to the right-wing newspapers (see Tables 5.1 and 5.2).

In the reporting of the student protests, the debates over tuition fees and other student issues, such as the quality of higher education, and public services in general, was quite prominent in the newspapers. Figure 5.7 offers a proportional representation of the shifts in the main focus of the articles across the period of analysis. The data analysis shows that the proportion of articles (mainly) focusing on the political process gradually increased as the date of the vote on increasing tuition fees approached, and declined after the vote (on 9 December 2010). Articles focusing mainly on violence by protesters were also numerous, especially in the early part of the period of analysis and immediately after the vote, when protests became very heated (see Chap. 4).

However, the attention paid to damage and violence in media representations did not affect the proportion of the coverage of the issues the students wanted to address, in a dramatic way; this remained relatively stable, except for the period of 27–30 November. What did occur in the context of the student protests was that the increase in the number of articles focusing on internal politics and conflicts within the movement did have a negative impact on the reporting of the issues, more so than the attention paid to damage and violence. Along the same lines, and focusing on the 1999 violent World Trade Organization (WTO) disruption in Seattle, DeLuca and Peeples (2002: 140) concluded that '[f]ar from discrediting or drowning out the message of the WTO protesters, the symbolic violence generated extensive media coverage and an airing of the issues'.

Over the long period covered by the content analysis of UK Uncut and Occupy LSX, the reproduction of anti-austerity frames in the mainstream media was mixed. Four core frames were coded. The first focused

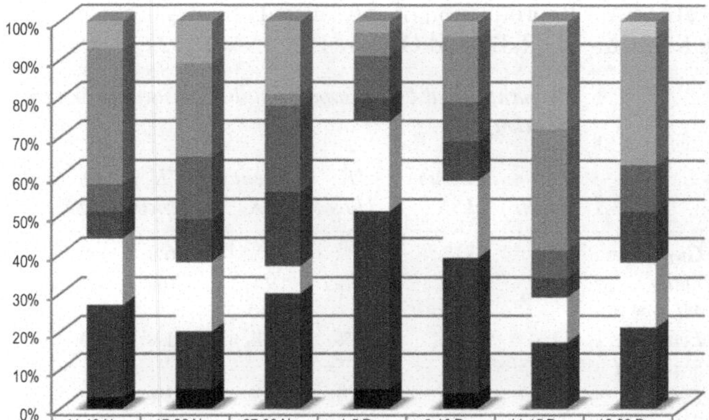

	11-16 Nov	17-26 Nov	27-30 Nov	1-5 Dec	6-10 Dec	11-15 Dec	16-23 Dec
Other	0	0	0	0	0	1	4
Police forces and actions	7	11	19	3	4	27	33
Violence by protesters	35	24	3	6	17	31	0
Protest tactics and internal politics	7	16	22	11	10	7	12
The culture of protest	7	11	19	6	10	5	13
The student issues	17	18	7	23	20	12	17
The political process	24	15	30	46	35	17	21
Factual accounts	3	5	0	5	4	0	0

Fig. 5.7 Shifts in main focus of the articles across time (proportional—%). Source: Own data

on corporate greed and on taxation more broadly; the second dealt with the unacceptably high levels of inequality; the third frame related to the stringent critique of austerity politics in the UK; and the fourth frame voiced a critique of democracy and its lack of representation.

Some of these movement frames are reproduced less than others in the reporting on the anti-austerity movement. Table 5.7 shows that the most frequently reproduced frame was the corporate greed and taxation frame. This applies in particular to the corpus on UK Uncut (between 60% and 80% of articles carry this frame), which is to be expected, since it represents its core message; however, it appears much less in Occupy LSX articles (between 30% and 50% of articles carry this frame). Messages regarding rising inequality and '*the 99% vs. 1%*' seem also to have achieved resonance; this rising inequality frame is present in many of the articles across the two cases, but, again, it is more pronounced in UK Uncut-related news articles. It seems that, proportionally, UK Uncut coverage tends to reproduce the main anti-austerity frames more than does the coverage of Occupy LSX.

Table 5.7 Reproduction of anti-austerity frames in the media representations of UK Uncut ($N = 532$) and Occupy LSX ($N = 1062$)

	Corporate greed & taxation		*Rising inequality*		*Austerity Britain*		*Broken democracy*	
	UK Uncut	*Occupy LSX*	*UK Uncut*	*Occupy LSX*	*UK Uncut*	*Occupy LSX*	*UK Uncut*	*Occupy LSX*
Guardian	60%	51%	47%	28%	36%	4%	15%	26%
Daily Mirror	68%	27%	50%	19%	50%	0%	18%	15%
Evening Standard	62%	48%	14%	17%	31%	3%	0%	19%
Daily Telegraph	67%	33%	31%	14%	13%	3%	7%	22%
Daily Mail	68%	42%	36%	19%	36%	6%	0%	17%
The Sun	86%	32%	41%	16%	14%	0%	0%	16%

Source: Own data ($p < 0.05$)

The other two frames—austerity Britain and broken democracy—were somewhat less present in the reporting of the anti-austerity movement. There are also other differences between the two cases. While the austerity Britain frame is reasonably present in reporting on UK Uncut (between 10% and 50% of articles carry this frame), it is largely absent from the Occupy coverage. Likewise, the broken democracy frame was very much part of Occupy LSX's message compared to that of UK Uncut, which is reflected in the media content analysis.

Overall, reproduction of the movement frames tended to be higher in the left-wing rather than in the right-wing press, but the right-wing media also carried the movement frames. So, whereas the tone of the article might be negative, the frame would be included. In a report on the street party held in front of the then Deputy Prime Minister Nick Clegg's house, organized by UK Uncut, *The Sun,* whose reporting of the anti-austerity movement was generally acerbic, gave a voice to a UK Uncut protester:

> One of the group's supporters, Jean Sandler, 42, said: 'Nick Clegg is one of the architects of austerity—he's a millionaire. The cuts are a political choice of this Government and the Cabinet of out-of-touch millionaires.' (quote from Elliott 2011)

Another example is Joan Bakewell's feature-length article, published in *The Daily Telegraph,* which noted that Occupy LSX 'helped fuel a public

Table 5.8 Temporal analysis of the reproduction of the corporate greed/taxation frame in the left-wing (LW) and right-wing (RW) media

	Greed/Taxation							
	UK Uncut		*Occupy*		*UK Uncut*		*Occupy*	
	LW (n = 384)		*LW (n = 767)*		*RW (n = 148)*		*RW (n = 295)*	
	%	*n*	%	*n*	%	*n*	%	*n*
Jan–Jun 2011	76	40	71	66	68	13	52	21
Jul–Dec 2011	54	74	47	186	61	31	28	36
Jan–Jun 2012	61	113	47	116	68	51	47	53
Jul–Dec 2012	73	8	58	15	67	2	43	6

Source: Own data ($p < 0.05$)

debate about money, ownership rights, and even capitalism itself' (Bakewell 2011). At the same time, as Lakoff (2004) reminds us, to challenge a frame, that frame needs to be invoked. As such, the contestation of a movement frame by the right-wing press can potentially end up strengthening it.

An analysis of the temporal dimension provides more detail about frame reproduction (see Table 5.8). In the left-wing media, the corporate greed and taxation frames were especially prominent in the early part of the period of analysis across the two cases; 76% ($n = 40$) of the UK Uncut, and 71% ($n = 66$) of the Occupy LSX coverage in the left-wing newspapers between January and June 2011 carried this frame (see Table 5.8). After June 2011, the presence of the frame reduced somewhat, but remained strong (at between 50% and 60%). In the right-wing media, the presence of the corporate greed and taxation frame remained relatively stable over the whole period of analysis (about 65% of the coverage for UK Uncut and about 50% for the Occupy LSX carried the frame).

The overall pattern for the inequality frame was similar (see Table 5.9); that is, more present in the first part of the period of analysis (January–June 2011) and more present also in the left-wing compared to the right-wing newspapers. The inequality frame was more present also in the UK Uncut coverage than in the Occupy LSX coverage.

The austerity Britain frame, which was confined mainly to UK Uncut articles, was fairly stable, but disappeared in the final part of the period of analysis (July–December 2012). Before July 2012, the austerity Britain

Table 5.9 Temporal analysis of the reproduction of the inequality frame in the left-wing (LW) and right-wing (RW) media

	Inequality							
	UK Uncut		*Occupy*		*UK Uncut*		*Occupy*	
	LW (n = 384)		*LW (n = 767)*		*RW (n = 148)*		*RW (n = 295)*	
	%	*n*	%	*n*	%	*n*	%	*n*
Jan–Jun 2011	76	40	56	52	42	8	10	10
Jul–Dec 2011	46	63	23	91	28	14	14	18
Jan–Jun 2012	42	77	25	61	28	21	16	18
Jul–Dec 2012	27	3	27	7	67	2	7	1

Source: Own data ($p < 0.05$)

frame was present in about 40% of left-wing media coverage of UK Uncut and about 25% of its right-wing media coverage. The broken democracy frame was present mainly in the Occupy LSX coverage, and was stable in the left-wing media (25%–30% of the coverage), but increased in the right-wing media. In the period January to June 2011, 10% (n = 4) of the coverage of Occupy LSX in the right-wing media included the broken democracy frame, compared to 23% (n = 26) of the coverage in the period January to June 2012.

5.2.4 *The Representation of Disruptive Protest Tactics*

As hinted at in the section on the overall tone of the articles (cf. Sect. 5.2.1), disruptive tactics played an important role in the anti-austerity protests and their media representations. In the case of the student protests, a substantial majority of articles addressed or alluded to violence in some way, even when the main focus was not violence per se. While some 20% (n = 72) of articles had violence from student protesters as the main focus, 63% (n = 210) of articles mentioned or addressed violence. As might be expected, the rightwing press emphasized violence more than the centre left media, with *The Daily Mail* and *The Daily Telegraph* mentioning violence in respectively 71% (n = 41) and 70% (n = 61) of their coverage of the tuition fees debate and the associated protests. Also in *The Guardian* and *The Independent* violence was addressed in a considerable amount of articles, respectively, 58% (n = 67) and 55% (n = 40).

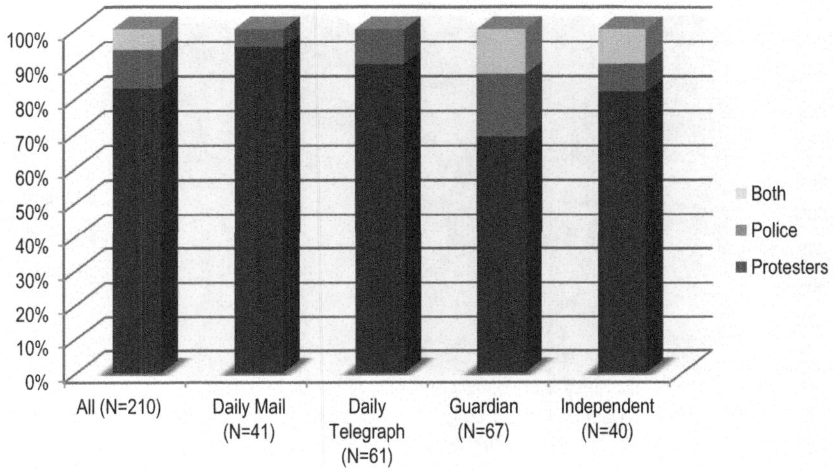

Fig. 5.8 When violence is mentioned, whose violence? Source: Own data ($p < 0.05$)

However, the violence was not limited to violence from protesters (cf. Fig. 5.8). While the right-wing press was focused almost exclusively on the damage inflicted by protesters, *The Guardian* and, to a lesser extent *The Independent*, also reported on police violence and took a more balanced approach. This applied, especially, to the later stages of the period of analysis, when critique of police brutality emerged as a distinct frame.

The way that the symbolic damage enacted by the student protesters was approached reveals a stark distinction between the right-wing and the left-wing press. While the typical liberal response was within a negative framing, describing the tactics of symbolic damage enacted by the protesters in a condemnatory tone, denoting it as illegitimate, orchestrated and unworthy of a democracy, the neutral stance implied that both positive and negative voices were given space in the article. A positive framing saw the tactics of symbolic damage as a legitimate form of resistance, as passionate politics, as a necessary evil that deserved a hearing, or as cheeky banter and teenage naughtiness. Figure 5.9 shows that the dominant framing of the tactics of symbolic damage enacted by the student protesters was negative, as might be expected.

While the right-wing newspapers condemned unequivocally the tactics of insurrectionary symbolic violence enacted by the students, the left-wing

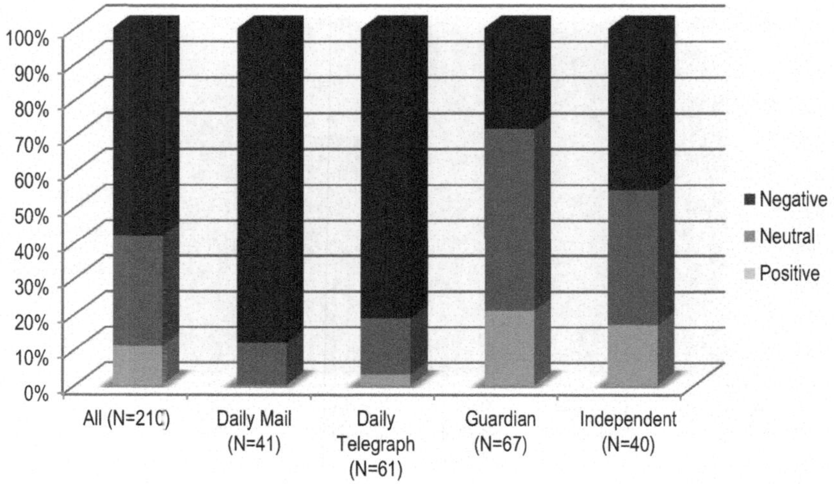

Fig. 5.9 Representation of the tactics of symbolic damage enacted by student protesters. Source: Own data ($p < 0.05$)

media took a more nuanced and neutral stance, sometimes even adopting a positive 'understanding' framing. However, this applied to only a minority of articles in the left-leaning media; 21% of articles in *The Guardian* mentioning violence adopted a positive frame, 17% of those in *The Independent*. In the rightwing media a positive framing of violence was almost totally absent; 3% of articles in *The Daily Telegraph* mentioning violence was somewhat understanding, compared to 0% of the *Daily Mail* reporting.

The tactics of damage and violent spectacle set a particular tone and, inevitably, all of the media tended towards a focus on the spectacular and the violent rather than the peaceful and the civic. All the front pages of the major UK newspapers on the day after the first student protest carried the same dramatic photo of a protester kicking in a window of the Tory HQ at 30 Millbank, as the *Daily Mail* front page in Fig. 5.10 shows.

At the same time, the overall amount of coverage was linked strongly to the spectacular nature of the actions organized by the student protesters, and the numbers they were able to mobilize. The first period of analysis started with the first major demonstration (11–16 November 2010). About 20% of all articles ($n = 71$) were published immediately after that first, and arguably most disruptive, demonstration. Another contentious moment was immediately before the vote on the tripling of tuition fees,

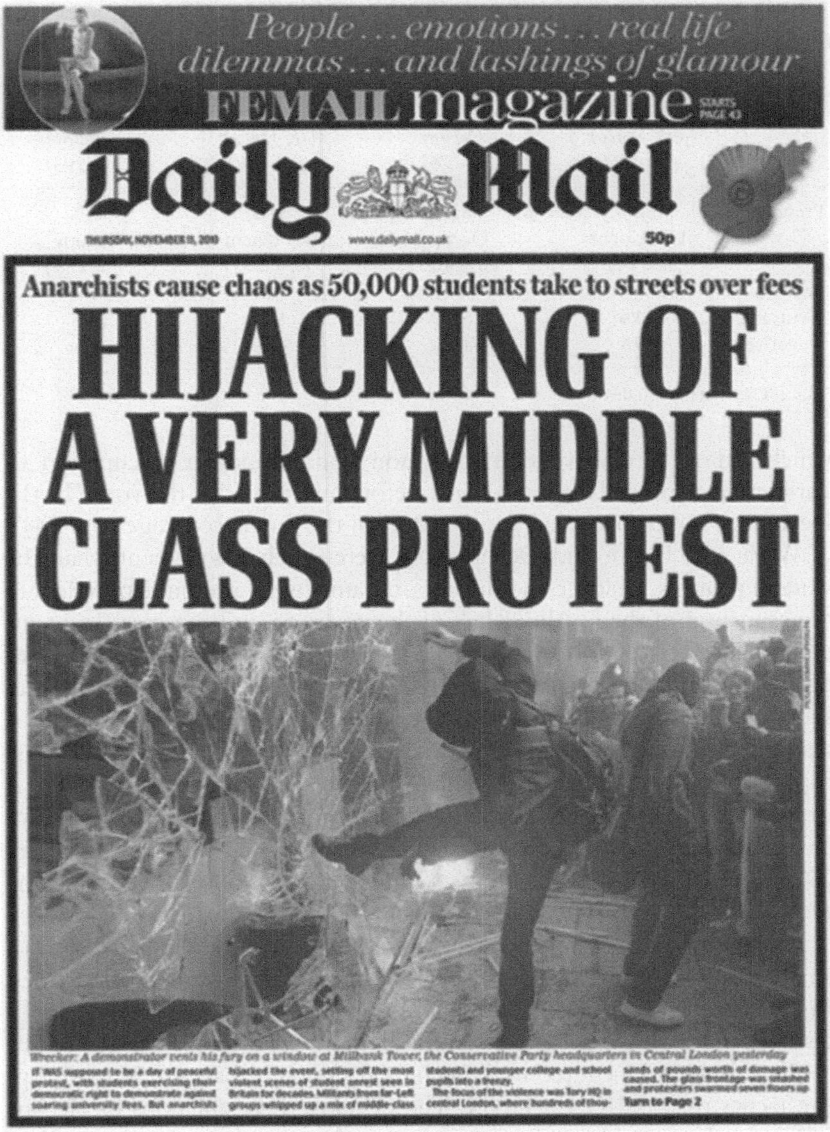

People . . . emotions . . . real life dilemmas . . . and lashings of glamour

FEMAIL magazine STARTS PAGE 43

Daily Mail

THURSDAY, NOVEMBER 11, 2010 www.dailymail.co.uk 50p

Anarchists cause chaos as 50,000 students take to streets over fees

HIJACKING OF A VERY MIDDLE CLASS PROTEST

Wrecker: A demonstrator vents his fury on a window at Millbank Tower, the Conservative Party headquarters in Central London yesterday

IT WAS supposed to be a day of peaceful protest, with students exercising their democratic right to demonstrate against soaring university fees. But anarchists hijacked the event, setting off the most violent scenes of student unrest seen in Britain for decades. Militants from far-Left groups whipped up a mix of middle-class students and younger college and school pupils into a frenzy.

The focus of the violence was Tory HQ in central London, where hundreds of thousands of pounds worth of damage was caused. The glass frontage was smashed and protesters swarmed seven floors up

Turn to Page 2

Fig. 5.10 Front pages of UK newspapers on 11 November 2010, the day after the first student demonstration against plans to triple tuition fees

Table 5.10 The presence and representation of the violence/disruption frame in the reporting on UK Uncut and Occupy LSX

	Left-wing newspapers		*Right-wing newspapers*	
	UK Uncut (n = 384)	*Occupy (n = 767)*	*UK Uncut (n = 148)*	*Occupy (n = 295)*
Presence	50%	52%	51%	54%
	UK Uncut (n = 192)	Occupy (n = 400)	UK Uncut (n = 75)	Occupy (n = 159)
Positive	7%	1%	0%	0%
Neutral	24%	57%	9%	55%
Negative	69%	42%	90%	45%

Source: Own data ($p < 0.05$)

which led to a massive demonstration and temporary occupation of Parliament Square. The periods just before and just after the vote (11–15 December 2010) occupied another 22% of the media coverage (n = 74).

While UK Uncut and Occupy LSX were much less 'violent' than the student protests, violence and disruption frames were also quite prevalent in the reporting of them. About half of the coverage, in both cases, contains the violence/disruption frame (see Table 5.10). The disruptive tactics of occupying public spaces (in the case of Occupy) or private spaces such as shops (in the case of UK Uncut), in particular, produced violence and/or disruption frames. A conflation between the two can be observed, with disruption being interpreted as a form of violence. In both cases, the activists were described as dangerous anarchists and/or as an unruly mob. For example, Occupy LSX was described as the 'tent city mob' (*The Sun* 16 November 2011) and the 'anti-capitalist mob' (*The Sun* 17 November 2011), while the *Daily Mail* described UK Uncut as 'a gang' (1 December 2011).

The percentages of positive, neutral and negative representations of violence and disruption in Table 5.10 refer to those articles carrying these frames. In the right-wing media, we found no positive representations of violence or disruption, but this was largely absent also in the left-wing media. The results confirm that UK Uncut received much more criticism as a result of its disruptive tactics than did Occupy LSX. The negative representations of Occupy LSX tended to emphasize the nuisance caused by the occupation of the steps of St Paul's Cathedral, and health and hygiene issues. In one of its headlines, *The Sun* quoted from legal papers filed by the City of London Corporation, which defended the interests of the City of London and called the Occupy protest camp a 'hell of drugs and filth' (Nash 2011).

At the same time, as in the case of the student protest, some attention to aggressive legal cases and problematic police interventions can be observed in the reporting, especially regarding the more disruptive tactics of UK Uncut. For example, *The Guardian* reported on the mass arrest of 138 UK Uncut protesters following their occupation of Fortnum & Mason (26 March 2011) and the ensuing legal cases for aggravated trespass. The police began, increasingly, to act pre-emptively by sending scare-letters or arresting known activists. This led NCAFC's co-founder, Michael Chessum, to condemn the police for their engagement in:

> a cynical attempt to stop people from attending the demonstration and to pre-criminalise the protest (quoted in Malik and Shepherd 2011)

However, again, just as in the case of the student protests, disruptive actions and the logic of damage (even though little damage was done) increased media resonance significantly (see Fig. 5.11). Media attention in the case of Occupy LSX was concentrated in the second part of the period

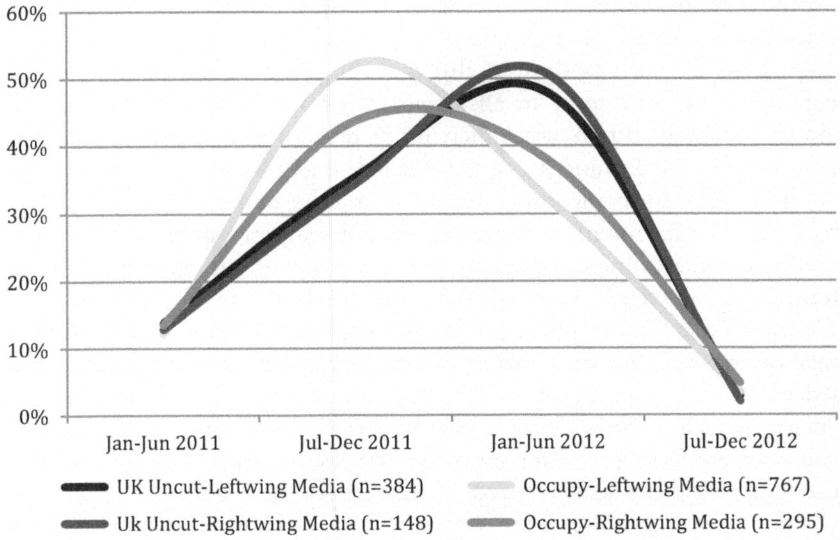

Fig. 5.11 Percentage of articles published in given periods in the left-wing and right-wing newspapers for UK Uncut ($N = 532$) and Occupy ($N = 1062$). Source: Own data

of analysis (July–December 2011) and focused on the occupation in front of St Paul's Cathedral (45%–50% of the coverage). Media attention on UK Uncut was similarly concentrated in the third period of analysis (January–June 2012), when it was most active and militant, engaging in disability protests, the occupation of Fortnum & Mason, a party in front of Nick Clegg's house, protests against 'sweetheart' tax deals for big companies (e.g. Goldman Sachs, among others) and exploitation of workers by supermarkets (e.g. Tesco, among others).

5.3 Conclusion

The data analysis presented in this chapter tends to confirm the protest and public nuisance paradigms, in showing the overall negative bias in the media towards militancy and radical protest. This is especially visible in the right-wing press. In contrast to the left-leaning press, reporting of the UK anti-austerity movement was substantially less in the right-wing press. This was especially so in the cases of UK Uncut and Occupy LSX, whose period of analysis was longer. The protests tended to be delegitimated and the protesters demonized. Above all, what emerges strongly in all three cases is the public nuisance paradigm.

Analysis of the data showed also that the protest and public nuisance paradigms did not apply in all instances, or across all publications. As already pointed out, it was much more pronounced in the right-wing compared to left-leaning press; there is a clear ideological bias, with right-wing newspapers being more negative in tone and giving (much) less space to the movement compared to the left-wing newspapers.

While establishment voices in the reporting of the student protests tended to outweigh activists' voices in all but one publication (*The Guardian* was the exception), militant voices were not only more numerous, on average, but they also received more article space than moderate voices. In the reporting on UK Uncut and Occupy LSX there are discrepancies regarding the relevance of the protest paradigm. Establishment sources were more predominant in the articles on UK Uncut published in the right-wing press, compared to activist sources, but, in the case of Occupy LSX there are more activists' voices than establishment ones across both the left- and right-wing newspapers. When UK Uncut and Occupy LSX activists were quoted, they tended to receive more article space on average.

It should be noted that being allowed a voice does not lead, necessarily, to positive exposure, but, importantly, it also does not mean exclusively negative exposure. Even right-wing newspapers expressed some degree of understanding for the anger of the students towards the government and its tripling of tuition fees. Also, there was some qualified sympathy *vis-à-vis* the aims and goals of UK Uncut and Occupy LSX from the right-wing newspapers. In other words, the reporting was not unequivocally negative and disparaging.

Despite those negative representations, which were visible mainly in the right-wing newspapers, many of the activists' frames were reproduced. The issues the students wanted to address regarding higher education, student debt, tuition fees and cuts to public services were fairly present, as a main focus, and remained so for most of the period of analysis. In both cases, the inequality and the corporate greed/taxation frames were frequently reproduced by the newspapers. Furthermore, the austerity Britain frame in the case of UK Uncut, and the broken democracy frame in the case of Occupy LSX, were also reproduced fairly often.

Arguably, as history teaches us, without some degree of disruption, nuisance and/or discomfort, political elites are unlikely to change or compromise (see Tilly 2000; della Porta and Diani 2006). In their own ways, each of the movements—the student organization NCAFC, UK Uncut and Occupy LSX—were disruptive and caused discomfort, mainly through blockades and the occupation of semi-public (church property) and private spaces (shops). This engendered high degrees of negative representations, but again more so in the right-wing than in the left-leaning press.

Our analysis, however, showed that the use of such tactics led to considerable spikes and increases in the amount of coverage of the movement, and thus the issues it aimed to address. It seemed that the creation of disruptive protest spectacles and the logic of damage leads to increased media exposure for the protesters and is not necessarily as detrimental to a given cause as often is claimed.

In the cases of UK Uncut and Occupy LSX, the use of spectacular protest tactics, such as occupations and street theatre, generated considerable media attention and, while at the same time they also engendered media dissonance, it did not stop many frames from being reproduced. As Koopmans (2004: 374) also points out, negative media resonance or dissonance is not necessarily bad: 'even the rejection of a demand has to reproduce that demand and thereby diffuses it further'.

Notes

1. The results of this content analysis were published earlier, in Cammaerts 2013.
2. Cohen's kappa (k) method for calculating intercoder reliability was used.
3. Idem ditto.
4. As a result of this, *The Guardian* articles on UK Uncut and Occupy greatly outnumber articles published in other newspapers across the exhaustive sample. This skewed the totals heavily; hence, for the UK Uncut and Occupy content analysis, the totals are not presented since they are not significant.
5. *Daily Mail* (2010) 'Standing Firm in the Face of Protests'. Editorial: 11 November.
6. *Daily Telegraph* (2010) 'The right to be angry is no excuse for violence'. Editorial: 11 December.

CHAPTER 6

The Reception of Anti-Austerity Discourses and Frames

This chapter addresses the *reception* moment of the Circuit of Protest, and thus implicates the audiences of the movements' self-mediation practices, and of the mainstream media representations of the movement. The audiences social movements aim to reach are heterogeneous. They consist of state actors, which are able to implement legal change, as well as non-state actors, which can achieve social and cultural change from below (Van Dyke et al. 2004). However, I would argue that they also include the public at large—'ordinary', non-activist citizens, those not manning the barricades or participating in direct action.

In some ways, this moment is the most opaque one in the circuit, precisely because of the difficulty involved in isolating the precise relationship between mediation and the formation of opinions and attitudes across society. While citizens' views and attitudes *vis-à-vis* social movements' goals and tactics are crucial for the movements' success and resonance, the way in which ordinary non-activist citizens receive, appropriate, or indeed reject, social movement discourses and frames is often a black box in current research on social movements, and the role of media and communication in protest. In much of the research so far, the focus has been on either the activists and their media and communicative practices, or on the ways in which mainstream media represent social movements and protest actions. The relationship between activists' practices or mainstream media reporting and the opinions of non-activist citizens is all too often assumed rather than researched in an in-depth manner. A notable exception here is

B. Cammaerts, *The Circulation of Anti-Austerity Protest*,
https://doi.org/10.1007/978-3-319-70123-3_6

Gamson's (1992) book entitled *Talking Politics*, which presents a triad of influences on opinion formation—experiential knowledge, popular wisdoms and media discourse. I concur here with Gamson (1992: 117) when he writes:

> From the standpoint of the wanderers, media discourse is a cultural resource to use in understanding and talking about an issue, but it is only one of several available. Nor is it necessarily the important one on some issues, compared, for example, with their own experience and that of significant others in their lives. Frequently, they find their way through the forest with a combination of resources, including those they carry with them.

By combining the results of a representative survey and a limited number of focus groups, I shall present an analysis of the reception of the anti-austerity movement's discourses and their constituent frames. I shall approach the moment of reception and the impact of mediation on non-activist audiences in a multi-dimensional way, attempting to unearth and expose the 'heterogeneous properties of audience discourses about media experiences' (Schrøder 2000: 242) and, in the context of this study, also the properties of audiences' attitudes towards the ideas and imaginaries put forward by the anti-austerity movement.

The theorization and understanding of the influence or impact of media on citizens and society at large, are, at best, fractured and highly contested. This is unsurprising, for two main reasons. On the one hand, given the sheer complexity and multifaceted nature of the process of reception and opinion formation, there is a temptation to simplify things. On the other hand, the question of the precise nature and degree of the impact and influence of the media and, by extension, of communication tools such as the internet, represents what Corner (2000) rightfully describes as 'the contested core of media research'. Were the questions of reception and impact not to matter, it would make no sense to study the media or the communicative practices enacted by various actors.

Given the contentious nature of assessing the relationship between media consumption and the formation of opinions, it is essential first to theorize the reception side of the Circuit of Protest, and position ourselves in the ongoing debates regarding the process of opinion formation and the role of mediation in it.

6.1 From Effects to Negotiated Decoding

The media effects tradition is the dominant way to address the relationship between media, on the one hand, and the opinion formation process on the other. Broadly speaking it is mainly interested in the (measurable) effects of media on audiences. Early versions of the effects model assumed that the mediated connection between transmitter and receiver resulted in a linear effect on audiences' behaviours and/or attitudes, in the form of a stimulus-response reaction. Lasswell (1927) famously wrote that *the* key question to understand a communicative process can be summarized as: 'Who says what to whom, with what effect?'

6.1.1 The Effects Tradition

One of the early responses to this effects questions was the so-called Hypodermic Needle or Magic Bullet theory. These theories attribute to mass media the potency to affect behaviours directly and shape the opinions of a gullible and malleable audience. It is perhaps not surprising that the emergence of these theories coincided with the birth and quite rapid diffusion of radio during the interbellum period. Important in this regard was the facility offered by radio to reach beyond the literate elites and how, subsequently, this new mass medium assumed a pivotal role in the propaganda efforts of the USA, the UK, Nazi Germany, and Soviet Russia in the run-up to, and during, the Second World War. The classic case embodying this direct effects model was the dramatic impact on US audiences of the 1938 broadcast of H. G. Wells' *The War of the Worlds*, an ironically realistic radio play directed by Orson Welles.

One of the main problems of the direct effects model was that, apart from Cantril et al.'s (1940) study on *The War of the Worlds* case,[1] there was a lack of sound empirical support for the bold claims made by this model. Attempts to prove a direct effect empirically exposed the model's inherent weaknesses and tended to highlight the complexity of media consumption and its impact on audiences. The famous study by Lazarsfeld et al. (1944) on the factors determining citizens' choices during a US presidential election campaign set out to prove the hypothesis of the direct effect of media on the voting intentions of citizens. Instead, the evidence pointed in another direction, namely that citizens have more agency and do not necessarily change their values or behaviours simply because the media tells them to do so.

On the basis of Lazarsfeld and his colleagues' results, a two-step flow model (sometimes called a limited effects model) was deemed more credible. The media influence opinion leaders, who follow the news consistently. These opinion leaders subsequently influence others by alerting them to certain content and ideas, while also providing their own schemata of interpretation or framing. This limited effect was confirmed by Klapper's (1960) selective exposure thesis, which concluded that people not only avoid contact with content that contradicts their own predispositions but they also develop selective perception and retention patterns when confronted with views or information that counter their own.

The advent of television saw theories of powerful media re-emerge and challenge the no effects and limited effects theories. Two important shifts were behind this return to a belief in the existence of strong and pervasive media effects. First, the influence of social psychology on the field of audience studies (rather than political science) and the shift this provoked from attempts to measure immediate behavioural effects on audiences to a focus on more long-term cognitive processes and longitudinal effects. Second, and of less interest here, was the shift in focus from the effects on media-consuming audiences to the political economy of media institutions themselves, their ownership structures, and the power of the media to embody hegemony and reinforce the status quo.

In relation to the first shift from political science to social psychology, Lang and Lang's (1959) study of the influence of mass media and voting in the USA was highly influential. In contrast to the limited effects model, this study repositioned mass media as a forceful actor in the shaping of public opinion. In doing so, long-term cultural influences that are transmitted through media were emphasized without necessarily being involved in purely behavioural change. Somewhat reminiscent of the concept of framing, as discussed in Chaps. 2 and 3, Lang and Lang (1959: 232) concluded that:

> The mass media force attention to certain issues. They build up public images of political figures. They are constantly presenting objects suggesting what individuals in the mass should think about, know about, have feelings about.

Later, McCombs and Shaw (1972) described this as the agenda-setting power of the media. In their article, they quoted Cohen (1963: 13), who famously stated that the media 'may not be successful much of the time in telling people what to think, but it is stunningly successful in telling its readers what to think about'. McCombs and Shaw identified patterns of influence between what is being reported in the media and what voters consider to be the campaign's key issues. This occurs in the form, not of a direct correlation or 'effect', but rather as a somewhat negotiated media influence. This is concurrent with the concept of priming, which introduces a longitudinal perspective. Priming theory posits that offering audiences a prior context enhances the power of mass media, since that context then is used to interpret subsequent communication (Iyengar and Kinder 1987).

As this brief and incomplete overview shows, perception of media power tends to vary over time and, like a pendulum, swings from all-powerful to not powerful at all, and back again (Katz 1980). However, some critics have also attacked the effects/transmission model at an epistemological level (Lewis and Cruz 1994; Gauntlett 1995). They reject the very possibility that media effects are measurable; and that they can be isolated from the many other factors that impact the formation of the public's opinions. Furthermore, they also contest the assumption that imbued meaning is singular and unambiguous at the level of both production and reception.

6.1.2 *Decoding and the Active Audience*

In contrast, many studies showed that mediated content is intrinsically polysemic and that, also at the level of reception, a variety of different interpretations of media content are being made by audiences. Hall's (1980 [1973]) encoding/decoding essay was hugely influential in this regard. It rejected the behaviourism inherent in many of the effects approaches: a television programme, Hall wrote, 'is not a behavioral input, like a tap on the knee' (ibid.: 131). He pointed also to the need to reconnect the process of reception or *decoding* to the discursive power relations embedded in the production or *encoding* of media texts.

Hall argued that the communicative process needed to be rearticulated 'without lapsing into one or other variant of low-flying behaviourism' (ibid.: 131), but, at the same time, he also stressed that, contrary to what many orthodox Marxist theories lead us to believe, those doing the decoding of media texts are discursive subjects rather than passive receivers of dominant ideology. As a result of this, the interpretation of media texts by audiences needs to be articulated as varied and contingent, but without denying the dominant and hegemonic nature of the encoding process.

Audiences have agency, and their interpretative frameworks can potentially play a disruptive role in the way that media content and information are decoded and contextualized:

> Audiences, like broadcasters, also stand in their own (very different) positions, relations and situations, have their own (again, different) relationship to power, to information, to sources, and bring *their* own frameworks of interpretation to bear in order to get a meaning, or *decode* the message. (Hall 1981 [1973]: 280; emphasis in original)

However, these decoding processes operate in conjunction or in opposition, and thus are relational to a preferential, a dominant or a hegemonic encoding process. Hall distinguishes three main ways in which audiences potentially decode and receive mediated information:

1. Via a compliant or *preferred reading*, whereby the dominant/hegemonic meaning encoded in the text is decoded in similar ways, the sender and the receiver share the same assumptions and biases. In other words, the decoder operates 'inside the dominant code' (Hall 1980 [1973]: 137), and thus it could be argued that, from one perspective, the communicative process, in this case, is successful;
2. Via a *negotiated reading*, whereby the dominant/hegemonic reading is deciphered broadly correctly and understood by the decoder, but tends to be applied in slightly different and at times contradictory ways, giving rise to a negotiated code—a 'mixture between adaptive and oppositional elements', both accepting the legitimacy of the hegemony, while reserving the 'right to make a more negotiated application' (ibid.). Here, we can envisage much scope for misunderstandings, contradictions and disjunctures in the communicative process; and
3. Via a resistant or *oppositional reading*, which identifies the dominant/hegemonic encoding for what it is, but at the same time rejects it and superimposes on it a critical oppositional code—thereby, retotalizing 'the message within some alternative framework or reference' (ibid.: 138). Here, it could be argued, the communicative process is, at the same time, successful and not successful, since the preferential reading is contested.

One of the many important contributions made by Hall, and cultural studies more generally, relates to having made audiences '*visible*, theoretically, empirically and politically' (Livingstone 1998: 195; emphasis in original). Also, opening up the possibility of various readings and interpretations strengthened and promoted the idea of active and, in particular, creative audiences (Morley 1993). Furthermore, Hall's work constitutes a clear critique of the effects models and behaviourism, precisely because variation in interpretations 'works against the idea of any uniform influence' (Corner 1995: 137). In addition, from a social movement perspective, the reception of movement frames and the role of media discourse in this process was being recognized increasingly as 'complicated and bidirectional' (Gamson 1992: 180).

However, there are some important critiques that have been levelled against the ways that Hall's theoretical exploration was appropriated and used subsequently in the cultural studies tradition. Some criticized cultural studies approaches for failing to explain 'how ideology works in and through the communications system' (Murdock 1989: 439). However, it also has to be acknowledged that cultural studies, and Hall in particular, has from its inception been deeply concerned with questions of ideology and dominance. Part of the problem here, according to some, was an overly uncritical celebritization of the polysemic nature of reception, and in particular the danger of equating polysemic reception with oppositional meanings. Morley (1992: 30; emphasis in original), for instance, criticized this 'tendency to find (and celebrate) traces of *opposition* everywhere'.

Many audience researchers who adopted Hall's encoding/decoding model in their qualitative empirical research found more nuance and greater heterogeneity in audiences' alternative decoding practices, many of which did not fit neatly within the negotiated, resistant or oppositional categories as theorized by Hall (see, among others, Lindlof 1991; Morley 1992; Lewis and Cruz 1994; Deacon et al. 1999; Schrøder 2000). This led Chen (1996: 318) to note that the encoding/decoding model fails to 'adequately account for the complex flow of social forces and its various conditions of possibility'.

Alongside these criticisms, questions relating to the uses and gratification of media and technology re-emerged, accompanied by issues about personal influences. In the field of social movement studies, Gamson and Modigliani (1989) studied opinion formation in the context of nuclear energy and concluded that personal experiences, predispositions, social networks, and 'life histories' matter a great deal in the process of meaning-making. This is in line with Katz and Lazersfeld's (1955) personal influence thesis, which at its core argues that 'processes of media influence are mediated by social contexts, including community and face-to-face interactions' (Livingstone 2006: 243), an argument that was also foregrounded by Gamson (1992) in the context of social movements.

Another important and more recent aspect that influences what we understand audiences to be in an arguably quite major way, is the changing technological landscape encompassing the various networked devices that audiences use to read, watch and listen. As mentioned briefly in Chap. 2, Silverstone (1994) rightly argued that mediation is not just about media texts—that is, the symbolic; it also has a material/technological component. This technological component has undergone astonishing changes in recent decades. For example, we could refer to the impact of the video cassette recorder (VCR) on television viewing habits, the role of the Sony Walkman in changing the way we listen to music, or the consequences of digitalization and the internet on pretty much everything to do with communication and media consumption. As a result of this double articulation of mediation—as symbolic text and as material object—audiences are, similarly, doubly articulated. They are seen to (re)produce both:

> 1. Meanings by negotiating the mutual interface of text and reader; and
> 2. Social relations by negotiating the material/social determinations that structure their everyday contexts of action.
>
> (Livingstone and Das 2013: 105)

Indeed, it is crucially important to consider the everyday contexts in which citizens read, listen, watch, and, increasingly, also interact and communicate. Thus, reception becomes an ever more complex phenomenon, characterized by a wide variety of media and communication platforms, of circulating conflicting meanings, and of diverse media and communicative practices. At the same time, we should not forget that, despite most people spending the majority of their daily media time online, and despite the diversity of content and meanings accessible through the internet, most of the content that circulates, and meaning-making that occurs online, are produced by the same media and communication organizations/companies/elites that produce and shape offline content.

Despite its flaws, I am drawn to Hall's encoding/decoding model, as it negotiates a position between compliance and resistance, acknowledging hegemony, but also leaving room for counter-hegemony, accounting for structural power, without denying the possibility of agency. In the context of this study, we can identify two main encoders: social movement actors, and mainstream media. However, it would be fair to assume that most 'ordinary' citizens receive their information about social movements and protest, not directly from a social movement's website, Facebook page or

Twitter account, but from the mainstream representations of protest. As shown in the previous chapter, this representation was a combination of hegemonic condemnation and some degree of reproduction of the counter-hegemonic frames.

At the level of the decoding by citizens, things become a bit complicated and less straightforward than Hall's model. Since I am examining the nature of the reception of social movements' frames and ideas circulating through society, the preferred decoding is an oppositional counter-hegemonic one, aligned with the social movement encodings. In order not to confuse things even further, I would juxtapose this with a hegemonic decoding that rejects social movement frames and aligns with hegemonic interests in society. A negotiated decoding then combines features of both hegemonic and counter-hegemonic decodings. Thus, I concur also with those who claim that the encoding/decoding model needs to be nuanced and complicated. Given the complex nature of mediation and opinion formation, the ways in which social movement encodings, through discourse or through framing, are decoded, is bound to be varied and, at times, contradictory, especially in ideological terms.

6.2 Citizens' Attitudes Towards the Anti-Austerity Movement and Its Discourse

To assess the way in which movement discourses are decoded by audiences, the focus here is mainly on non-activist citizens, those who do not attend demonstrations on a regular basis and are not active members of political organizations or social movements. First, a number of questions relating to the movement frames, knowledge of the movement, sympathy with the movement, and media consumption were put to a representative sample of 1651 UK citizens. The survey was conducted via a representative online panel from 12 December 2014 to 5 January 2015. The credibility interval of this survey was ±2.41%. Quotas were used for gender, age, and geographical distribution. We do have to acknowledge, however, that while online polling is much cheaper than traditional polling, it also has serious limitations (Zukin 2015). An important limitation is that online surveys use non-probability sampling, and those who are attracted to participate in online panels are not fully representative of the general population; they opt-in and we do not know who opted out. Furthermore, respondents need to have internet access and posess internet skills which in itself could induce biases. However, despite these weaknesses, non-probability-based samples can be useful 'for identifying issues, defining ranges of alternatives, or collecting other sorts of non-inferential data' (Fricker 2017: 167). As such, I shied away from correlation and regression analyses in this chapter and we need to treat the survey data with some caution, as the results are probably more indicative of certain trends rather than being truly statistically representative of the UK population.

A survey, much like an unfocused photograph, can provide a vague insight into what respondents think about the movement frames, and their attitudes towards the movement, but it does not provide much depth into answering questions as to why the respondents think the way they do, and this is where focus groups come in (Kitzinger 1995). Three focus groups, comprised of average non-activist citizens who agreed broadly with the anti-austerity frames and discourses, were conducted. I decided I wanted to understand better the complexity of reception within a group of people who were not very politically active, but who broadly agreed with the anti-austerity movement frames, rather than focusing on those who completely disagreed with or rejected their framings. I also privileged gender and generational difference over class differences, since all the focus group participants were middle-class (C1 and C2 category).

As already mentioned in Chap. 2, the focus groups were held on 2 and 3 June 2015. Two were held in London—one with a group of young women aged between 18 and 29 years, and the other with a group of women aged between 30 and 49 years. The third focus group was held in Birmingham with a group of older men aged between 50 and 65 years. The groups were mixed in terms of voters and non-voters, political persuasion and ethnicity. The focus group discussions were analysed with a thematic analysis using the movement frames identified in Chap. 3, attitudes for and against UK Uncut, Occupy, and the student protests and role of media/mediation.

I am acutely aware that three focus groups is insufficient, and that this weakens my analysis. This fact, together with the use of an online panel comprising a non-probability-based sample, warrants some care and prudence in terms of the claims we can derive from this data. Nevertheless, I do think that the combination of the survey and focus group data provided some fascinating insights into the complexity of the reception process of social movement and protest frames, as will become apparent in this chapter.

First, I shall discuss alignment with the movement frames. Second, knowledge about the UK anti-austerity movement, and support for the movement, will be assessed. The role and potential impact of the media and of mediation is analysed in the final section of this chapter.

6.2.1 Degree of Resonance of Movement Frames

Before mentioning the movement to the respondents, they were prompted to agree or disagree with a set of statements, which concurred with or contradicted the anti-austerity movement frames. It should be noted that a sizeable proportion of respondents chose the neutral option when asked for their opinion on these statements; between 20% and 30% stated that they had no opinion on these statements. Despite this relatively high proportion of 'don't knows', it seems that many of the anti-austerity movement's frames are supported by a considerable majority of respondents (cf. Table 6.1). The focus-group data, however, provided some important nuances to this overall picture of high frame resonance.

Table 6.1 Agreement and disagreement with the following statements[a]

	The financial sector should abide by much more stringent rules and regulations—% AGREE	*Inequality has risen to unsustainable proportions—% AGREE*	*The privatization of public services such as the NHS and schools is a good thing—% DISAGREE*	*Companies and multinationals should be allowed to use loopholes and profit from generous tax-rules—% DISAGREE*
Male ($n = 814$)	81	65	50	66
Female ($n = 837$)	76	59	52	63
16–24 ($n = 231$)	63	56	39	43
25–39 ($n = 397$)	70	60	42	48
40–54 ($n = 434$)	82	69	55	67
55–64 ($n = 311$)	88	59	60	80
65+ ($n = 278$)	87	64	59	85
No Qual. ($n = 104$)	75	65	56	61
O/A Levels ($n = 830$)	78	63	50	66
BA/Voc. ($n = 569$)	81	61	52	66

(*continued*)

Table 6.1 (continued)

	The financial sector should abide by much more stringent rules and regulations—% AGREE	*Inequality has risen to unsustainable proportions—% AGREE*	*The privatization of public services such as the NHS and schools is a good thing—% DISAGREE*	*Companies and multinationals should be allowed to use loopholes and profit from generous tax-rules—% DISAGREE*
MA/PhD (*n* = 148)	74	61	51	59
Regular Newspaper Readers (*n* = 1013)	82	67	64	66
Non- or Low Newspaper Readers (*n* = 638)	73	61	60	61
Total (*n* = 1651):	78	62	51	65

Source: Own data (for *Gender* and *Age*, all cross-tabulations are significant, respectively at the 0.05 and the 0.001 levels; for *Education*—only financial rules and inequality are significant at the 0.05 level; for *Newspapers*, cross-tabulations for privatization, tax loopholes and financial rules are significant at the 0.001 level, but there is no statistical association between newspaper reading and views on inequality)

[a]All the percentages in this chapter were rounded up in the case of those >0.5%, and rounded down in the case of those <0.5%

Overall, men tended to be more supportive of the anti-austerity frames than the women, with the exception of privatization of the NHS and schools; here the differences are within the credibility interval of ±2.41%. Generational differences can also be observed; counter-intuitively, older generations tend to be more progressive and align themselves more with the anti-austerity movement frames than those who are younger (and this is statistically significant at the 0.001 level). Education level seems to have little impact, and is also less significant statistically.

Stricter regulation of the financial sector received strong support across the UK population, regardless of socio-demographic characteristics—almost 80% of respondents agreed with the introduction of more stringent rules and regulations. An anti-bankers discourse could also be discerned in the focus groups:

> The bankers—nothing happens to them, they get millions as a bonus and workers are laid off. (Focus Group 3, older male, June 2015)

Over 60% of respondents agreed with the statements that inequality has risen to unsustainable levels, and that our 'representative' democratic system protects the interests of the few over the many. In the focus groups, inequality was an important topic, which generated much discussion, but inequality was interpreted broadly in terms of fairness/unfairness, and as inevitable and something that cannot be changed:

> The social circles individuals were brought up in matter; if you come from a poorer family your life expectancy is much shorter and you don't have the educational support. (Focus Group 1, young female, June 2015)

> There was an unfair distribution of wealth. There's a small minority of people that are very wealthy and the wealth is contained in that minority. (Focus Group 2, middle-aged female, June 2015)

> It's always been that the top 10% earn 90% of the wealth …You are never going to change that whether it's an austere environment or not. (Focus Group 3, older male, June 2015)

Concern regarding inequality, and seen through the prism of unfairness, was directed not only to the top end of the social ladder, but also to the bottom end. In discussions about rising inequality, those in receipt of benefits, and immigrants, were also blamed by some focus group members:

> I think it's [inequality] always been there. But Labour bringing in all these benefits, making people feel comfortable, then the crash. (Focus Group 1, young female, June 2015)

> They [immigrants] haven't paid tax. They come in, they say they've got illness, there's nothing wrong with them. They're just staying in the bed; we can't get rid of them because they want a house. (Focus Group 2, middle-aged female, June 2015)

This is not entirely surprising, given how much of the UK's media reports on immigration, and how they represent the poor and disadvantaged in society. A recent study on how the poor, and recipients of welfare,

are represented in UK, Danish and Swedish print media, concluded that the UK's conservative and tabloid newspapers consistently portray the able-bodied poor and those on benefits in a negative and punitive way, 'often constructed around the stereotypes about the deviance of the poor' (Larsen and Dejgaard 2013: 298). There is, in the UK, a long tradition of what has been called 'scroungerphobia' (Golding and Middleton 1982). Similarly, immigrants are depicted in very negative, and some would argue racist, ways by the British media, exhibiting implicit as well as explicit xenophobia (KhosraviNik 2010: 23). The tabloid media in particular, but also the right-wing broadsheets, often conflate refugees, asylum seekers, immigrants and migrants, and they can be deemed to be 'responsible for creating and maintaining a moral panic' regarding immigrants and asylum seekers (Gabrielatos and Baker 2008: 33).

Regarding privatization of the British National Health Service (NHS) and schools, the degree of support for this was higher than expected; younger people, especially, do not find privatization of these quintessential 'public' services overly problematic (cf. Table 6.1). While a third of 16–24-year-olds agreed with the statement that privatization of the NHS and schools would be a good thing, only around one in six of the over-40-year-olds agreed. It has to be said in this regard that the neoliberal discourse of privatization and the rejection of an interventionist state goes back to the end of the 1970s in the UK and has been very dominant ever since; as Mizen (2002: 18) concludes in his piece on the impact of monetanism on youth:

> under the guise of the 'Third Way', in rejecting the interventionist state and endorsing the strategy of depoliticization, New Labour have succeeded in going beyond previous governments in their determination to restructure youth.

Given that focus group participants were recruited on the basis of their support for anti-austerity frames, however, it was not surprising to find that public sector cuts were seen to be among the most obvious and visible effects of the economics crisis:

> They're closing three of the hospitals near me so it's had a horrible impact, everyone has to go to one A&E, so, yeah, I'm really worried about that. (Focus Group 1, young female, June 2015)

There also was fairly widespread disagreement, both in the survey and in the focus groups, with the statement that companies and multinationals should be allowed to use loopholes to avoid paying taxes. Fair taxation is a significant anti-austerity movement frame, especially for UK Uncut. About 78% of respondents (*n* = 1284) claimed to have knowledge about companies, multinationals, and the rich engaging in aggressive tax avoidance.

When asked for their views on this, the overall sentiment was negative. Table 6.2 shows that a large majority of respondents, across all socio-demographic variables, believe that rich individuals, companies and multinationals should contribute more to society. It has to be noted here that cross-tabulations with age were not statistically significant. This support for higher taxes for the rich and for companies was supported by the focus groups, where the notion of fairness re-emerged:

> I think the rich should pay a bit more tax because they can afford it. I have to pay £150 a month for my council tax, and someone who's got way more has to pay the same as me, it's not fair. (Focus Group 2, middle-aged female, June 2015)

Table 6.2 Attitudes towards taxation

	Rich and wealthy individuals should pay more taxes—% AGREE	*Companies should pay more taxes—% AGREE*
Male (*n* = 814)	77	77
Female (*n* = 837)	71	69
16–24 (*n* = 231)	72	71
25–39 (*n* = 397)	74	73
40–54 (*n* = 434)	74	75
55–64 (*n* = 311)	72	69
65+ (*n* = 278)	77	76
No Qual (*n* = 104)	70	71
O&A Level (*n* = 830)	74	73
BA/Voc (*n* = 569)	72	73
MA/PhD (*n* = 148)	81	76
Regular Newspaper Readers (*n* = 1013)	74	76
Non- or Low Newspaper Readers (*n* = 638)	73	65
Total (*n* = 1651):	74	73

Source: Own data (for *Gender* and *Newspaper*, all cross-tabulations are significant, respectively at the 0.001 and 0.05 levels; for *Education*, only statement on individuals is significant at 0.05 level; cross-tabulations for *Age* are not statistically significant)

However, to nuance this somewhat, when asked about their own taxes only 3% ($n = 50$) of respondents considered that their personal tax bill was too low. Similarly, in the focus group with middle-class participants, who described themselves explicitly as 'the squeezed middle', there was no appetite for higher taxes: 'I don't want to pay more tax!', one participant exclaimed (Focus Group 1, young female, June 2015).

Democracy, it seems, has become an empty signifier for many people—'I'm probably going to sound like a right idiot but what do you mean by democracy? I don't understand', a focus-group participant asked (Focus Group 1, Young female, June 2015). In the survey, the statement that democracy is geared towards protecting the interests of the rich rather than those of ordinary working people, resonated fairly strongly (cf. Table 6.3). Almost two-thirds of respondents believed that the current democratic system does not represent their interests. Education level has a considerable impact on whether this systemic critique of the democratic system is shared (which is statistically significant at the 0.05 level). Age is also statistically significant (at 0.05 level), with older people being more critical of democracy than younger ones.

Table 6.3 Critique of the representative model of democracy

	Our democratic system protects the interests of rich people over and above those of ordinary working people—% AGREE
Male ($n = 814$)	63
Female ($n = 837$)	57
16–24 ($n = 231$)	56
25–39 ($n = 397$)	60
40–54 ($n = 434$)	61
55–64 ($n = 311$)	59
65+ ($n = 278$)	64
No Qual. ($n = 104$)	54
O/A Levels ($n = 830$)	59
BA/Voc. ($n = 569$)	62
MA/PhD ($n = 148$)	66
Regular Newspaper Readers ($n = 1013$)	62
Non- or Low Newspaper Readers (n = 638)	58
Total ($n = 1651$):	60

Source: Own data (for *Gender*, the cross-tabulation is significant at the 0.001 level; For *Age* and *Education*, the cross-tabulations are significant at the 0.05 level; cross-tabulation with *Newspapers* is not statistically significant)

In the focus groups, this critique of the representative model of democracy, something stressed particularly by Occupy LSX, resonated strongly with participants. There seemed to be a general feeling amongst the focus group participants that politicians do not represent 'ordinary' folk:

> I think they [politicians] make up their own mind anyway and I don't think whatever we say matters, it doesn't have an impact. (Focus Group 2, middle-aged female, June 2015)

> The latest elections show it's not very representative, is it? …a quarter of people who bothered to vote voted for the Tories and they're in a majority. So where's the democracy in that? (Focus Group 3, older male, June 2015)

> I think you need more people in politics who have been in the real world than have been to high education and this, that and the other, I don't think they understand. (Focus Group 2, middle-aged female, June 2015)

As in the case of inequality, there seems to be a degree of complacency and 'giving up' in relation to the potential to be able to change things: 'I heard so many people say this election like "What's the point of voting—they are all the same anyway"' (Focus Group 1, young female, June 2015). However, many of the participants in the focus groups themselves felt that it was, nevertheless important to participate and to be involved

> I don't know if it makes a difference, but I think you have to be involved, otherwise shut up basically. (Focus Group 2, middle-aged female, June 2015)

While it is, in my view, impossible to isolate the precise impact of media consumption or mediation from the multiple other factors affecting opinion formation, the data about media consumption does suggest that citizens who have a high degree of media use, especially of reading newspapers, are more likely to agree with the most common frames of the anti-austerity movement, but this tends also to relate to higher levels of education.

6.2.2 *Knowledge of the Anti-Austerity Movement*

To assess knowledge about the anti-austerity movement, it was decided to focus on three organizations/mobilizations that had come to symbolize the UK anti-austerity movement in recent years. First, UK Uncut, a direct action organization that uses flash-mob tactics to mobilize against, and raise awareness of, companies evading taxation in the UK. Second, Occupy LSX, a loosely organized group of people, who in 2011 occupied the steps of St Paul's Cathedral and a square north of London's financial district to protest against the lack of regulation of the financial system, and against austerity. Third, the NCAFC, a direct-action organization that emerged out of the 2010 student protests against the tripling of tuition fees in the UK, but, from the outset had extended its agenda also to protest against cuts to public services more broadly.

The survey results show that only a relative minority of respondents had heard of these anti-austerity organizations or mobilizations (cf. Table 6.4). A third of respondents knew about Occupy LSX, but only around 15% had heard of UK Uncut and NCAFC. There was a clear generational effect (statistically significant at the 0.001 level); the younger respondents were more likely to know about the anti-austerity movement. For example, about 40% of the respondents between 16 and 39 years old knew about Occupy LSX, compared to only 26% of the respondents over 65 years old. There was also a significant gender difference (statistically

Table 6.4 Knowledge of the movements

	Occupy LSX %	*UK-Uncut* %	*NCAFC* %
Male (n = 814)	41	21	10
Female (n = 837)	25	11	19
16–24 (n = 231)	39	29	30
25–39 (n = 397)	40	21	22
40–54 (n = 434)	30	12	9
55–64 (n = 311)	30	10	7
65+ (n = 278)	26	10	6
No Qual (n = 104)	16	11	10
O&A Level (n = 830)	28	14	14
BA/Voc (n = 569)	39	16	15
MA/PhD (n = 148)	49	26	22
Regular Newspaper Readers (n = 1013)	39	19	19
Non- or Low Newspaper Readers (n = 638)	24	10	8
Regular TV Viewers (n = 1444)	33	15	14
Non or Low TV Viewers (n = 207)	35	20	19
Total (n = 1651):	33	16	15

Source: Own data (for *Gender*, *Age* and *Media Use*, all cross-tabulations are significant for all cases at the 0.001 level; for *Education*, UK Uncut cross-tabulations are significant at 0.001, NCAFC at 0.05, and Occupy is not significant)

significant at the 0.001 level), with men much more likely to know about Occupy LSX and UK Uncut, whereas women were more likely to have heard of the NCAFC. Education also seems to play an important role as an indicator of whether the individual had prior knowledge of these organizations and mobilizations. Respectively, 16% and 11% of people without educational qualifications had heard about Occupy LSX and UK Uncut, compared to almost 50% and 26% of those with a masters or a doctoral degree. It has to be noted here, though, that the cross-tabulations for Occupy with educational level were not statistically significant.

Despite being aligned with the movement frames, participants in the focus groups were not really aware of particular cases. However, when prompted with a media image of St Paul's Cathedral, many did recall these protests, but some also referred to the nuisance they created:

> I remember when they were at St Paul's and it felt like they were there for ages, and it was a real inconvenience for people who worked around there and visited St Paul's. (Focus Group 2, middle-aged female, June 2015)

In addition to probing respondents' knowledge about the movement, they were also asked if they had heard of the slogan '99% versus 1%'. This slogan encapsulates much of what the anti-austerity movement is about. In many ways, the '99% versus 1%' slogan can be seen as an attempt to build class alliances or a 'chain of equivalence' (Laclau and Mouffe 1985) among various struggles, a prevalent tactic of many social movements in the history of social change.

However, considering the extensive circulation of this slogan online as well as in the mainstream media, relatively few respondents said they were familiar with it. Slightly more than 40% of people claimed have heard of it (n = 695). Education level is clearly a strong indicator in this regard (significant at the 0.05 level). While slightly less than 30% of those with no higher education qualification had heard of the '99% versus 1%', a large majority of those with a masters or doctoral degree indicated that they were familiar with it (about 65%). Also, age is an important factor (significant at the 0.05 level)—the younger the individual, the more likely it is that they will be familiar with the slogan (57% of 16–24-year-olds compared to only 32% of those aged 65+).

Among those aware of the '99% versus 1%' slogan, there was a tendency also to support its premise (about 65%). Interesting, here, is that those with no higher education qualification, who had heard about the slogan, were as likely to agree with it as those with a higher education qualification who were aware of the slogan (both about 75%). However, as pointed out earlier by the focus group data, the notion of inequality is related not just to the 1%. When discussing taxation as a way to redistribute and lower inequality, some participants focused on clamping down on immigration and benefits as integral to solving the 'fairness' problem: one focus group participant was adamant that 'if you come to the country you shouldn't be able to get benefits straight away' (Focus Group 1, young female, June 2015).

The degree of media consumption plays an important role here (statistically significant for all cases at the 0.001 level). Knowledge of the movement was considerably higher among people who read a newspaper regularly, compared to those who only occasionally or never read one (cf. Table 6.4). Paradoxically, those who watched little or no television were significantly more knowledgeable about the movement than those who regularly watched television, in particular in the case of knowing about UK Uncut and NCAFC, but rather less so in the case of Occupy LSX. This might potentially be explained by more time spent online, which is used prolifically by these movements to self-mediate.

Respondents who had prior knowledge of the slogan '99% versus 1%' (n = 695) and of aggressive tax evasion (n = 1285), were asked where they had come across the slogan and the information on tax evasion (cf. Table 6.5). This revealed the continuing importance of mainstream media

Table 6.5 Where did you hear about '99% versus 1%' or 'aggressive tax evasion'? (multiple answers were possible)

	The Slogan '99% versus 1%' *(n = 695/42%)* %	*Aggressive tax evasion* *(n = 1285/78%)* %
Protest event	11	6
Family or friends	16	12
Newspaper	26	46
Radio	12	18
TV	25	63
Surfing online	15	17
Social media	10	7

Source: Own data

(especially newspapers and television, but, to a lesser extent, also radio), as well as the internet and social media for learning about movement frames and politics more generally. However, as also shown by previous studies (e.g. Gamson 1992), family, friends and protest events also provide information, but in a somewhat less pronounced way compared to the media and communication tools taken together.

6.2.3 *Sympathy with the Aims and Goals of the Anti-Austerity Movement*

After explaining to the respondents what UK Uncut, Occupy LSX and the NCAFC stood for,[2] they were asked if, and to what extent, they sympathised with the anti-austerity movement. Many respondents had no opinion (between 25% and 30%), but among those who did, a clear majority sided with the movements. Unsurprising given the sampling criteria, this relatively high level of support was also observed in the focus groups:

> Some of these kids we should take a leaf from them, because they are passionate, sometimes when you get older you get a bit down trodden, but these kids they have a fire in their belly, maybe we should listen to them. (Focus Group 2, middle-aged female, June 2015)

> I think it is great that there are ethical people who will stand up. (Focus Group 3, older male, June 2015)

Slightly more than half of the respondents agreed with Occupy LSX (53%) and with NCAFC (56%), but almost 65% agreed with the aims and goals of UK Uncut (cf. Fig. 6.1). Overall, more male than female respondents were sympathetic to the anti-austerity movement (significant at the 0.001 level). However, there were generally no stark generational differences, except in the case of the student protest organization NCAFC, which was supported by 64% of respondents aged 16–24 years, compared to about 50% of those aged over 55 years. This can be explained, of course, by NCAFC's emphasis on tuition fees, quality of higher education, and student interests.

Education played an important predictive role (significant at the 0.001 level). Across the board, the higher the level of education, the higher the support for the anti-austerity movement. UK Uncut received 72% support

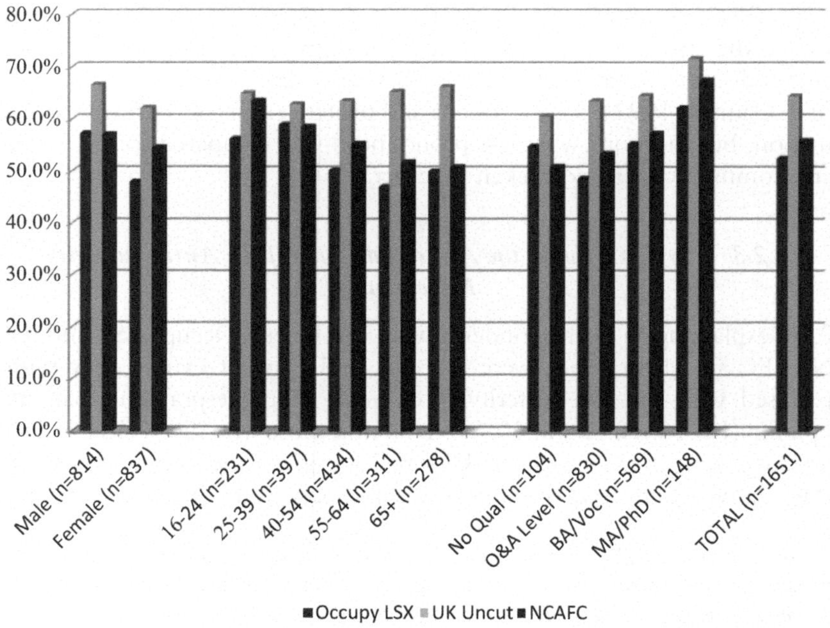

Fig. 6.1 Degree of sympathy and support for the anti-austerity movement. Source: own data (all cross tabulations are significant at the 0.001 level)

among those with a higher education degree, compared to 61% of those without one. Similarly, Occupy received 62% support among those with a MA/PhD degree, compared to around than 50% support from those without qualifications, or those educated to A Level and undergraduates. The NCAFC too scored much higher among those with a higher education (68% support among those with a MA/PhD degree) compared to those with only upper secondary education (51% of those with no university-level qualification).

The focus group participants were sampled from those who expressed broad agreement with the movement frames; thus it could be expected that these participants would align themselves generally with the anti-austerity movement (sometimes to their own surprise). At the same time, serious doubts were raised regarding the effectiveness of these movements and their radical image. One participant praised the fact that protest movements raise awareness, but referred also to the difficulty of sustaining protest: 'I think they bring more awareness of what is happening, but it often seems to die out' (Focus Group 3, older male, June 2015).

Across the three focus groups, the disruptive tactics enacted by the movement were not supported, and some considered such activities to be more damaging to the public or ordinary working people than to the actual targets of the protests:

> I do agree with some of the things they are fighting for, but I get a bit scared with organizations like that, that they are going to take it a bit far, like, I'm all for some things, but don't go mad and, you know, try and be Guy Fawkes. (Focus Group 1, young female, June 2015)

> I think they seem more aggressive, so sitting in Vodafone [in the case of UK Uncut], that's actually in someone's workspace. So you might be impacting the company but you're also being confrontational with the staff. (Focus Group 2, middle-aged female, June 2015)

> There is a lot of thuggery, don't get me wrong, I'm not saying everybody is, there are intelligent people in them, but a lot of these people want to go out for a fight. (Focus Group 3, older male, June 2015)

Compared to knowledge about the movement, the influence of newspaper reading on sympathy with the movement was less obvious (cf. Table 6.6), which indicates that the movement frames resonate quite broadly among the UK population. In this regard, newspaper readership is associated statistically with sympathy for the movements. TV use (whether high or low), however, is not.

Table 6.6 Sympathy with the movement related to degree of media use

	Occupy LSX %	*UK-Uncut* %	*NCAFC* %
Regular newspaper readers (n = 1013)	55	67	59
Non- or low newspaper readers (n = 638)	49	61	51
Regular TV viewers (n = 1444)	53	65	57
Non- or low TV viewers (n = 207)	52	57	50
Total (n = 1651):	52	64	56

Source: Own data (for newspapers, all cross-tabulations are significant at the 0.001 level; for TV there is a marginal significance for Occupy (0.052), but not for the other cases)

6.2.4 *The Role of Media and Mediation*

Overall, we can observe that higher degrees of, in particular, newspaper consumption tends to increase knowledge about political issues, which seems a reasonable assumption. Being more and better informed as well as having higher levels of education also impact positively on support for the movement frames and sympathy for the movement.

In the focus groups, media was discussed from several angles. However, very few participants were able to recall news stories about the anti-austerity movement without some explicit prompting. When prompted by newspaper headlines and photos, many participants declared that the media did not represent the anti-austerity protests fairly. At the same time, the participants were self-reflexive and exhibited quite high degrees of lay knowledge about media representation of these groups and, in particular, relative to the participants' fairly low or sporadic use of the media. Selection biases and misrepresentations by the media were identified, alongside a tendency for the media to focus on the violent and spectacular:

> They make them all seem like hippies and whacky crazy people or really aggressive people. (Focus Group 1, young female, June 2015)

> Sometimes at marches you do get one person who's going to kick off and they concentrate on that. It's not fair. (Focus Group 2, middle-aged female, June 2015)

> I think the media's selective about what they choose to focus on. Even after the election there were a few protests but it was really bitty, the coverage I saw. (Focus Group 2, middle-aged female, June 2015)

When prompted by real news stories on the anti-austerity movement from the *Daily Mail* and *The Guardian,* focus group participants also recognized the inherent ideological biases prevalent in the UK's mainstream media. One participant reacted negatively to the *Daily Mail* piece on Occupy LSX, which had used thermal cameras to show that most of the tents at St Paul's were empty, another commented on the much fairer coverage in *The Guardian* as being logical:

> It's not fair they are trying to pick holes and find something bad. Why are they going out with thermal imaging cameras? They want to find something bad. (Focus Group 2, middle-aged female, June 2015)

> I think it will depend on which media ... I would expect to read about UK Uncut in *The Guardian*; I wouldn't expect to read about it in the *Daily Mail*. (Focus Group 3, older male, June 2015)

Given the focus on the (mainstream) media, the internet was mentioned less in the focus groups. However, it came up in a discussion on the difference between traditional and contemporary movements. Regarding the former, unions and student protest demonstrations were mentioned, but the latter related mainly to internet activism, and especially to online petitions:

> We were saying we both sign petitions because they land in your inbox and it says it'll take two minutes and you think 'yeah ok then I'll just do it' and it's easy with social media and Twitter. (Focus Group 2, middle-aged female, June 2015)

What is, however, less evident and straightforward to assess on the basis of the data presented in this chapter, is the precise relationship between news consumption on the one hand, and opinion formation about politics and the anti-austerity movement on the other. What our data does reveal, however, is that opinion formation occurs, as Gamson (1992) also concluded, through a combination of experiential knowledge (e.g. being distraught that a local hospital is closing down), popular wisdoms (e.g. the popular myth that immigrants are abusing the welfare system), and media discourse (e.g. how people get to know about companies aggressively evading tax obligations). This, as well as the relatively low level of knowledge of the movement, also means that popular support for the frames of the movement found in the survey data cannot be attributed solely to the efforts of activists to circulate their frames, either independently or through mainstream media representations.

6.3 Conclusion

As argued at the outset of this chapter, the reception or decoding process is a complex phenomenon. The precise nature of the impact or influence of the mediation process on opinion formation is opaque, and remains somewhat elusive in terms of isolating it from other factors such as friends and family, personal political persuasions, personal experiences, and stereotypes.

It also has to be acknowledged that the data presented in this chapter are not unproblematic. The use of an online panel for the survey and the low number of focus groups engenders the need to express prudence *vis-à-vis* the claims that can be made on the basis of this data. As discussed earlier, I would consider the survey data indicative of certain trends rather than being fully representative, and the focus group data served primarily to probe deeper on certain trends exposed by the survey.

Despite these difficulties and caveats, the survey demonstrated that most UK citizens broadly supported many of the frames of the anti-austerity movement, and seemed to accept the preferred reading from the perspective of the anti-austerity movement. This was especially the case when it came to the more stringent regulation of the financial sector, a fairer taxation system, reducing inequalities, and critiques of the liberal representative model of democracy and of mainstream politics.

The focus group data provided a deeper understanding of the complex nature of that support and revealed important nuances in this regard. When discussing the crisis, inequality and fairness, not just the wealthy elites (or in other words 'the 1%') are implicated, but immigrants, and the poor and the vulnerable in society, who are seen as profiteering, are also blamed. Thus, to an extent, we can observe here a decoding that also aligns with some dominant/hegemonic frames of bashing the poor, and negative representations of 'the other', which are backed up by popular wisdoms and stereotypes, and fanned by a xenophobic and poor-bashing right-wing press in the UK.

Taking the survey and the nuances provided by the focus groups into account, it would be fair to conclude that the decoding of the oppositional frames and discourses encoded by the anti-austerity movement conforms largely to a negotiated reading combining oppositional with dominant/hegemonic readings. The preferred readings of the social movement frames were, to some extent, decoded correctly, and even supported, but they intersect with a set of dominant/hegemonic encodings and frames that are also present.

When assessing knowledge of and support for the anti-austerity movement, a similar nuanced picture emerges after combining the survey results with the focus group data. The level of knowledge about these movements seemed relatively low, but once prompted, respondents tended to align themselves with many of the movements' goals and aims. However, the focus groups also revealed that while goals and aims might be shared, the means used by protest movements to achieve them often are not. The disruptive tactics used by activists to attract attention and to contest the powers that be are seen as undermining their message. Some of these views are, again, very much in line with a dominant/hegemonic position *vis-à-vis* protest and disruption—for example, anti-strike discourses or a liberal emphasis on civility and the requirement to reduce nuisance when protesting.

As a result, few citizens can identify themselves with those active in the anti-austerity movement, since the latter are generally considered to be far too weird, radical and aggressive. Misgivings about whether the anti-austerity movement has the ability to really change anything could also be observed. Politicians, banks and large corporations were argued to be more prone to protecting the status quo than listening to the concerns raised by these movements. It seems that the post-2008 period has accentuated the existing deep-seated distrust towards representative politics, as was witnessed in the focus groups.

The role of the media and mediation situates itself at various levels when it comes to the reception of movement frames. One of the most important ways through which non-activist citizens gain knowledge about social movements and the issues they address is through the media, online as well as offline. It emerged strongly that reading newspapers on a regular basis had a positive influence on knowledge about the movements. Knowledge about the Occupy slogan '99% versus 1%' and about aggressive tax evasion, was gleaned predominantly through traditional media channels as well as the internet. Likewise, it is also conceivable that the long-term negative depictions and framings in the UK media of the poor and of immigrants has a significant impact on many citizens' negative views and attitudes regarding these vulnerable and disadvantaged groups in society.

It has to be clear, though, that opinion formation about political issues cannot be reduced merely to exposure to mediated discourses and frames, regardless of whether they are hegemonic or counter-hegemonic. As mentioned previously, experiential knowledge, life paths, social class, views of peers and family, but also ideology, so-called popular wisdoms, myths, and stereotypes also shape our political opinions greatly.

As result of this, isolating the precise impact of media discourse on people's attitudes towards the anti-austerity movement and its frames is tricky, and impossible to do with the kind of data that was gathered. The difficulty here is also that most people do not consider themselves to be influenced all that much by the media or social media. Almost all the participants in the focus groups claimed to have only sporadic contact with the news media, but at the same time they proved to be quite media-savvy and to have considerable lay knowledge about the different media. Certainly, the media and mediation play significant, and I would say central roles, but an important point is to also recognize the complexity of this process, and the presence of many non-media-related factors in the ways that people form their political opinions, and the extent to which social movements have an impact on this.

Social movements show us that the status quo is not fixed for ever, and that change, even radical change, is always a distinct possibility. However, many 'ordinary', non-activist citizens are not optimistic about this possibility of change. They exhibit a high degree of complacency, and feelings of powerlessness, which could be seen as one of the outcomes of neoliberal post-democracy and post-politics (Crouch 2004; Mouffe 2013; Brown 2015). These feelings are strengthened by a common adherence to the hegemonic antipathy towards and rejection of the conflictual, which is arguably essential for, and constitutive of, social change. This delegitimization of conflictual and disruptive tactics to achieve aims that are considered noble, takes the sting out of contentious politics and activism, but is widespread among ordinary, non-activist citizens.

Notes

1. Cantril's study was criticized, though, for exaggerating the actual audience numbers as well as the claims of widespread panic (Bartholomew 2001).
2. Respondents were given the following explanations before being asked whether they sympathised with them or not: (1) Occupy LSX protests against the banks as the main culprits of the financial crisis, and questions the legitimacy of Westminster Parliament; (2) UK Uncut protests against large corporations not paying their taxes, and wanting these taxes to be used to support public services; and (3) NCAFC protest against the rise in tuition fees for higher education and cuts to social services more generally.

CHAPTER 7

Conclusion: Closing the Circuit

In this concluding chapter, I address the *mediation opportunity structure*, which is characterized by the dynamic interplay between the agentic opportunities and the structural constraints aiming to thwart these opportunities (Cammaerts 2012). This represents the dialectic relationship between agency and structure, between generative and restrictive power, and between empowerment and domination, in the context of the various connections identified between media, communication and contentious politics. This interplay speaks to the productive nature of power, as articulated by Foucault, whereby forces of domination always and unavoidably engender a variety of resistances.

This dialectic between strategies of domination and of resistance can be discerned at each of the four moments comprising the Circuit of Protest. This chapter will unpack this dialectic further and discuss how it played out in relation to the UK's anti-austerity movement, at the level of: (1) the production of movement discourses, movement frames and a collective identity; (2) the movement's communicative practices to self-mediate these discourses, frames and identity; (3) the mainstream media representation of these discourses, frames and identity; and (4) the reception of these discourses, frames and identity by non-activist citizens.

In addition, I will relate this to an assessment of the successes and failures of the UK anti-austerity movement, suggesting that we need a more open, and in particular a longer-term, perspective on what constitutes success for a social movement. Finally, I reflect on the usefulness and novelty

B. Cammaerts, *The Circulation of Anti-Austerity Protest*,
https://doi.org/10.1007/978-3-319-70123-3_7

of the Circuit of Protest as a framework to study social movements and their efforts to achieve social change. This also addresses the broader question regarding the extent to which studying the mediation of and by a movement constitutes a productive prism to achieve a deeper and more varied understanding of the processes of social change in which movements are embroiled.

At the same time, it is important to understand that the metaphors of the circuit and circulation do not allow for total closure. The circuit metaphor implies a certain dynamism; there is no ultimate conclusion, precisely because circulation is an ongoing, and ultimately conflictual, process, which takes place continuously, and in which oscillations in one moment have inevitable consequences for the other moments. This leads to different actors changing/adapting their strategies and means of operation and, at times, results in unforeseen and surprising outcomes:

> Meaning is not simply sent from one autonomous sphere—production, say—and received in another autonomous sphere—consumption. Meaning-making functions ... more like the model of a dialogue. It is an ongoing process. It rarely ends at a pre-ordained place. (Du Gay et al. 1997: 10)

Let me first, however, address the mediation opportunity structure and thus the dialectic interplay between opportunities and constraints situated in each of the different moments discussed in the previous chapters.

7.1 Production of Movement Discourses, Frames and Identity

The anti-austerity movement in the UK did not emerge out of the blue (see also Zamponi and Daphi 2014). It emerged, in part, out of prior anti-capitalist, global justice and radical environmental movements, but it also reached out beyond these, creating what we can call an intersectional *chain of equivalence* among a variety of agendas and struggles (Laclau and Mouffe 1985). The anti-austerity movement in the UK was also heavily influenced by events in other countries happening around the same period (2010–11). Noteworthy in this regard are: the Arab Spring and in particular the occupation of Tahrir Square in Cairo; the occupation of squares in several major cities in Spain by the Indignados movement; and Occupy Wall Street in the USA.

Discursively, the UK's anti-austerity movement capitalized on the growing levels of discontent concerning the economic and political backlash from the 2008 banking crisis, and the inadequate responses of Western liberal democracies to these. The perception that the poor and ordinary working people were being made to pay for it, while those considered to be responsible for the crisis were profiting from it, enabled the anti-austerity movement to mobilize a set of moral frames of indignation, unfairness and injustice. In this regard, the re-emergence of a politics of redistribution, and of economic and social issues—such as fair taxation and a plea for strong public services—were central, as was the stringent criticism of the representative liberal democratic system. Democracy as we know it was deemed to be unrepresentative, leading to calls to 'democratize democracy'. These discursive and framing efforts also led to the expression of a powerful collective identity frame aimed at building class alliances and symbolizing the chain of equivalence mentioned earlier; it was argued that, ultimately, it was an existential struggle, pitting the 99% against the 1%.

It must be acknowledged, however, that at a time when the political opportunity structure was arguably most favourable to a stringent critique of neoliberalism, the dominant ideology managed to hegemonize itself further (see Cammaerts 2015). This can be explained in large part by an aggressive discursive war of position, with a view to ensuring that neoliberalism itself remained beyond criticism, and that the extension of capitalism and the commodification of every aspect of the populace's everyday lives continued unabated (Crouch 2015). As Hall (1988: 8) pointed out some time ago, '[t]he hope of every ideology is to naturalise itself out of History and into Nature and thus to become invisible, to operate unconsciously'. Arguably, this is what the neoliberal project has managed to achieve—the ultimate stage of hegemony.

The broader theoretical point this raises is to which extent the counter-frames, as articulated by the anti-austerity movement, were able to challenge and de-naturalize the invisibilized hegemonic discourse of neoliberalism, and expose it for the ideological project that it is. What we can observe, however, is very much the reverse of this. As Cairns et al. (2016: 10) point out, for many 'the public presence of political unrest is a sign that austerity measures are functioning correctly rather than an indication of policy failure'. From this perspective, the struggles for visibility by those critiquing neoliberalism and the politics of austerity are instrumental in the strategies of invisibility of the hegemony. As I argue elsewhere:

> neoliberal ideology has been very successful in making itself invisible as an ideology and presenting itself to us as a natural state of affairs, as entirely innocent of power … However, this invisibility or negation—to put it in Hegelian terms—is sustained through the struggles of visibility waged by the antagonistic constitutive outsides. (Cammaerts 2015: 533)

In addition to this, if we assess the nature of the counter-frames of the UK anti-austerity movement contesting neoliberalism and advocating for a renewed politics of redistribution and 'real' democracy, we have to conclude that these frames were, all in all, quite reformist and 'reasonable'. Without disputing their worth and usefulness as concepts and policies, redistribution through progressive taxation, and a deliberative style of horizontal democracy, are both products of the post-Second World War era, as witnessed by the expansion of the Keynesian welfare state and the rise of New Left participatory ideals (Esping-Anderson 1990; Pateman 1970). Likewise, calls for the regulation of capitalism by a democratic state also fit within a long history of state interventions to make capitalism work and workable, rather than to criticize it per se (Torfing 1998). The anti-austerity movement was not neo-anarchist or revolutionary at all—its aim was to re-democratize the state through 'the reassertion of popular sovereignty via a more empowered citizenry' (Gerbaudo 2017: 237).

Given the radical antecedents to the anti-austerity movement in the UK, this reformist agenda was to some extent surprising. Gone were calls for bourgeois democracy to be overthrown, for an anti-capitalist revolution, for full participation, and for the genuine democratization of the means of production. Rather, what we saw was, at best, an adherence to what Seymour (2014: 169) called 'anarcho-reformism'. This is characterized by (1) scathing criticism of elite politics and democratic institutions; (2) an abject rejection of the left-right divide as being empty and useless political categories pertaining to the past; and, (3) a platform of relatively tame and reformist demands for change. To some extent this was a conscious choice, made so as not to antagonize internally, and to attempt to align the frames of the movement with a larger constituency—that is, the 99%. As Dave from Occupy LSX explained:

> Not being framed as left was important to us, the media didn't seem to want to frame us as left and we certainly weren't framing ourselves as left. We felt that 'left' was a diversionary label and that our solutions were humane and represented common sense economically, ecologically and socially … At the

Fig. 7.1 Banner at Occupy LSX, St Paul's Cathedral, London, 16 October 2011. Source: Neil Cummings: https://commons.wikimedia.org/wiki/File:Occupy_London_banner.jpg

> beginning we had a banner saying *'Capitalism is Crisis'* [see Fig. 7.1] and this was quickly replaced by a banner saying *'All Power to the 99%'*. That was a conscious decision and I think it was the right one. If we as Occupy had come out full guns blazing saying 'we are anti-capitalists', it would have played into the mainstream frame, which would have led to fewer people listening to us. (personal interview, 10 October 2016)

In other words, there were clear attempts made to de-ideologize the anti-austerity discourse, and thus to naturalize the movement discourse by presenting the movement frames as quintessentially hegemonic, as plain common sense. At the same time, the movement shied away from being too antagonistic *vis-à-vis* the object of its criticism. An important strategic reason for doing so was frame-bridging and the construction a long chain of equivalence, implicating as many people as possible. This went hand in hand with a reluctance to articulate the boundaries of the movement and a rejection of the left-right political cleavage as something that was unhelpful, and potentially even damaging to their political struggle.

However, the difficulty encountered by the anti-austerity discourse in truly unsettling neoliberalism could be explained in part by its explicit refusal to position itself ideologically; because of that it arguably also failed to re-discursify the neoliberal hegemony or to make it contingent again. As such, arguably, it operated within the neoliberal hegemony, rather than aiming to unsettle it fundamentally. In this regard we should probably also ask the question to what extent building a very long and almost endless chain of equivalence leads to the constitution of a chain that is weak, ephemeral and easily breakable (see later comments on sustainability).

All this points also to the conclusion that mere political momentum, which clearly was present in the post-2008 period, is not enough to break a movement, or to denaturalize the hegemony of neoliberalism. What I would suggest here is that a powerful political opportunity structure needs to dovetail with a strong and very favourable ***mediation opportunity structure,*** which has discursive implications, as discussed in this section, but it also has a material side to it, in terms of the self-mediation practices. It also addresses the dynamic interplay between the encoding of movement frames, implicating these self-mediation practices, but also mainstream media representations, and the way these encodings are decoded by citizens.

Let me first focus on the nature of the self-mediation practices pertaining to the movement, and how they impacted on their repertoires of contentious action.

7.2 Self-Mediation Practices of Movement Discourses, Frames and Identity

Through a set of self-mediation practices, linked conceptually to a logic of disclosure, of examination and of remembrance, the UK anti-austerity movement managed to disseminate its movement frames widely, to mobilize for direct action, to coordinate these direct actions, to organize themselves internally, to record and archive mediated protest artefacts, and to document acts of police violence. Whereas the production moment is related more to the symbolic and discursive realm of a contentious struggle, the self-mediation practices relate more to its material and action-oriented aspects.

As was shown in Chap. 4, social media played a central—even constitutive—role in the context of the UK's anti-austerity movement, as they have done for other contemporary movements. Registering a Twitter account, coining a hashtag, setting-up a Facebook page/event are among the first things any movement *does,* before contemplating the organization of direct action. However, communication tools and self-mediation practices are not relevant only at the start of a movement—they remain essential throughout its existence. As such, self-mediation practices play a crucial role in sustaining a struggle through the ability to communicate independently the symbolic and action frames, and the collective identity of the movement.

The mobilization efforts of the UK's anti-austerity movement were highly mediated and could in part be characterized by what Bennett and Segerberg (2013) call 'connective action' through self-organizing networks, in which digital technologies and, in particular, social media became pivotal 'organizing agents'. However, at the same time, there is also ample evidence of the presence of mobilization efforts following 'old-style' collective action patterns. For example, UK Uncut is coordinated in a much more top-down manner than Occupy LSX, and even in Occupy LSX there was a distinction between 'the periphery' and the core of the movement. Also, as pointed out in the analysis, the presence of collective—rather than connective—action frames was apparent and strong across all three cases. What might have started as connective action, gradually shifted to become (offline) collective action, with varying degrees of success (see Sect. 7.5). As such, I concur here with Gerbaudo (2017: 136–37) when he argues that an over-emphasis of the connective tends to:

> overlook the persistence of collectivity in digital protest and the fact that the use of social network sites has been accompanied by the rise of new forms of leadership.

From the interviews with activists and the analysis of the types of actions that the UK anti-austerity movement organized, it became clear that media and mediation play constitutive roles in addition to instrumental ones. By this, I mean that, to a large extent, lay knowledge of media routines and news values is shaping the kinds of protest spectacles being performed by the movement. The anti-austerity movement's protest performances aimed to 'distress and mildly inconvenience the rich', as Seymour (2014: 166) put it, but their protest events were also, broadly speaking, mediagenic, and as such thought through with the explicit aim of maximizing media resonance, but at the same time 'not rock the boat too much', as Maggie from Occupy LSX put it (personal interview, 17 October 2016). Apart from the student protests, the actions of the UK anti-austerity movement were mainly spectacle-driven and moderately disruptive, rather than violent. This amounts to what could be called the mediatization of protest, not as a meta-process, but rather as a second-order process, in which knowledge about how media and journalists operates greatly influenced radical contentious action (cf. Livingstone and Lunt 2014).

However, the technologies of self-mediation do not operate in a vacuum. As Burkitt (2002: 235) posits, 'technologies of the self are forms of production as well as means of domination'. In other words, we cannot address the former without also considering the latter, and in particular the dynamic between both.

In the context of the use of social media to disseminate counter-hegemonic discourses and to mobilize for contentious action, there is a set of systemic limitations that must be acknowledged. While social media platforms are often heralded as liberal spaces—advocating freedom of speech, facilitating democratic struggles against authoritarian regimes, and supposedly even fuelling revolutions, when it comes to radical protest in Western democracies, social media platforms can readily become illiberal and highly restricted spaces. The justification usually offered by internet companies for such repressive actions relates to breaches of their opaque terms and conditions of use.

An example of such a corporate clampdown and purge was the sudden and unannounced removal by Facebook of a large number of political groups that rallied against the UK government's austerity measures (see Table 7.1).

This happened prior to the wedding of Prince William and Catherine Middleton in 2011, but Facebook denied that their intervention was political. Instead, Facebook justified the removal of these political groups by stating that profiles can only represent individuals, not (anonymous) organizations:

> As you may know, Facebook profiles are intended to represent individual people only. It is a violation of Facebook's Statement of Rights and Responsibilities to use a profile to represent a brand, business, group, or organization. As such, your account was disabled for violating these guidelines. (quoted in Andrews 2011)

Table 7.1 List of deactivated political Facebook groups (28–29 May 2011)

Anarchista Rebellionist	Free Ricardo Palmera group	Ourland FreeLand
Anti-Cuts Across Wigan	Freedom Isa StateofMind	PROUD TO BE A MEMBER OF THAT
ArtsAgainst Cuts	Frfi Students	LEFT-WING FRINGE GROUP CALLED WOMEN[a]
Beat'n Streets	Goldsmiths Fights Back	Rochdale Law Centre[a]
BigSociety Leeds	IVA Womensrevolution	Rock War
Bootle Labour	Jason Derrick	Roscoe 'Manchester' Occupation[a]
Bristol Anarchist Bookfair[a]	Leeds City College Against Fees and Cuts	Save NHS
Bristol Ukuncut	London Student Assembly	Sheffield Anti-libdemconference
Camberwell AntiCuts	NETWORK X	Sheffield Occupation[a]
Canadians Against Proroguing Parliament	Newcastle Occupation[a]	Slade Occupation[a]
Canadians don't care about the Royal Wedding[a]	No Cuts	Socialist Unity
Canadians Rallying to Unseat Harper	No Quarter Cutthewar	Southwark Sos
Central London SWP[a]	NO STEPHEN HARPER WE WON'T SHUT THE Fuck UP	SWP Cork
Chesterfield Stopthecuts	North East Walkout	Teampalestina Shaf
Claimants Fightback	North London Solidarity	Tower Hamlet Greens[a]
Cockneyreject	Not Stephen Harper 2011[a]	UWE Occupation[a]
Comrade George Orwell	Notts-Uncut Part-of UKUncut	Westminster Trades Council
Don't Break Britain United	Occupied Oxford	Whospeaks Forus[a]
Ecosocialists Unite[a]	Occupy Monaco	WOMEN WHO R CREEPED OUT BY STEPHEN HARPER[a]
First of May band	Open Birkbeck	York Anarchists

Source: Open Rights Group (http://wiki.openrightsgroup.org/wiki/FB_takedowns)

[a]These groups were up again by May 2011

Furthermore, in the context of anti-systemic protest and contestation, there always looms the threat of state surveillance of the communication by and between activists, which also implicates the vulnerabilities of mobile phones. The ways in which the state can surveil activists have become ever more sophisticated in a digital age. We are living in a surveillance society, in which, in essence, full privacy is no longer possible (Lyon 2015). In this regard, social media platforms, internet service providers, and mobile phone operators are easy targets for the state in the context of gathering intelligence about activists and protest movements (Trottier and Fuchs 2015).

All this illustrates the vulnerability of radical activism when relying so heavily on the corporate structures that own the internet; the popular social media platforms and the companies that facilitate financial transactions online. At any time, these companies can decide to close down spaces of contention, and ban activists from using their platforms. This also impedes remembrance, since movement content online can disappear without prior warning.

The process of examination and, linked to this, a degree of self-reflexivity, have led to increased awareness among activists of surveillance, and the dangers of over-reliance on social media and mobile communications. Activists who were interviewed attested to being very careful about sharing sensitive information online or through mobile phones, and there is also an acute awareness of the tensions relating to a reliance on corporate social media, as this quote from a student activist, enrolled at University College London at the time, attests:

> Ultimately, the anti-cuts movement in the UK will need to start organising through self-hosted, open source platforms to avoid reliance upon the very corporate power structures we are aiming to challenge. (Aitchison 2011: np)

This exposes one of the main contradictions of the increased reliance of social movements on social media, namely that, 'while distancing themselves from the values and exploitation of digital capitalism, protesters rely on its products to organize and mobilize' (Milan 2015: 5). In this regard, I concur with Chouliaraki (2010: 229), who argues that social media are deeply implicated in the neoliberal project. Self-mediation through social media is 'a deeply ambivalent process', implicating a set of tensions 'between politics and the market, expressive citizenship and consumerist authenticity, activism and therapy, solidarity and narcissism'.

Switching to independent, non-commercial open-source platforms is, however, difficult to achieve. The very reason why the popular social media platforms are so attractive for contentious politics lies in their high penetration levels, and their potential to reach mass audiences directly without the need to own the mass media required to do so.

Activists also rely on commercial digital platforms to produce an archive of protest artefacts, which serves to record positive self-representations, and to construct a visual and textual memory of the movement, but also to document and expose police violence. While these movement archives are increasingly accessible for more people, and potentially globally, they are also vulnerable, as the storage of content long-term often comes with a cost, and content can also be erased, as shown above. At the same time, the mediation practice of sousveillance or the surveilled watching the surveillers, enabled by the affordances of mobile phones, proved to be a very powerful weapon in the hands of the weaker parties.

The power and reach of social media should, however, not be exaggerated. Whereas the penetration of social media in the UK might indeed be relatively high,[1] it is far from universal and, typically, social media require citizens to opt-in by 'liking' or by 'following' a particular feed or account. As such, the use of social media, especially in terms of disclosure, could be considered a form of *narrowcasting*—which would be justifiable given the relatively low number of followers and likes on Facebook and Twitter for the anti-austerity movement. Thus there is a high probability that activists who use social media exclusively reach only those who are already more-or-less aligned with the movement's aims and goals. Movements using social media are thus preaching mainly to the converted. This is also linked to the phenomenon of the so-called filter bubble, or the idea that social media algorithms lead to people engaging only with those with whom they are ideologically aligned (Pariser 2012; Beer 2017).

All this explains why many social movement scholars and activists also point to the continuing importance of the mainstream media for communicating beyond the like-minded, in particular when it comes to the logic of disclosure and efforts to circulate movement discourses and frames (see Rucht 2013). However, mainstream media have their own issues and constraints.

7.3 Representation of Movement Discourses, Frames and Identity

Prior to the 2008 financial crisis, McCurdy (2010) observed within the UK's radical anti-globalization movement that militant left-wing politics had reluctantly come to terms with the need to adapt, at least *partially*, to the media, and subsequently to develop strategies to manage it. This seems to have been perfected in recent years. Journalistic connections were central to UK Uncut. Occupy LSX immediately established a media centre, where people with communication skills and media/PR experience were active. However, it has to be said that this occurred with much less internal contention than in the case studied by McCurdy. Radical activists today are much more pragmatic and less belligerent towards the mainstream media. They have not only become much more aware of the importance of mainstream media resonance, but they also have more knowledge about how the media operate, and what journalists need in order to produce a good story. As a result of all this, they are also far more prone to, and skilled at, providing this to (some) journalists.

Despite all these attempts to manage the movement's own media visibility and increase its resonance, the media representation of the UK's anti-austerity movement was, however, mixed at best. Some was fair and balanced, even positive, but much of the media representation was quite negative and critical of the movement, for a variety of reasons. Here we see the importance of voice for protest movements, and the pivotal role of the mainstream media as gatekeepers for a mass audience, which movements cannot reach merely through social media and narrowcasting. It is clear that media and symbolic power are deeply implicated in the ways in which 'broader forms of organization may subtly undermine or devalue voice' (Couldry 2010: 2).

Unsurprisingly, an ideological bias can be observed in this regard, with the right-wing press being most negative, and in addition not paying much attention to the anti-austerity movement. Despite this (as outlined in Chap. 5), across all media a certain degree of understanding could be observed in relation to the frustrations and anger underpinning the anti-austerity movement. The protests organized by British students in 2010 were, on the whole, considered to be justified and reasonable, given the tripling of university tuition fees, and the broader sentiment that younger generations were being short-changed. At the same time, however, the student protests were positioned as a middle-class protest, which was subsequently negatively framed. Along the same lines, UK Uncut's fair taxation frames were widely shared and deemed totally legitimate by most media. Also, Occupy LSX received some degree of support when it came to its harsh criticism of the recklessness and greed displayed by the banking and financial sectors, an opinion that, at the time, was shared by some of the right-wing newspapers.

However, there was also clear evidence of both the *protest* and *public nuisance paradigms* being activated in the reporting of the anti-austerity movement (McLeod and Hertog 1999; Di Cicco 2010). This related in particular to a very negative depiction of the mildly disruptive tactics employed by the movement. The smashing of windows and subsequent occupation of the Tory headquarters by student protesters was condemned almost unanimously and derided by the British media. A dichotomy was constructed by the media between the good civic students protesting in an orderly manner, and the bad uncivic students who were violent and deemed to be infiltrated by anarchist 'thugs' and 'professional' troublemakers. Whereas UK Uncut received fairly positive coverage of its ludic, neo-Situationist protest performances, this changed quite radically after it occupied the Fortnum & Mason luxury flagship store. Suddenly, the tone in the reporting on UK Uncut became more negative and condemnatory. Also, in the case of Occupy LSX, after the early media enthusiasm dissipated, attention in many newspapers shifted towards the disruption that the encampment caused, the (legal) conflicts with the City of London, and the overall nuisance created by the occupation on the steps of St Paul's Cathedral.

The broader question that emerges here is to what extent the activation of the protest paradigm in the reporting of contentious action and resistance necessarily represents a hindrance to a movement achieving its aims? First and foremost, it has to be acknowledged that the protest paradigm did not apply across the board, nor at all times. As discussed above, there are ideological differences, with the left-wing media giving more voice to, and being more positive towards, the movement, than is the case with the right-wing media. However, the latter is more dominant in the UK media landscape. There is also a temporal dimension, whereby the diagnostic frames of the movement might be recognized and deemed to be valid, but the prognostic and motivational frames are rejected forcefully. Second, if the repertoire chosen by activists includes the use of aggressive, disruptive or violent tactics, then it is not surprising that the protest paradigm is activated in the liberal establishment media. The British media have a long history of reacting virulently and in a scathing manner in such instances, as has been shown by past research (Halloran et al. 1970; Philo 1995; Curran et al. 2005). At the same time, we also need to acknowledge the point raised by Lakoff (2004) and others, namely that, in order to challenge and deligitimate a (movement) frame, it also needs to be activated.

Furthermore, positive media resonance and the absence of the protest paradigm are not in themselves prerequisites for a movement's success. There are many empirical cases of social and political struggles that received predominantly negative coverage in the mainstream media, but still achieved social and political change. Media resonance of the UK's anti-austerity movement was mixed and fairly negative, but this did not prevent their frames from permeating public debate and public consciousness, as I shall discuss in the next section. Furthermore, protest movements are in some ways stuck between a rock and a hard place in this regard. They must organize spectacular protest performances to gain visibility and to become newsworthy, but this risks negative media resonance because of their disruption and nuisance.

7.4 Reception of Movement Discourses, Frames and Identity

While needing to be prudent because of methodological limitations in terms of online panels and a small number of focus groups, the outcome of the reception study arguably yielded some of the most interesting and valuable insights into the circulation of anti-austerity protest. The formation of citizens' political opinion is a complex matter, however, and determining the precise weight of the different factors influencing opinion formation is, at best, elusive. Thus the exact role of social movements in this process is difficult to isolate. Here, I concur with Giugni (1998: 373), who asserts that one of the main difficulties in the study of social movements and contentious politics lies in establishing:

> a causal relationship between a series of events that we can reasonably classify as social movement actions and an observed change in society, be it minor or fundamental, durable or temporary.

Similarly, the precise nature of the impact or the 'effect' of the media, and of mediation on opinion formation, is equally difficult to establish and pinpoint. Whereas it cannot be denied that the media have influence and play a crucial role in the formation of people's opinions, 'media are rarely likely to be the only necessary or sufficient cause of an effect, and their relative contribution is extremely hard to assess' (McQuail 2010: 369). At the same time, the very idea of a somewhat passive audience receiving movement and media frames is outdated in an age of multiple platforms, an abundance of channels, screens, and a hyper-saturated media landscape, both on- and offline (Livingstone 2015).

While keeping these important caveats in mind, it is abundantly clear that the UK anti-austerity movement and its discourse resonated within broader public opinion. Whereas media representations of the movement were often very negative, most of the anti-austerity frames received considerable to strong support among the British population. In particular, calls for a renewed politics of redistribution, fair taxation of the rich and of large companies, and more stringent regulation of the financial sector, were shared by a majority of British citizens, as was the movement's critique of liberal democracy as being unrepresentative of the interests of ordinary citizens. Along the same lines, while knowledge about the movement was rather low, when it was explained what NCAFC, UK Uncut and Occupy LSX stood for, popular support for them was relatively high.

The nature of this support, as was apparent from the survey, needs to be qualified in several ways, however. First, it would be foolish to consider this support akin to ideological alignment with the movement. As Martín-Barbero (1993: 76) argued, 'not every assumption of hegemonic power by the underclass is a sign of submission and not every rejection is resistance'. This came to the foreground in the focus group discussions with people who broadly supported the movement frames. Non-activist citizens supporting anti-austerity frames, tended to kick at the top—the 1%—and be critical of elites, but they also kicked at the bottom of society, holding up immigrants and the undeserving poor also as ones to blame.

Second, contradictions were observed in relation to media representations of the UK anti-austerity movement, and how they impacted on people's opinion formation, but also, crucially, how public opinion impacts on media framing. What we might be observing here is an oscillation of influence between media and public opinion. The strong support for the anti-austerity frames from the general population might have prompted the (mainly right-wing) media in the UK to adopt a stance which to some extent was supportive of some of the criticisms voiced by the anti-austerity movement. However, equally, we could also observe that the activation of the protest and, in particular, the public nuisance paradigm by the media, impacted on public perceptions of the movement as a whole as being aggressive and disruptive. George, who was active in the student movement, points to this interplay between police reaction, media representation, public opinion, and self-reflexivity within the movement: 'Our reaction against police intimidation was quite forceful and was perceived as quite threatening to people outside of the activist milieu, and that created tensions within the movement' (personal interview, 23 February 2017).

What the reception study also revealed was a deep sense of frustration and powerlessness felt by many citizens. It exposed what Fisher (2014: np) calls a 'collective depression':

> We must understand the fatalistic submission of the UK's population to austerity as the consequence of a deliberately cultivated depression. This depression is manifested in the acceptance that things will get worse (for all but a small elite), that we are lucky to have a job at all (so we shouldn't expect wages to keep pace with inflation), that we cannot afford the collective provision of the welfare state.

Many ordinary citizens voiced this sense of despair and submission. It can be paraphrased as 'we know we are being exploited, but we are aware also that there is absolutely nothing we can do about it'. This sentiment of powerlessness is accompanied by a degree of complacency, but also, unfortunately, with an anger and sense of victimhood which desperately looks for others to blame (cf. immigrants or those on benefits). It would be too simplistic to blame all this on an orthodox understanding of false consciousness. Instead, Lukes' (2005: 150; emphasis in original) reflections on false consciousness are more useful in this regard:

> It would be simplistic to suppose that willing and unwilling compliance to domination are mutually exclusive: one can *consent* to domination and *resent* the mode of its exercise. Furthermore, internalised illusions are entirely compatible with a highly rational and clear-eyed approach to living with them.

* * *

On the basis of the analysis presented above, we can conclude that the *mediation opportunity structure* for the anti-austerity movement was characterized by the clever exploitation of the discursive opportunities created by the UK government's response to the 2008 crisis, as well as the material self-mediation opportunities that print, social media, the internet, and mobile technologies afford activists. These discursive opportunities and self-mediation affordances were mitigated, however, by the invisibility of the neoliberal ideology's war of position, and by corporate as well as state repression, respectively. In addition to this, self-mediation practices constitute narrowcasting, which means that the mediation opportunity structure also includes the mainstream media as a central actor to achieve the circulation of movement discourses and frames beyond the already converted, and to impact broader public opinion. Lay knowledge by activists and adaptation strategies create a set of opportunities at this level, and the repertoire of contentious action today is greatly shaped by what is perceived to be the prevailing journalistic routines and news values. Part of that repertoire is also geared towards creating protest spectacles contesting elites, creating disruption, and at times even the use of symbolic violence. This leads to negative media representations, demonization, and invokes tropes of protesters as deviants and as folk devils. Finally, the mediation opportunity structure is not merely a matter of production of discourses and frames by activists and journalists, and of the materiality of self-mediation practices. Circulation also implicates a reception process and opinion formation among citizens. This was revealed to be influenced only partially by the mediated discourses by activists and mainstream media. We could also observe a complex mix of alignments with both movement and hegemonic frames.

7.5 The Successes and Failures of the UK's Anti-Austerity Movement

Studying a movement through the Circuit of Protest, and through the interplay between generative and constraining power dynamics, as outlined above, enables, in my view, a more nuanced and varied understanding of the ways in which a movement has been successful or not. This study concurs with Diani (1997: 132) in moving away from an overemphasis on 'causal attribution' to determine the success or failure of a social movement. Following from this, as also argued by Flesher Fominaya (2010: 400), movement success 'should not be judged solely by the achievement of explicit political goals'.

In terms of the UK's anti-austerity movement, we can identify failures, but also a series of marked successes. I shall address some of the failures first. Arguably, in terms of its main aims and political demands, we would need to conclude that not many (if any) of these were realized (at the time of writing). As Gerbaudo (2017: 234) also concludes, 'after spring came winter'. The ruthless casino capitalist system, which was at the heart of the financial crisis, is pretty much intact, and the City of London has, by and large, managed to avert a more stringent regulatory regime. In stark contrast to most ordinary 'salaried' people, who pay their fair share of tax, large companies and rich individuals are still able to reduce their tax bills massively, through all sorts of (legal and illegal) loopholes and fiscal magic. As a result, inequality has continued to increase unabated in recent years (Piketty 2015). The liberal democratic system continues to be seen by many people as not delivering on its representative promise, and little or nothing has been done to address this in terms of democratic reform or a pushback of economic power, rather the contrary, in fact (Brown 2015). A glaring example is the continued and relentless neoliberalization of the education sector (Giroux 2015). If anything, rather than being reduced or abolished as the NCFAC demanded, university tuition fees are set to rise again in England.

We should also highlight issues of sustainability and the movement's lack of stamina as being among its main failures. Seen from a longer-term and comparative perspective, the anti-austerity movement was a powerful and colourful 'flash in the pan', but a flash nevertheless. From this historical perspective, the anti-austerity movement constituted a brief outpouring of activist enthusiasm and readiness to organize and participate in protest spectacles, but the public outcry, indignation, and frustration arguably failed to galvanize into sustained political contestation and long-term commitment to the cause (as has been the case for other movements, such as those fighting for workers' rights, civic rights, environmentalism, and feminism). This might be a sign of the times, which are characterized by political fragmentation and short attention spans. Dave, from Occupy, referred to *The Shallows*, a book by Carr (2010), to decry this contemporary phenomenon:

> The fact that Occupy burst on the stage and then subsequently disappeared is arguably related to the so-called shallows and to the fact that attention spans and how we relate to the world have been fundamentally altered by the internet. And there is something in that, there is such a proliferation of things and issues for which you can have a fascination for a little while, but because there is so much other stuff to care about, it can fade away quite rapidly too. (Dave, personal interview, 10 October 2017)

At the same time, we can also approach this as abeyance or intermediate moments between periods of high intensity of activism and direct action. During periods of abeyance 'pockets of movement activity may continue to exist and can serve as starting points of a new cycle of the same or a new movement at a later point in time' (Taylor and Crossley 2013: 1).

In spite of these failures, it can also be concluded that the UK's anti-austerity movement struck a popular chord in the context of the post-2008 financial crisis, and managed to voice a sense of moral indignation that was, and is, shared broadly by the citizenry (Kaldor and Selchow 2013). Though not many British citizens were aware of these organizations and mobilizations driving the movement, a majority of UK citizens supported the movement frames and had sympathy for the organizations themselves. As a result, the movement managed to shift debate in relation to inequality, globalization, taxation and democracy—the popularization of the slogan 99% versus 1% being a good illustration of this.

What the results point out, furthermore, is that success is not always a matter of change here and now, nor of immediate and tangible policy shifts. Success can also be situated at the level of shifts in public discourse or the articulation of stringent and compelling critiques of the powers that be (Touraine 1981). A lawyer, working in London's financial sector, commented on these longer-term impacts of the Occupy movement in an open letter addressed to the Occupy protesters and published in *The New Statesman*:

> the great achievement of 'Occupy LSX' was never the physical camp. It was the realisation that those in power can be wrong-footed, and that their bullshit can be exposed, by those who are serious and thoughtful about promoting a better world. This can be done anywhere, and not just in a churchyard of a Cathedral. (Green 2012)

This is reminiscent of the slogan *You Can't Evict an Idea*, used by many Occupy LSX protesters after police forcefully ended the occupations (in June 2012). This need for a longer-term perspective is apparent also in the ways in which the ideas and ethos of the anti-austerity movement, and Occupy in particular, lived on in terms of local self-empowerment, new ways of movement organizing and decision making, innovative exchange and sharing models, new media initiatives, etc. which sprang up in the aftermath of Occupy. From this perspective, it could be argued that the anti-austerity movement has led to a considerable degree of what is commonly referred to as movement spill-over (Gerbaudo 2017; Flesher Fominaya 2017).

The militant student protest organization NCAFC also has a lasting legacy, but as student protester George expressed it in a more understated way: 'we had a myriad of knock-on effects that I guess are less obvious and visible in society, but it keeps percolating' (personal interview, 23 February 2017). The student protests against the tripling of higher education tuition fees not only highlighted the fierce resistance among students against the impact of neoliberalism on the university sector, but it also politicized a considerable number of young people, who subsequently became active in other political organizations and mobilizations, including, among others, UK Uncut and Occupy, but also in the Labour Party led by Jeremy Corbyn:

> The student protests created a deeply politicised generation that still has networks and links today. Many people active in the activist milieu in the last few years came out of the student protests in 2010. Also, many young people currently engaged in supporting the Corbyn campaign are people that were also involved in the NCAFC. (George, personal interview, 23 February 2017)

This brings us to the impact of the anti-austerity movement on political life, more broadly, in the UK. Despite advocating a new kind of horizontal democratic politics, fuelled by autonomist Marxism (cf. Katsiaficas 2006), arguably it has been on traditional representative politics that the anti-austerity movement in the UK has had the most profound impact for the better, but also for the worse. This impact is most pronounced in the context of its influence on progressive social democratic politics. Many on the left saw the 2008/9 financial crisis, and the ensuing politics of austerity, as the final nail in the coffin of so-called 'third way' politics, or the deluded view that a progressive politics could be achieved from within the premises and values of neoliberalism.

This growing awareness led, ultimately, to the unexpected victory of Jeremy Corbyn becoming leader of the Labour Party, replacing Ed Miliband after his defeat in the 2015 general election. Corbyn, a long-time political maverick and anti-establishment figure, won on a distinctly left-wing anti-austerity platform, which proved to be fairly popular, as also shown by the results of the survey presented in Chap 6. His election and, even more so, his re-election after a leadership challenge a year later (in September 2016), followed by his near-victory in the 2017 general elections, represented the political mainstreaming of the anti-austerity discourse. As Flesher Fominaya (2017: 14) also points out, the emergence of Corbyn 'cannot be understood without factoring in the influence of the Occupy movements'.

The political impact of the anti-austerity movement is not limited only to left-wing progressive politics, however. 'Where are the Liberal Democrats now?', George asked rhetorically when discussing the successes of the student protests (personal interview, 23 February 2017). The Liberal Democrats who approved the tripling of the tuition fees during their coalition with the Tories were almost decimated in the 2015 elections. At the level of policy making, changes can also be observed, moving away from a politics and discourse of austerity. At the national level, the Tory-led government quietly dropped its explicit austerity agenda. George

Osborne, the main architect of austerity Britain, was relegated to the back benches by the new Prime Minister, Theresa May, who replaced David Cameron after the referendum on membership of the European Union (EU) let to a win for Brexit–i.e. for the UK leaving the EU.

At the EU level, we can refer to the conviction of Apple by the European Commission, which ruled that the tax arrangements the technology giant had negotiated with Ireland amounted to illegal state aid. As such, Apple was ordered by the EU Commission to pay €13 billion, which a prominent left-wing commentator saw as a vindication of the protest:

> Tax justice is only on the agenda because movements forced it there. It was an issue that once only excited those on the fringes of political debate. Years of campaigning changed that. Those in a position of authority are responding to pressure from below … Social change is often a story of defeat followed by setback, followed by defeat followed by setback—and then success. (Jones 2016: np)

These modest shifts can, in my view, be attributed in large part to the mobilizations and protests set in motion by the anti-austerity movement in 2010–11.

What has also become apparent in recent years, however, is that the anti-austerity discourse—especially the valid criticisms of globalization, of an out-of-touch political elite, and the ideas encapsulated by the 99% versus 1% slogan—have been appropriated not only by a progressive politics but also by a populist right-wing agenda across Europe and in the USA. This phenomenon is not entirely new, and is part of what could be seen as a long-term process of normalization of the radical populist right (Berezin 2013).

The rising popularity of the populist right in the UK, exemplified by UKIP—the United Kingdom Independence Party—and the political discourse of its one-time leader, Nigel Farage, but also by populist political actors within the Conservative Party—for example, Boris Johnson, now Foreign Secretary—can be explained, in part, by their partial appropriation of the populist features of the anti-austerity discourse. This became apparent in the efforts of the Leave Europe campaign to appeal to working-class voters in the EU referendum, which, as mentioned above, the pro-Brexit camp ultimately won. In the words of student protester George:

> The optimism post-2010 that new possibilities for change were possible has been thrown into serious doubt in recent times in the sense that we now know that this openness which the movement created can go both ways. (personal interview, 23 February 2017)

In other words, the high levels of support for the anti-austerity discourse, as shown by the survey data, as well as the nuances highlighted by the focus group discussions in terms of voicing discontent towards the establishment, but also towards immigrants and the so-called 'undeserving' poor, have been exploited efficiently and successfully by right-wing populists to promote and further an anti-progressive and illiberal politics of exclusion. Such populist right-wing politics are, as Offe (2013: 216) argues, the 'only political agents in the decades since 1990 who have managed to broaden their political base and enhance participation, if not the kind of participation envisaged by liberal democratic theory'. In recent years, it has achieved this through the partial appropriation of the anti-austerity discourse.

This calls into question the strategic reluctance of the anti-austerity movement to position itself more clearly ideologically, and to remain vague when it came to articulating the boundaries of the movement in relation to its collective identity (see also Kavada 2015). This discursive strategy arguably made it too easy for right-wing populism to coopt and pervert part of the anti-austerity discourse. This was especially apparent in the campaign advocating for Brexit, which successfully constructed a false schism between the interests of ordinary people (the 99%), better off outside the EU, and the interests of the power-elites (the 1%), wanting to stay inside the Union. The Brexit campaign catered also to a dark, racist, anti-immigrant sentiment, and thus exploited the ambiguity exposed by the focus group discussions on notions of inequality and fairness.

It has to be noted though that many within the radical left in the UK were also in favour of Brexit, but more from the perspective of a stringent critique of the EU as a neoliberal project (King 2015; Davidson 2016; Moreno 2016). In line with Laclau's (2005: 19) passionate plea to rescue populism, many within the left argue that left-wing politics should also embrace populism as an agonistic political strategy. Podemos in Spain and Syriza in Greece are seen as contemporary examples of this strategy, as are figures such as Bernie Sanders in the USA and Jeremy Corbyn in the UK, albeit to a lesser extent.

Important in this regard is the urgent need to reconstitute 'the people' in an inclusive and open way, thereby contesting right-wing populism, which constructs 'the people' in an exclusionary and xenophobic manner. In addition, democracy needs to be invigorated and juxtaposed with neoliberalism and the elites that espouse it. For this to happen, new connections and links will need to be built between a variety of progressive social movements and left-wing parties. As Mouffe (2016: np) points out, in this regard, movements must constitute:

> a collective will that establishes a synergy between the multiplicity of social movements and political forces and whose objective is the deepening of democracy … what is needed is a politics that reestablishes the agonistic tension between the liberal logic and the democratic logic.

This was echoed by Dave's statement that, 'At Occupy we have always talked about the need to find feasible ways to turn protest into genuine political leverage and clout' (personal interview, 10 October 2016). The question remains, in my view, as to whether populism is the most productive and lasting way to achieve this?

7.6 The Circulation of Protest: A Useful Metaphor and Framework?

In this book, I adopted the Circuit of Protest as both a conceptual metaphor and a methodological approach to analyse and assess a specific social movement through the prism of mediation. The circuit addresses simultaneously: (1) the production of symbolic meaning and a collective identity; (2) a set of self-mediation practices; (3) a variety of media representations; and (4) the ways in which all of this subsequently influences citizens. I argued also that a dynamic interplay between agentic opportunities and structural constraints operates at each of these moments, which, taken together, constitutes a mediation opportunity structure for movements and activists.

Given the increased importance and centrality of the media, and in particular of communication in this digital age, it seems apt to use the various ways in which media and communication are both instrumental in and constitutive of protest, as a productive prism to study a social movement and protest from a variety of angles. A focus on the circulation of movement discourses and frames by activists, as well as mainstream representations of protest, producing its own frames, addresses in conjunction with each other: (1) the symbolic and the material aspects of a political struggle;

(2) the appropriation of alternative media by social movements and the mainstream media representations of protest; and (3) the production of meaning and its reception by citizens. The metaphors of circulation and a circuit imply something circular and dialectic rather than one side or a moment dominating or determining the other(s). As such, by adopting circulation as a metaphor, determinisms in terms of privileging one moment over and above another, or one side of a dichotomy over another, are avoided. Instead, the tensions as well as the interconnections between the two sides of the dichotomy, and between the different moments, are of interest.

I shall now briefly assess each of the above-mentioned mediation dialectics from the perspective of the Circuit of Protest, and their relevance to debates in social movement studies, as well as media and communication studies.

The production of the symbolic was influenced and partly shaped by material circumstances and affordances. The material, in this regard, relates to the material conditions underlying the political opportunity structure, out of which the movement emerged, as well as the media and communication technologies it used to communicate the symbolic. The political opportunity structure has a material foundation, namely the real consequences of austerity for many people. The symbolic side of the struggle mobilized these material consequences to increase its resonance and induce moral indignation. Media practices and the affordances (hidden as well as explicit) embedded in the media and communication technologies also have a distinct materiality, which increasingly shapes the way a social and political struggle is waged.

At the same time, however, the symbolic impacts also on the material, and this was especially apparent in terms of the kinds of direct actions and protest displays the movement created, which had highly performative, and thus symbolic, aspects to them. The strategies of mild disruption enacted by the movement also aptly combined the symbolic as well as the material aspects of its struggle. Here we can observe how media-savviness and lay knowledge among activists of how the media operates shape direct action, which could be denoted as the mediatization of protest; but this occurs, I would argue, as part of a much broader and more complex mediation process.

By highlighting this dialectic between the material and the symbolic aspects of protest, the Circuit of Protest also speaks to debates in social movement studies between those highlighting resources (Resource

Mobilization approach) and those highlighting the cultural aspects of a social and political struggle (Culturalist approach). At the same time, the Circuit of Protest also addresses tensions within media and communication studies between those privileging the study of media texts and content, and those focusing on practices. The symbolic and the material work in conjunction with each other. At times, the material shapes the symbolic, and at other times the symbolic shapes the material.

The dialectic between alternative media—used by activists to self-mediate their diagnostic, prognostic, and motivational frames, and mainstream media—which presents its own mediation of protest is at the centre of the movement under study and, I would argue, of all contemporary social movements. Setting up social media accounts, deciding on which hashtags to adopt, and using these to mobilize for direct action and to assert a collective identity, are generally the first actions activists take. These should be seen in terms of the long-standing efforts of movements to establish independent or alternative means of communication—to *be* the media. Alongside alternatives, we can observe a high degree of what Rucht (2004) called adaptation strategies. In the anti-austerity movement, this could be observed in terms of the repertoire of contentious action and the types of direct action enacted, as well as the ways in which activists attempted to manage journalists and their media representations.

Another way in which this dialectic between alternative and mainstream manifests itself is through the ambiguity of the internet as an alternative independent public space. Whereas social media are widely used as alternative channels of communication by activists, exploiting the potential of bypassing the mainstream media, these corporate online spaces are, of course, inherently mainstream and can be closed down at any point. This also demonstrates that we need to make a conceptual difference between alternative content and alternative channels of communication (Cammaerts 2016). Online platforms are not truly independent platforms at all; they are corporate spaces, and dependence on them makes activists vulnerable. This can also be linked to a long-standing debate within (alternative) media studies regarding the nature and the boundaries between alternative and mainstream media, which ultimately are relational concepts. Alternative media is that which is not mainstream, but empirical reality is often more complex (Bailey et al. 2008). This complexity also operates at the level of the relationship between social movements producing alternative content, and the channels through which they distribute this content.

In addition to this, the dialectic between alternative and mainstream, in the context of the Circuit of Protest, highlights a set of processes, mediation practices, repertoires and resources that are internal to the movement (as highlighted by the Resource Mobilization approach), and the opportunity structures that situate themselves outside the movement (as foregrounded by the Political Process approach). The latter relate, for instance, to: surveillance by the state, potentially hostile media organizations, social media platforms taking editorial decisions, and the very nature of the affordances of networked communication technologies and platforms. The former has relevance for skills of activists, access to knowledge and technologies, creativity, and innovation to circumvent the barriers put in place by those outside and operating against the movement.

The third and final mediation dialectic of relevance here focuses on the relationship between the production of meaning and its reception. As indicated at several points throughout the book, this is an elusive dialectic. The aim of this study was not to 'prove' conclusively causal effects, but rather to try to understand the intricacies of the reception process, as well as the various ways in which citizens negotiate, adopt or resist the circulation of movement discourses, frames, and collective identities. This revealed a complex interplay between hegemony and counter-hegemony, and between dominant meanings and resistant ones.

It suggests a move away from the classic Gramscian view of power and hegemony towards a more Foucauldian view, which not only rejects a simplistic bifurcation between domination and subordination but also complicates the nature of what Gramsci called consent. We can refer back here to the notion of the technologies of the self, which was adopted to study the self-mediation practices, but which implicates technologies of domination and compliance, as well as self-reflection and resistance.

This Foucauldian approach to political discourse, hegemony and resistance is above all relevant in the context of the vivid debate in social movement studies regarding the role that ideology plays in the formation and sustainability of social movements (Diani 2000; Klandermans 2000; Oliver and Johnston 2000). This debate exposes a tension between two main ways of articulating ideology within social movement studies. First, ideology as the belief system underpinning a movement, informing the collective framing efforts of movements, the construction of collective identities, and the fostering of actions. This links neatly to the discussion above about the cultural and symbolic aspects of social and political struggles, and thus of agency and contingency. Second, ideology as social order and common sense against which social movements fight, as the symbolic resources which legitimate domination. This second—more Marxist—way of approaching ideology points to the more stable societal structures that tend to be contested by movements. As the analysis of the interplay between the production and reception of meaning implies, these two ways of mobilizing ideology in view of social struggles are not mutually exclusive; rather, they interact and constantly influence each other. A movement develops its own ideology, but at the same time it needs also to unsettle and expose the ideological nature of the political order and of common sense, something the UK's anti-austerity movement has arguably attempted to do, with mixed success.

* * *

The Circuit of Protest, as presented and developed in this book, constitutes a productive conceptual and methodological framework to study a particular movement, and has yielded interesting results. As well as providing an empirical model to study the various ways in which media and communication are relevant for activists and protest, the circuit enables us to bridge, or at the very least, to address, some important tensions within social movement as well as media and communication theory.

It enables us to think about the symbolic and material sides of a contentious struggle in conjunction with each other. It stresses the interplay between a set of processes that occur internally to a movement, but accounts also for the movement's external context. It explicitly implicates public opinion and non-activist citizens in the process of contentious politics. Furthermore, it positions a dialectic and productive articulation of power centrally at each of the different moments of the circuit. This avoids determinisms, and leads, I suggest, to a more sophisticated and nuanced perspective on the nature of the success and failure of a movement and the struggle waged.

Mediation, as also discussed at length by Martín-Barbero (1993), is a very apt and productive theoretical concept to study contentious politics. Silverstone's double articulation of mediation allows the linking of the symbolic aspects of media and the materiality of communication technologies. It also enables the consideration of the usage of communication technologies and the resulting mediation practices, on the one hand, and media/journalistic representations on the other. By linking mediation and opportunity structure conceptually, a dialectical position is taken *vis-à-vis* one of the core dichotomies in the social sciences: namely, between structure and agency. In terms of contentious politics, the concepts of alternative and mainstream media are highly relevant in equal measure—the former in view of the self-mediation practices of the movement; and the latter in view of the circulation of its frames beyond the like-minded. This brings us to the complex nature of reception and the notion of active audiences. As this study showed, researching the reception of movement frames is worthwhile, and a crucial component to understand and discuss the ambivalent nature of the circulation of protest. As Silverstone (2006: 42) put it, mediation is:

> not just a matter of what appears on the screen, but is actually constituted in the practices of those who produce the sounds and images, the narratives and the spectacles, as well as, crucially, those who receive them.

Finally, the circuit is a holistic conceptual and methodological framework which enables the study of the 'processes of production, content, reception and circulation of social meaning simultaneously' (Philo 2007: 175). The Circuit of Protest needs to be applied to a wide variety of social and political struggles, and as a result of this, inevitably be improved and built upon. Be my guest!

Notes

1. In 2016, half of the UK population, and more than 60% of internet users in the UK, used Facebook, and a quarter of the UK population and almost 40% of internet users were active on Twitter (eMarketer 2016).

Bibliography

Aitchison, Guy. 2011. Political Purge of UK Facebook Underway. *Open Democracy*, April 29. https://www.opendemocracy.net/ourkingdom/guy-aitchison/political-purge-of-uk-facebook-underway. Accessed Aug 2017.

Albrekt Larsen, Christian, and Thomas Engel Dejgaard. 2013. The Institutional Logic of Images of the Poor and Welfare Recipients: A Comparative Study of British, Swedish and Danish Newspapers. *Journal of European Social Policy* 23 (3): 287–299.

Altheide, David. 1985. *Media Power*. London: Sage.

Altheide, David, and Robert Snow. 1991. *Media Worlds in the Post-journalism Era*. New York: Aldine de Gruyter.

Altman, Roger C. 2009. The Great Crash, 2008: A Geopolitical Setback for the West. *Foreign Affairs*. January/February Issue. https://www.foreignaffairs.com/articles/united-states/2009-01-01/great-crash-2008. Accessed Aug 2017.

Anderson, Alison. 1993. Source–Media Relations: The Production of the Environmental Agenda. In *The Mass Media and Environmental Issues*, ed. A. Hansen, 51–68. Leicester: Leicester University Press.

———. 2003. Environmental Activism and the News Media. In *News, Public Relations and Power*, ed. Simon Cottle, 117–132. London: Sage.

Andrews, Julie D. 2011. U.K. Activists Gripe Facebook Unfairly Removed Profiles. *AD Week*, May 2. http://www.adweek.com/digital/u-k-activists-gripe-facebook-unfairly-removed-profiles/. Accessed Aug 2017.

Anstead, Nick. 2017. The Idea of Austerity in British Politics, 2003–2013. *Political Studies*: Online First.

Atton, Chris. 2002. *Alternative Media*. Edinburgh: Edinburgh University Press.

Bailey, David. 2014. Contending the Crisis: What Role for Extra-Parliamentary British Politics? *British Politics* 9 (1): 68–92.

B. Cammaerts, *The Circulation of Anti-Austerity Protest*,
https://doi.org/10.1007/978-3-319-70123-3

Bailey, Olga, Bart Cammaerts, and Nico Carpentier. 2008. *Understanding Alternative Media*. Maidenhead: Open University Press/McGraw-Hill.

Bakardjieva, Maria, and Georgia Gaden. 2012. Web 2.0 Technologies of the Self. *Philosophy & Technology* 25 (3): 399–413.

Baker, Sam. 2010. Vodafone Protest Shows Tweets Can Get People on the Streets. *The Guardian*, November 1. http://www.theguardian.com/commentisfree/2010/nov/01/vodafone-protest-social-media. Accessed 10 Feb 2017.

Bakewell, Joan. 2011. The Meek Are on Your Doorstep. *The Daily Telegraph*, November 6.

Bartholomew, Robert E. 2001. *Little Green Men, Meowing Nuns, and Head-Hunting Panics: A Study of Mass Psychogenic Illness and Social Delusion*. Jefferson, NC: McFarland.

Bateson, Gregory. 1955 [2006]. A Theory of Play and Fantasy. In *The Game Design Reader: A Rules of Play Anthology*, ed. Katie Salen and Eric Zimmerman, 314–328. Cambridge, MA: MIT Press.

Bauer, Martin W. 2007. Classical Content Analysis: A Review. In *Qualitative Researching with Text, Image and Sound*, ed. Martin Bauer and George Gaskell, 131–151. London: Sage.

BBC. 2008. UK Banks Receive £37bn Bail-Out, October 13. http://news.bbc.co.uk/1/hi/business/7666570.stm. Accessed 10 Feb 2017.

———. 2010. Students March … and March … in Central London. November 30. http://www.bbc.co.uk/news/education-11882582. Accessed 10 Feb 2017.

———. 2012. UK Uncut Protesters Cleared of Fortnum and Mason Trespass. March 23. http://www.bbc.com/news/uk-england-london-17496073. Accessed 10 Feb 2017.

Beckett, Charlie. 2011. Saturday's Demonstrations Showed the Media's Difficulties in Reporting the Issues and the Actions of a Small Group of Protesters at the Same Time. POLIS Director's Blog. March 26. http://www.charliebeckett.org/?p=4220. Accessed 10 Feb 2017.

Beer, David. 2017. The Social Power of Algorithms. *Information, Communication & Society* 20 (1): 1–13.

Belfield, Chris, Jonathan Cribb, Andrew Hood, and Robert Joyce. 2015. *Living Standards, Poverty and Inequality in the UK: 2015*. London: Institute for Fiscal Studies. http://www.ifs.org.uk/uploads/publications/comms/R107.pdf. Accessed 10 Feb 2017.

Benford, Robert D., and David A. Snow. 2000. Framing Processes and Social Movements: An Overview and Assessment. *Annual Review of Sociology* 26: 611–639.

Bennett, Lance W. 1990. Toward a Theory of Press–State Relations. *Journal of Communication* 40 (2): 103–125.

———. 2003. New Media Power: The Internet and Global Activism. In *Contesting Media Power*, ed. Nick Couldry and James Curran, 17–37. Lanham, MD: Rowman & Littlefield.

Bennett, Lance W., and Alexandra Segerberg. 2013. *The Logic of Connective Action: Digital Media and the Personalization of Contentious Politics.* Cambridge: Cambridge University Press.

Berezin, Mabel. 2013. The Normalization of the Right in Post-Security Europe. In *Politics in the Age of Austerity*, ed. Armin Schäfer and Wolfgang Streeck, 239–261. Cambridge: Polity Press.

Bertens, Hans. 2014. *Literary Theory: The Basics.* 3rd ed. Abingdon: Routledge.

Beuchler, Steven M. 1993. Beyond Resource Mobilization? Emerging Trends in Social Movement Theory. *The Sociological Quarterly* 34 (2): 217–235.

Bimber, Bruce, Andrew J. Flanagin, and Cynthia Stohl. 2005. Reconceptualizing Collective Action in the Contemporary Media Environment. *Communciation Theory* 15 (4): 365–388.

Birks, Jen, and John Downey. 2015. 'Pay Your Tax!' How Tax Avoidance Became a Prominent Issue in the Public Sphere in the UK. In *Media, Margins and Civic Agency*, ed. Einar Thorsen, Daniel Jackson, Heather Savigny, and Jenny Alexander, 166–181. London: Palgrave Macmillan.

Blumer, Herbert. 1951. Collective Behavior. In *Principles of Sociology*, ed. A.M. Lee, 67–121. New York: Barnes & Noble.

Blumler, Jay G., and Elihu Katz, eds. 1974. *The Uses of Mass Communications: Current Perspectives on Gratification Research.* Beverly Hills, CA: Sage.

Bobbio, Norberto. 1987. *Which Socialism?* Cambridge: Polity Press.

Bourdieu, Pierre. 1977. *Outline of a Theory of Practice.* Cambridge: Cambridge University Press.

Boyce, George. 1978. The Fourth Estate: The Reappraisal of a Concept. In *Newspaper History: From the 17th Century to the Present Day*, ed. George Boyce, James Curran, and Pauline Wingate, 19–40. London: Constable and Company Ltd.

Boyle, M.P., D.M. McLeod, and C.L. Armstrong. 2012. Adherence to the Protest Paradigm: The Influence of Protest Goals and Tactics on News Coverage in US and International Newspapers. *The International Journal of Press/Politics* 17 (2): 127–144.

Brewer, Paul R. 2001. Value Words and Lizard Brains: Do Citizens Deliberate About Appeals to Their Core Values? *Political Psychology* 22 (1): 45–64.

Brown, Wendy. 2010. We Are All Democrats Now…. *Theory & Event* 13 (2): online.

———. 2015. *Undoing the Demos: Neoliberalism's Stealth Revolution.* New York: Zone Books.

Brummer, Alex. 2010. This Plunder of Our Heritage. *Daily Mail*, December 6. http://www.dailymail.co.uk/money/article-1335974/ALEX-BRUMMER-New-York-Fed-comes-clean.html. Accessed 10 Feb 2017.

Burgess, Stephen. 2011. Measuring Financial Sector Output and Its Contribution to UK GDP. *Bank of England Quarterly Bulletin* Q3: 234–246.
Burkitt, Ian. 2002. Technologies of the Self: Habitus and Capacities. *Journal for the Theory of Social Behaviour* 32 (2): 219–237.
Cairns, David, Nuno de Almeida Alves, Ana Alexandre, and Augusta Correia. 2016. *Youth Unemployment and Job Precariousness. Political Participation in the Austerity Era*. Basingstoke: Palgrave Macmillan.
Calhoun, Craig. 1998. Community Without Propinquity Revisited: Communications Technology and the Transformation of the Urban Public Sphere. *Sociological Inquiry* 68 (3): 373–397.
Cammaerts, Bart. 2005. ICT-Usage Among Transnational Social Movements in the Networked Society—To Organise, to Mobilise and to Debate. In *Media, Technology and Everyday Life in Europe: From Information to Communication*, ed. Roger Silverstone, 53–72. Aldershot: Ashgate.
———. 2012. Protest Logics and the Mediation Opportunity Structure. *European Journal of Communication* 27 (2): 117–134.
———. 2013. The Mediation of Insurrectionary Symbolic Damage: The 2010 UK Student Protests. *International Journal of Press/Politics* 18 (4): 525–548.
———. 2015a. Technologies of Self-Mediation: Affordances and Constraints of Social Media for Protest Movements. In *Civic Engagement and Social Media—Political Participation Beyond the Protest*, ed. Julie Uldam and Anne Vestergaard, 97–110. Basingstoke: Palgrave Macmillan.
———. 2015b. Movement Media as Technologies of Self-Mediation. In *The Routledge Companion to Alternative and Community Media*, ed. Chris Atton, 445–456. London: Routledge.
———. 2015c. Neoliberalism and the Post-hegemonic War of Position: The Dialectic Between Invisibility and Visibilities. *European Journal of Communication* 30 (5): 522–538.
———. 2016. Overcoming Net-Centricity in the Study of Alternative and Community Media. *Journal of Alternative and Community Media* 1 (1): 1–3.
———. forthcoming. Discourse and Framing in Social Movement Theory: Connecting the Nodes. *Communication Theory*.
Cammaerts, Bart, and Nico Carpentier. 2009. Blogging the 2003 Iraq War: Challenging the Ideological Model of War and Mainstream Journalism? *Observatorio* 3 (2): 1–23.
Cammaerts, Bart, and César Jiménez-Martínez. 2014. The Mediation of the Brazilian V-for-Vinegar Protests: From Vilification to Legitimization and Back? *Liinc em Revista* 10 (1): 44–68.
Cantril, Hadley, Hazel Gaudet, and Herta Herzog. 1940. *The Invasion from Mars: A Study in the Psychology of Panic (with the Complete Script of the Famous Orson Welles Broadcast)*. Princeton, NJ: Princeton University Press.
Carey, James W. 1989. *Communication as Culture: Essays on Media and Society*. Boston, MA: Unwin Hyman.

Carpentier, Nico. 2005. Identity, Contingency and Rigidity: The (Counter-)hegemonic Constructions of the Identity of the Media Professional. *Journalism* 6 (2): 199–219.

———. 2010. Deploying Discourse Theory. An Introduction to Discourse Theory and Discourse Theoretical Analysis. In *Media and Communication Studies Intersections and Interventions*, ed. Nico Carpentier, Ilija Tomanic Trivundza, Pille Pruulmann-Vengerfeldt, Ebba Sundin, Tobias Olsson, Richard Kilborn, Hannu Nieminen, and Bart Cammaerts, 251–266. Tartu: Tartu University Press.

Carr, Nicholas. 2010. *The Shallows: How the Internet Is Changing the Way We Think, Read and Remember*. London: Atlantic Books.

Castells, Manuel. 1997. *The Power of Identity*. Oxford: Wiley.

Chadwick, Andrew. 2007. Digital Network Repertoires and Organizational Hybridity. *Political Communication* 24 (3): 283–301.

Chen, Kuan-Hsing. 1996. Post-Marxism: Between/Beyond Critical Postmodernism. In *Stuart Hall: Critical Dialogues*, ed. David Morley and Kuan-Hsing Chen, 309–325. Abingdon: Routledge.

Chomsky, Noam. 2012. *Occupy*. London: Penguin Books.

Chouliaraki, Lilie. 2010. Self-Mediation: New Media and Citizenship. *Critical Discourse Studies* 7 (4): 227–232.

Christians, Clifford G., Theodore L. Glasser, Denis McQuail, Kaarle Nordenstreng, and Robert A. White. 2009. *Normative Theories of the Media: Journalism in Democratic Societies*. Chicago, IL: University of Illinois Press.

Cohen, Bernard C. 1963. *The Press and Foreign Policy*. Princeton, NJ: Princeton.

Cohen, Stanley. 1972. *Folk Devils and Moral Panics: The Creation of the Mods and Rockers*. London: MacGibbon & Kee.

Colonel, Sheila S. 2001. The Media, the Market and Democracy: The Case of the Philippines. *Javnost/The Public* 8 (2): 109–124.

Conboy, Martin. 2004. *Journalism: A Critical History*. London: Sage.

Corner, John. 1991. Meaning, Genre and Context: The Problematics of 'Public Knowledge' in the New Audience Studies. In *Mass Media and Society*, ed. James Curran and Michael Gurevitch, 217–230. London: Methuen.

———. 1995. *Television Form and Public Address*. London: Arnold.

———. 2000. 'Influence': The Contested Core of Media Research. In *Mass Media and Society*, ed. James Curran and Michael Gurevitch, 3rd ed., 376–397. London: Arnold.

Costanza-Chock, Sasha. 2003. Mapping the Repertoire of Electronic Contention. In *Representing Resistance: Media, Civil Disobedience, and the Global Justice Movement*, ed. A. Opel and D. Pompper, 173–191. London: Praeger.

Cottle, Simon. 2008. Reporting Demonstrations: The Changing Media Politics of Dissent. *Media, Culture and Society* 30 (6): 853–872.

Couldry, Nick. 2004. Theorising Media as Practice. *Social Semiotics* 14 (2): 115–132.

———. 2010. *Why Voice Matters: Culture and Politics After Neoliberalism*. London: Sage.

Crossley, Nick. 2006. *Contesting Psychiatry*. London: Routledge.
Crouch, Colin. 2004. *Post-Democracy*. Cambridge: Polity Press.
———. 2012. *The Strange Non-Death of Neoliberalim*. Oxford: Polity.
———. 2015. *The Knowledge Corrupters: Hidden Consequences of the Financial Takeover of Public Life*. Cambridge: Polity Press.
Curran, James. 2005. Mediations of Democracy. In *Mass Media and Society*, ed. James Curran and Michael Gurevitch, 4th ed., 122–149. London: Hodder Arnold.
Curran, James, Julian Petley, and Ivor Gaber. 2005. *Culture Wars: The Media and The British Left*. Edinburgh: Edinburgh University Press.
Dale, Stephen. 1996. *McLuhan's Children: The Greenpeace Message and the Media*. Toronto: Behind the Lines.
Dalton, Russell J. 1996. *Citizen Politics: Public Opinion and Political Parties in Advanced Industrial Democracies* - 2nd Edition. Chatham, NJ: Chatham House Publishers.
Daphi, Priska. 2013. Collective Identity Across Borders: Bridging Local and Transnational Memories in the Italian and German Global Justice Movements. In *Understanding European Movements: New Social Movements, Global Justice Struggles, Anti-Austerity Protest*, ed. Cristina Flesher Fominaya and Laurence Cox, 158–171. London: Routledge.
Darnton, Robert. 1982. *The Literary Underground of the Old Regime*. Cambridge, MA: Harvard University Press.
Davidson, Neil. 2016. The Socialist Case for Leave. *Jacobin Magazine*, June 22. https://www.jacobinmag.com/2016/06/leave-european-union-brexit-ukip-corbyn-cameron/. Accessed 10 Feb 2017.
Dayan, Daniel. 2013. Conquering Visibility, Conferring Visibility: Visibility Seekers and Media Performance. *International Journal of Communication* 7: 137–153.
De Sade, Donatien Alphonse François. 1968 [1799]. *Juliette* – trans. By Austryn Wainhouse. New York, NY: Grove Press.
Deacon, David, Natalie Fenton, and Alan Bryman. 1999. From Inception to Reception: The Natural History of a News Item. *Media, Culture & Society* 21 (1): 5–31.
Deel, Sean, and Tamsin Murray-Leach. 2015. Political Blockage and the Absence of Europe: Subterranean Politics in London. In *Subterranean Politics in Europe*, ed. Mary Kaldor and Sanine Selchow, 168–199. London: Palgrave Macmillan.
della Porta, Donatella. 2015. *Social Movements in Times of Austerity: Bringing Capitalism Back into Protest Analysis*. Oxford: Polity Press.
della Porta, Donatella, and Mario Diani. 2006. *Social Movements: An Introduction*. 2nd ed. Oxford: Blackwell.
della Porta, Donatella, and Herbert Reiter, eds. 1998. *Policing Protest: The Control of Mass Demonstrations in Western Democracies*. Minneapolis, MN: University of Minnesota Press.

DeLuca, Kevin Michael. 1999. *Image Politics: The New Rhetoric of Environmental Activism*. New York: Guilford Press.

DeLuca, Kevin Michael, and Jennifer Peeples. 2002. From Public Sphere to Public Screen: Democracy, Activism, and the 'Violence' of Seattle. *Critical Studies in Media Communication* 19 (2): 125–151.

Derrida, Jacques. 1978. *Writing and Difference*. London: Routledge & Kegan Paul.

———. 1997. *Politics of Friendship*. London: Verso Books.

Diani, Mario. 1997. Social Movements and Social Capital: A Network Perspective on Movements Outcomes. *Mobilization: An International Quarterly* 2 (2): 129–147.

———. 2000. The Relational Deficit of Ideologically Structured Action. *Mobilization* 5 (1): 17–24.

———. 2001. Social Movement Networks: Virtual and Real. In *Culture and Politics in the Information Age: A New Politics?* ed. Frank Webster, 117–128. London: Routledge.

Diani, Mario, and Doug McAdam, eds. 2003. *Social Movements and Networks: Relational Approaches to Collective Action*. Oxford: Oxford University Press.

Di Cicco, Damon T. 2010. The Public Nuisance Paradigm: Changes in Mass Media Coverage of Political Protest Since the 1960s. *Journalism and Mass Communication Quarterly* 87 (1): 135–153.

Donohue, George A., Phillip J. Tichenor, and Clarice N. Olien. 1995. A Guard Dog Perspective on the Role of Media. *Journal of Communication* 45 (2): 115–132.

Donson, Fiona, Graeme Chesters, Ian Welsh, and Andrew Tickle. 2004. Rebels with a Cause, Folk Devils Without a Panic: Press Jingoism, Policing Tactics and Anti-capitalist Protest in London and Prague. *Internet Journal of Criminology*. http://www.internetjournalofcriminology.com/. Accessed 10 Feb 2017.

Downey, John, and Natalie Fenton. 2003. New Media, Counter Publicity and the Public Sphere. *New Media & Society* 5 (2): 185–202.

Downing, John D. 2008. Social Movement Theories and Alternative Media: An Evaluation and Critique. *Communication, Culture and Critique* 1 (1): 40–50.

Downing, John D., with Tamara Villareal Ford, Genève Gil, and Laura Stein. 2001. *Radical Media: Rebellious Communication and Social Movements*. London: Sage.

Du Gay, Paul, Stuart Hall, Linda Janes, Hugh Mackay, and Keith Negus. 1997. *Doing Cultural Studies: The Story of the Sony Walkman*. London: Sage.

Dyer-Witheford, Nick. 1999. *Cyber-Marx: Cycles and Circuits of Struggle in High-Technology Capitalism*. Urbana and Chicago, IL: University of Illinois Press.

Eldridge, John. 1995. *Glasgow Media Group Reader, Volume One: News Content, Language and Visuals*. London: Routledge.

Elliott, Amber. 2012. Mob's Protest Party Outside Clegg House. *The Sun*, May 27.

eMarketer. 2016. More than Half of UK Population Will Log on to Facebook This Year. February 25. https://www.emarketer.com/Article/More-Than-Half-of-UK-Population-Will-Log-on-Facebook-This-Year/1013627. Accessed 10 Feb 2017.

Esping-Anderson, Gøsta. 1990. *The Three Worlds of Welfare Capitalism*. Princeton, NJ: Princeton University Press.

Eurostat. 2015. *Unemployment Statistics*. Brussels: Eurostat. http://ec.europa.eu/eurostat/statistics-explained/index.php/Unemployment_statistics. Accessed 10 Feb 2017.

Ferree, Myra Marx, and David A. Merill. 2000. Hot Movements and Cold Cognition: Thinking about Social Movements in Gendered Frames'. *Contemporary Sociology* 29 (3): 454–462.

Ferree, Myra Marx, William Anthony Gamson, Juergen Gerhards, and Dieter Rucht. 2002. *Shaping Abortion Discourse: Democracy and the Public Sphere in Germany and the United States*. Cambridge: Cambridge University Press.

Fisher, Mark. 2014. Good for Nothing. *The Occupied Times*, March 19. https://theoccupiedtimes.org/?p=12841. Accessed 10 Feb 2017.

Flesher Fominaya, Cristina. 2010. Creating Cohesion from Diversity: The Challenge of Collective Identity Formation in the Global Justice Movement. *Sociological Inquiry* 80 (3): 377–404.

———. 2015. Debunking Spontaneity: Spain's 15-M/Indignados as Autonomous Movement. *Social Movement Studies* 14 (2): 142–163.

———. 2017. European Anti-Austerity and Pro-Democracy Protests in the Wake of the Global Financial Crisis. *Social Movement Studies* 16 (1): 1–20.

Foucault, Michel. 1972. *The Archeology of Knowledge*. London: Tavistock.

———. 1978. *The Will to Knowledge: The History of Sexuality*. Vol. 1. London: Penguin Books.

———. 1979. *Discipline and Punish: The Birth of the Prison*. Harmondsworth: Penguin Books.

———. 1981. The Order of Discourse. In *Untying the Text: A Post-Structuralist Reader*, ed. Robert Young, 48–78. Boston, MA and London: Routledge & Kegan Paul.

———. 1988. Technologies of the Self. In *Technologies of the Self: A Seminar with Michel Foucault*, ed. Luther H. Martin, Huck Gutman, and Patrick H. Hutton, 16–49. London: Tavistock Publications.

———. 2002. *The Order of Things*. London: Routledge.

Fraser, Nancy. 1996. Social Justice in the Age of Identity Politics: Redistribution, Recognition, and Participation. The Tanner Lectures on Human Values, Stanford University, April 30–May 2.

———. 2000. Rethinking Recognition. *New Left Review* 3 (May–June): 107–120.

Freeman, Jo. 1979. Resource Mobilization and Strategy: A Model for Analyzing Social Movement Organization Action. In *The Dynamics of Social Movements*, ed. Mayer N. Zald and John D. McCarthy, 167–189. Cambridge, MA: Winthrop Publishers.

Fricker, Ronald D. 2017. Sampling Methods for Online Surveys. In *The SAGE Handbook of Online Research Methods*, ed. Nigel G. Fielding, Raymond M. Lee, and Grant Black, 162–183. London: Sage.

Gabrielatos, Costas, and Paul Baker. 2008. Fleeing, Sneaking, Flooding: A Corpus Analysis of Discursive Constructions of Refugees and Asylum Seekers in the UK Press, 1996–2005. *Journal of English Linguistics* 36 (1): 5–38.

Gallie, Walter B. 1956. Essentially Contested Concepts. *Proceedings of the Aristotelian Society* 56: 167–198.

Galloway, Robin. 2011. Pathetic Protest. *The Sun*, October 28.

Galtung, Johan, and Mari Holmboe Ruge. 1965. The Structure of Foreign News. The Presentation of the Congo, Cuba and Cyprus Crises in Four Norwegian Newspapers. *Journal of Peace Research* 2 (1): 64–91.

Gamson, William A. 1992. *Talking Politics*. Cambridge: Cambridge University Press.

———. 1995. Constructing Social Protest. In *Social Movement and Culture*, ed. Hank Johnston and Bart Klandermans, 85–106. Minneapolis, MN: University of Minnesota Press.

Gamson, William A., and David Meyer. 1996. Framing Political Opportunity. In *Comparative Perspectives on Social Movements*, ed. Doug McAdam, John D. McCarthy, and Mayer N. Zald, 275–290. Cambridge: Cambridge University Press.

Gamson, William A., and A. Modigliani. 1989. Media Discourse and Public Opinion on Nuclear Power: A Constructionist Approach. *American Journal of Sociology* 95 (1): 1–37.

Gamson, William A., and Gary Wolfsfeld. 1993. Movements and Media as Interacting Systems. *Annals of the American Academy of Political and Social Science* 526: 114–127.

Gauntlett, David. 1995. *Moving Experiences: Understanding Television's Influences and Effects*. London: John Libbey.

Gerbaudo, Paolo. 2017. *The Mask and the Flag: Populism, Citizenism and Global Protest*. London: Hurst & Co.

Gerbaudo, Paolo, and Emiliano Treré. 2015. In Search of the 'We' of Social Media Activism: Introduction to the Special Issue on Social Media and Protest Identities. *Information, Communication & Society* 18 (8): 865–871.

Gibson, James J. 1977. The Theory of Affordances. In *Perceiving, Acting, and Knowing: Toward an Ecological Psychology*, ed. Robert Shaw and John Bransford, 67–82. Hillsdale, NJ: Lawrence Erlbaum Associates.

———. 1979/1986. *The Ecological Approach to Perception*. Hillsdale, NJ: Lawrence Erlbaum Associates.

Giddens, Anthony. 1979. *Central Problems in Social Theory: Action, Structure and Contradiction in Social Analysis*. Berkeley, CA: University of California Press.

Gill, Stephen. 2000. Toward a Postmodern Prince? The Battle in Seattle as a Moment in the New Politics of Globalisation. *Millennium: Journal of International Studies* 29 (1): 131–140.

Gillan, Kevin, Jenny Pickerill, and Frank Webster. 2008. *Anti-war Activism: New Media and Protest in the Information Age*. Basingstoke: Palgrave Macmillan.

Giroux, Henry A. 2015. Public Intellectuals Against the Neoliberal University. In *Qualitative Inquiry—Past, Present, and Future: A Critical Reader*, ed. Norman K. Denzin and Michael D. Giardina, 194–222. London: Routledge.

Gitlin, Todd. 1980. *The Whole World Is Watching: Mass Media in the Making & Unmaking of the New Left*. Berkeley and Los Angeles, CA: University of California Press.

Giugni, Marco G. 1998. Was It Worth the Effort? The Outcomes and Consequences of Social Movements. *Annual Review of Sociology* 24: 371–393.

Goffman, Erving. 1974. *Frame Analysis: An Essay on the Organization of Experience*. London: Harper & Row.

Golding, Peter, and Sue Middleton. 1982. *Images of Welfare: Press and Public Attitude to Poverty*. Oxford: Blackwell.

Goodwin, Jeff, and James M. Jasper, eds. 2004. *Rethinking Social Movements: Structure, Meaning and Emotion*. Lanham, MD: Rowman & Littlefield.

Goodwin, Jeff, James M. Jasper, and Francesca. Polleta, eds. 2001. *Passionate Politics: Emotions and Social Movements*. Lanham, MD: Rowman & Littlefield.

Graber, Doris. 2005. Political Communication Faces the 21st Century. *Journal of Communication* 55 (3): 479–507.

Gramsci, Antonio. 1971. *Selections from the Prison Notebooks*. London: Lawrence & Wishart.

Green, David Allen. 2012. An Open Letter to the St Paul's Protesters: What Is the Significance So Far of "Occupy LSX"? *The New Statesman*, February 24. http://www.newstatesman.com/blogs/david-allen-green/2012/02/city-cathedral-camp-occupy. Accessed 10 Feb 2017.

Greene, Jennifer C., Valerie J. Caracelli, and Wendy F. Graham. 1989. Toward a Conceptual Framework for Mixed-Method Evaluation Designs. *Educational Evaluation and Policy Analysis* 11 (3): 255–274.

Habermas, Jürgen. 1989. *The Structural Transformation of the Public Sphere: An Inquiry into a Category of Bourgeois Society*. Cambridge, MA: MIT Press.

Halbwachs, Maurice. 1980 [1950]. *The Collective Memory*. New York: Harper & Row.

Hall, Stuart. 1980 [1973]. Encoding/Decoding. In *Culture, Media, Language: Working Papers in Cultural Studies, 1972–79*, ed. Centre for Contemporary Cultural Studies, 128–138. London: Hutchinson.

———. 1981 [1973]. The Structured Communication of Events. In *Society and Social Sciences: An Introduction*, ed. David C. Potter and James Anderson, 269–289. London/Henley: Routledge & Kegan Paul/Open University Press.

———. 1988. *The Hard Road to Renewal: Thatcherism and the Crisis of the Hard Left*. London: Verso.

———. 1997a. *Representation: Cultural Representations and Signifying Practices*. London: Sage.

———. 1997b. *Representation & the Media. Lecture Transcript*. Northampton, MA: Media Education Association. http://www.mediaed.org/transcripts/Stuart-Hall-Representation-and-the-Media-Transcript.pdf. Accessed 10 Feb 2017.

Hallin, Daniel C. 1986. *The "Uncensored War"*. New York: Oxford University Press.

Halloran, James D., Philip Elliott, and Graham Murdock. 1970. *Demonstrations and Communication: A Case Study*. Harmondsworth: Penguin Books.

Harlow, Summer. 2011. Social Media and Social Movements: Facebook and an Online Guatemalan Justice Movement that Moved Offline. *New Media & Society* 14 (2): 225–243.

Haythornthwaite, Caroline. 2002. Strong, Weak, and Latent Ties and the Impact of New Media. *The Information Society* 18 (5): 385–401.

Herman, Edward S., and Noam Chomsky. 1988. *Manufacturing Consent: The Political Economy of the Mass Media*. New York: Pantheon.

Hermanns, Heike. 2008. Mobile Democracy: Mobile Phones as Democratic Tools. *Politics* 28 (2): 74–82.

HM Treasury. 2010. Spending Review 2010. October 20. https://www.gov.uk/government/publications/spending-review-2010. Accessed 10 Feb 2017.

Honderich, Ted. 1989. *Violence for Equality: Inquiries in Political Philosophy*. 3rd ed. London/New York: Routledge.

Honneth, Axel. 2001. Recognition or Redistribution? Changing Perspectives on the Moral Order of Society. *Theory, Culture & Society* 18 (2–3): 43–55.

———. 2012. *The I in We: Studies in the Theory of Recognition*. Cambridge: Polity Press.

House of Commons. 2009. Banking Crisis: Dealing with the Failure of the UK Banks. HC416. April 21. http://www.publications.parliament.uk/pa/cm200809/cmselect/cmtreasy/416/416.pdf. Accessed 10 Feb 2017.

Hutchby, Ian. 2001. Technologies, Texts and Affordances. *Sociology* 35 (2): 441–456.

Hutton, Patrick H. 1988. Foucault, Freud and the Technologies of the Self. In *Technologies of the Self: A Seminar with Michel Foucault*, ed. Luther H. Martin, Huck Gutman, and Patrick H. Hutton, 121–144. London: Tavistock Publications.

Iyengar, Shanto, and Donald D. Kinder. 1987. *News That Matters: Television and American Opinion*. Chicago, IL: University of Chicago Press.

Jasper, James. 1997. *The Art of Moral Protest: Culture, Biography, and Creativity in Social Movements*. Chicago, IL: Chicago University Press.

Jasper, James M., and Jane Poulsen. 1995. Recruiting Strangers and Friends: Moral Shocks and Social Networks in Animal Rights and Anti-nuclear Protests. *Social Problems* 42: 493–512.

Jessop, Bob. 1990. Regulation Theories in Retrospect and Prospect. *Economy & Society* 19 (2): 153–216.

Johnson, Richard. 1986. The Story So Far: And for the Transformations. In *Introduction to Contemporary Cultural Studies*, ed. D. Punter, 227–313. London: Longman.

Johnston, Hank, ed. 2009. *Culture, Social Movements, and Protest*. Farnham: Ashgate.

———. 2014. *What Is a Social Movement?* Cambridge: Polity Press.

Jones, Owen. 2016. Apple Must Now Pay Its Taxes. This Is a Vindication of Protest. *The Guardian*, August 30. https://www.theguardian.com/commentisfree/2016/aug/30/apple-tax-avoidance-vindication-protest-ttip. Accessed 10 Feb 2017.

Juris, Jeff S. 2012. Reflections on #Occupy Everywhere: Social Media, Public Space, and Emerging Logics of Aggregation. *American Ethnologist* 39 (2): 259–279.

Kahn, Richard, and Douglas Kellner. 2004. New Media and Internet Activism: From the "Battle of Seattle" to Blogging. *New Media & Society* 6 (1): 87–95.

Kaldor, Mary, and Sabine Selchow. 2013. The 'Bubbling Up' of Subterranean Politics in Europe. *Journal of Civil Society* 9 (1): 78–99.

Katsiaficas, Georgy. 2006. *The Subversion of Politics: European Autonomous Movements and the Decolonization of Everyday Life*. Oakland, CA: AK Press.

Katz, Elihu. 1980. On Conceptualising Media Effects. In *Studies in Communication*, ed. Thelma McCormack, vol. 2, 119–141. Greenwich, CT: JAI Press.

Katz, Elihu, and Paul F. Lazarsfeld. 1955. *Personal Influence: The Part Played by People in the Flow of Mass Communication*. Glencoe, IL: Free Press.

Kavada, Anastasia. 2015. Creating the Collective: Social Media, the Occupy Movement and Its Constitution as a Collective Actor. *Information, Communication & Society* 18 (8): 872–886.

Keane, John. 1991. *The Media and Democracy*. Cambridge: Polity Press.

———. 2004. *Violence and Democracy*. Cambridge: Cambridge University Press.

KhosraviNik, Majid. 2010. The Representation of Refugees, Asylum Seekers and Immigrants in British Newspapers: A Critical Discourse Analysis. *Journal of Language and Politics* 9 (1): 1–28.

King, John. 2015. The Left Wing Case for Leaving the EU. *New Statesman*, June 11. http://www.newstatesman.com/politics/2015/06/john-king-left-wing-case-leaving-eu. Accessed 10 Feb 2017.

Kitzinger, Jenny. 1995. Introducing Focus Groups. *British Medical Journal* 311: 299–302.

Klandermans, Bert. 1988. The Formation and Mobilization of Consensus. *International Social Movement Research* 1: 173–196.

———. 2000. Must We Redefine Social Movements as Ideologically Structured Action? *Mobilization: An International Journal* 5 (1): 25–30.

Klapper, Joseph. 1960. *The Effects of Mass Communication*. Glencoe, IL: Free Press.

Kluge, Alexander. 1982. On Film and the Public Sphere. *New German Critique* 24 (25): 211–212.

Koopmans, Ruud. 1999. Political. Opportunity. Structure. Some Splitting to Balance the Lumping. *Sociological Forum* 14 (1): 93–105.

———. 2004. Movements and Media: Selection Processes and Evolutionary Dynamics in the Public Sphere. *Theory and Society* 33 (3/4): 367–391.

Koopmans, Ruud, and Paul Statham. 1999. Political Claims Analysis: Integrating Protest Event and Political Discourse Approaches. *Mobilization: An International Journal* 4 (2): 203–222.

Krippendorff, Klaus. 2013. *Content Analysis: An Introduction to Its Methodology*. Thousand Oaks, CA: Sage.

Krugman, Paul. 2012. *End This Depression Now!* New York: W. W. Norton.

Laclau, Ernesto. 1996. *Emancipation(s)*. London: Verso.

———. 2005. *On Populist Reason*. London: Verso.

Laclau, Ernesto, and Chantal Mouffe. 1985. *Hegemony and Socialist Strategy. Towards a Radical Democratic Politics*. Verso: London.

Lakoff, George. 2004. *Don't Think of an Elephant! Know Your Values and Frame the Debate*. White River Junction, VT: Chelsea Green.

Lang, Kurt, and Gladys Engel Lang. 1959. The Mass Media and Voting. In *American Voting Behaviour*, ed. Eugene J. Burdick and Arthur J. Brodbeck, 217–235. New York: Free Press.

Larsen, Christian Albrekt, and Thomas Engel Dejgaard. 2013. The Institutional Logic of Images of the Poor and Welfare Recipients: A Comparative Study of British, Swedish and Danish Newspapers. *Journal of European Social Policy* 23 (3): 287–299.

Lasswell, Harold D. 1927. *Propaganda Technique in the World War*. New York: Alfred A. Knopf.

Lazarsfeld, Paul Felix, Bernard Berelson, and Hazel Gaudet. 1944. *The People's Choice: How the Voter Makes Up His Mind in a Presidential Campaign*. New York, NY: Columbia University Press.

Lester, Libby, and Brett Hutchins. 2009. Power Games: Environmental Protest, News Media and the Internet. *Media, Culture and Society* 31 (4): 579–595.

Lewis, Justin, and Jon Cruz, eds. 1994. *Viewing, Reading, Listening: Audiences and Cultural Reception*. Boulder, CO: Westview Press.

Lewis, Paul, Adam Gabbatt, Matthew Taylor, and Simon Jeffery. 2010. UK Uncut Protesters Spied Upon by Undercover Police. *The Guardian*, December 3.

http://www.theguardian.com/uk/2010/dec/03/uk-uncut-protests-undercover-police. Accessed 10 Feb 2017.

Liebes, Tamar, and Elihu Katz. 1990. *The Export of Meaning*. Oxford: Oxford University Press.

Lindekilde, Lasse. 2014. Discourse and Frame Analysis: In-depth Analysis of Qualitative Data in Social Movement Research. In *Methodological Practices in Social Movement Research*, ed. Donatella della Porta, 195–227. New York: Oxford University Press.

Lindlof, Thomas R. 1991. The Qualitative Study of Media Audiences. *Journal of Broadcasting and Electronic Media* 35 (1): 23–42.

Lipschutz, Ronnie D. 2005. Networks of Knowledge and Practice: Global Civil Society and Global Communications. In *Global Activism, Global Media*, ed. Wilma de Jong, Martin Shaw, and Neil Stammers, 59–80. London: Pluto Press.

Livingstone, Sonia. 1998. Audience Research at the Crossroads: The 'Implied Audience' in Media and Cultural Theory. *European Journal of Cultural Studies* 1 (2): 193–217.

———. 2006. The Influence of "Personal Influence" on the Study of Audiences. *The ANNALS of the American Academy of Political and Social Science* 608: 233–250.

———. 2007. On the Material and the Symbolic: Silverstone's Double Articulation of Research Traditions in New Media Studies. *New Media and Society* 9 (1): 16–24.

———. 2015. *Active Audiences? The Debate Progresses but It Is Far from Resolved. Communication Theory* 25 (4): 439–446.

Livingstone, Sonia, and Ranjana Das. 2013. The End of Audiences? Theoretical Echoes of Reception Amid the Uncertainties of Use. In *A Companion to New Media Dynamics*, ed. John Hartley, Jean Burgess, and Axel Bruns, 104–121. Oxford: Wiley-Blackwell.

Livingstone, Sonia, and Peter Lunt. 2014. Mediatization: An Emerging Paradigm for Media and Communication Studies. In *Mediatization of Communication*, ed. Knut Lundby, 703–724. Berlin: De Gruyter Mouton.

Lukes, Steven. 2005. *Power: A Radical View*. 2nd ed. Basingstoke: Palgrave Macmillan.

Lyon, David. 2015. *Surveillance After Snowden*. Cambridge: Polity Press.

Mackay, Hughie, and Gareth Gillespie. 1992. Extending the Social Shaping of Technology Approach: Ideology and Appropriation. *Social Studies of Science* 22 (4): 685–716.

MacPherson, C.B. 1977. *The Life and Times of Liberal Democracy*. Oxford: Oxford University Press.

Malik, Shiv, and Jessica Shepherd. 2011. Police Send Warning Letters to Activists Ahead of Student Protests. *The Guardian*, November 8.

Mansell, Robin. 2012. *Imagining the Internet: Communication, Innovation, and Governance*. Oxford: Oxford University Press.

Mansell, Robin, and Marc Raboy. 2011. *The Handbook of Global Media and Communication Policy*. Chichester: Wiley-Blackwell.

Martín-Barbero, Jesús. 1993. *Communication, Culture and Hegemony: From the Media to Mediation*. London: Sage.

Marx, Karl, and Friedrich Engels. 1848 [1969]. Manifesto of the Communist Party. In *Marx/Engels Selected Works*, vol. 1, 98–137. Moscow: Progress Publishers.

Mathiesen, Thomas. 1997. The Viewer Society: Michel Foucault's 'Panopticon' Revisited. *Theoretical Criminology* 1 (2): 215–234.

Mattoni, Alice, and Emiliano Treré. 2014. Media Practices, Mediation Processes, and Mediatization in the Study of Social Movements. *Communication Theory* 24 (3): 252–271.

McAdam, Doug, Sidney Tarrow, and Charles Tilly. 2001. *Dynamics of Contention*. Cambridge: Cambridge University Press.

McCammon, Holly J., Courtney Sanders Muse, Harmony D. Newman, and Teresa M. Terrell. 2007. Movement Framing and Discursive Opportunity Structures: The Political Successes of the U.S. Women's Jury Movements. *American Sociological Review* 72 (5): 725–749.

McCarthy, John D., and Mayer N. Zald. 1973. *The Trend of Social Movements in America: Professionalism and Resource Mobilization*. Morristown, NJ: General Learning Press.

McCombs, Maxwell E., and Donald L. Shaw. 1972. The Agenda-Setting Function of Mass Media. *Public Opinion Quarterly* 36 (2): 176–187.

McCurdy, Patrick. 2010. Breaking the Spiral of Silence: Unpacking the 'Media Debate' Within Global Justice Movements. A Case Study of Dissent! and the 2005 Gleneagles G8 Summit. *Interface: A Journal for and About Social Movements* 2 (2): 42–67.

———. 2012. Social Movements, Protest and Mainstream Media. *Sociology Compass* 6 (3): 244–255.

McDonald, Kevin. 2002. From Solidarity to Fluidity: Social Movements Beyond "Collective Identity"—The Case of Globalization Conflicts. *Social Movement Studies* 1: 109–128.

McKay, George. 2011. UK Uncut: A Very British Protest? Cultural Studies with a Soundtrack, February 10. http://georgemckay.org/uk-uncut-a-very-british-protest/. Accessed 12 Apr 2016.

McLeod, Douglas M., and James K. Hertog. 1999. Social Control and the Mass Media's Role in the Regulation of Protest Groups: The Communicative Acts Perspective. In *Mass Media, Social Control, and Social Change*, ed. David P. Demers and Kasisomayajula Viswanath, 305–330. Ames, IA: Iowa State University Press.

McQuail, Denis. 2010. *Mass Communication Theory*. 6th ed. London: Sage.

Melucci, Alberto. 1996. *Challenging Codes: Collective Action in the Information Age*. Cambridge: Cambridge University Press.

Mertes, Tom, ed. 2004. *A Movement of Movements: Is Another World Really Possible?* London: Verso.

Messenger, Terry. 2010. Vodafone Closure Campaign—Tax-Dodging Protest Began over a Pint in Nag's Head Pub. *Camden Review*, December 29. http://www.camdenreview.com/node/7776. Accessed 10 Feb 2017.

Meyer, David S., and Nancy Whittier. 1994. Social Movement Spillover. *Social Problems* 41: 277–298.

Milan, Stefania. 2015. When Algorithms Shape Collective Action: Social Media and the Dynamics of Cloud Protesting. *Social Media + Society* 1 (2): 1–10.

Mizen, Phillip. 2002. Putting the Politics Back into Youth Studies: Keynesianism, Monetarism and the Changing State of Youth. *Journal of Youth Studies* 5 (1): 5–20.

Moreno, Ebony. 2016. I'm Mixed Race, Female, Left-Wing, a 19-Year-Old Student—And Yes, I Really Am Voting for Brexit. *The Independent,* June 21. http://www.independent.co.uk/voices/im-mixed-race-female-left-wing-and-a-student-and-yes-i-really-am-voting-for-brexit-a7093221.html. Accessed 10 Feb 2017.

Morley, David. 1980. *The Nationwide Audience: Structure and Decoding.* In British Film Institute Television Monograph #11. London: British Film Institute.

———. 1992. *Television, Audiences and Cultural Studies.* London: Routledge.

———. 1993. Active Audience Theory: Pendulums and Pitfalls. *Journal of Communication* 43 (4): 13–19.

Morozov, Evgeny. 2009. The Brave New World of Slacktivism. *Foreign Policy*, 19/05. http://neteffect.foreignpolicy.com/posts/2009/05/19/the_brave_new_world_of_slacktivism. Accessed Aug 2017.

Mouffe, Chantal. 1979. Hegemony and Ideology in Gramsci. In *Gramsci and Marxist Theory*, ed. Chantal Mouffe, 168–204. London: Routledge & Kegan Paul.

———. 2005. *On the Political.* London: Routledge.

———. 2013. *Agonistics: Thinking the World Politically.* London: Verso.

———. 2016. The Populist Moment. *Open Democracy*, November 21. https://www.opendemocracy.net/democraciaabierta/chantal-mouffe/populist-moment. Accessed Aug 2017.

Murdock, Graham. 1981. Political Deviance: The Press Presentation of a Militant Mass Demonstration. In *The Manufacture of News: Deviance, Social Problems and the Mass Media*, ed. Jock Young and Stanley Cohen, 206–225. London: Constable.

———. 1989. Cultural Studies: Missing Links. *Critical Studies in Mass Communication* 6 (4): 436–440.

Nash, Emily. 2011. St Paul's Camp 'Hell of Drugs and Filth'. *The Sun*, November 22.

National Commission on the Causes of the Financial and Economic Crisis in the United States. 2011. *The Financial Crisis Inquiry Report.* Washington DC: US

Government Printing Office. http://www.gpo.gov/fdsys/pkg/GPO-FCIC/pdf/GPO-FCIC.pdf. Accessed Aug 2017.

NCAFC. 2010. No Confidence in Aaron Porter! December 15. http://anticuts.com/2010/12/15/nus-is-not-fit-for-purpose-we-need-a-fighting-union/. Accessed Aug 2017.

———. 2012/2014. NCAFC Constitution, Adopted on 8–9 December 2012 and Amended on December 14th 2014. http://anticuts.com/ncafc-constitution/. Accessed Aug 2017.

Negt, Oskar, and Alexander Kluge. 1993. *The Public Sphere and Experience: Toward an Analysis of the Bourgeois and Proletarian Public Sphere*. Minneapolis, MN: University of Minneapolis Press.

Nez, Héloïse. 2012. Délibérer au sein d'un mouvement social: Ethnographie des assemblées des Indignés à Madrid. *Participations* 3 (4): 79–102.

Nieburg, Harold Leonard. 1962. The Threat of Violence and Social Change. *American Political Science Review* 56: 865–873.

Oberschall, Anthony. 1973. *Social Conflict and Social Movements*. Englewood Cliffs, NJ: Prentice-Hall.

Occupy LSX. 2011a. The Initial Statement. October 17. http://occupylondon.org.uk/occupy-london-agreements/. Accessed 10 Feb 2017.

———. 2011b. Global Democracy Statement. October 15. http://occupylondon.org.uk/occupy-london-agreements/. Accessed 10 Feb 2017.

———. 2011c. Corporations Statement. November 25. http://occupylondon.org.uk/occupy-london-agreements/. Accessed 10 Feb 2017.

———. 2011d. Economics Statement. December 6. http://occupylondon.org.uk/occupy-london-agreements/. Accessed 10 Feb 2017.

———. 2011e. Safe Space Policy. November. http://occupylondon.org.uk/occupy-london-agreements/. Accessed 10 Feb 2017.

———. 2011f. Occupied Times of London—The Independent Newspaper of Occupy London Launches. Press Release, October 27. http://occupylondon.org.uk/occupied-times-of-london-the-independent-newspaper-of-occupy-london-launches-2/. Accessed 10 Feb 2017.

Offe, Claus. 2013. Participatory Inequality in the Austerity State: A Supply-Side Approach. In *Politics in the Age of Austerity*, ed. Armin Schäfer and Wolfgang Streeck, 196–218. Cambridge: Polity Press.

Oliver, Pamela E., and Hank Johnston. 2000. What a Good Idea! Ideologies and Frames in Social Movement Research. *Mobilization: An International Journal* 4 (1): 37–54.

Oliver, Pamela E., and Gregory M. Maney. 2000. Political Processes and Local News Article Coverage of Protest Events: From Selection Bias to Triadic Interactions. *American Journal of Sociology* 106 (2): 463–505.

Osborne, Peter. 2011. Time for HMRC to Settle Its Own Bill. *The Daily Telegraph*, December 20.

Pan, Zhongdang, and Gerald M. Kosicki. 1993. Framing Analysis: An Approach to Media Discourse. *Political Communication* 10 (1): 55–75.

Pariser, Eli. 2012. *The Filter Bubble: What the Internet Is Hiding from You*. London: Penguin Books.

Park, Robert Ezra, and Ernest W. Burgess. 1966 [1921]. *Introduction to the Science of Sociology*. 3rd ed. Chicago: University of Chicago Press.

Pateman, Carole. 1970. *Participation and Democratic Theory*. Cambridge: Cambridge University Press.

Peterson, Abby, Mattias Wahlström, and Magnus Wennerhag. 2015. European Anti-Austerity Protests—Beyond 'Old' and 'New' Social Movements? *Acta Sociologica* 58 (4): 293–310.

Philo, Greg, ed. 1995. *Glasgow Media Group Reader, Volume 2: Industry, Economy, War and Politics*. London: Routledge.

———. 2007. Can Discourse Analysis Successfully Explain the Content of Media and Journalistic Practice? *Journalism Studies* 8 (2): 175–196.

Piketty, Thomas. 1996. The Politics of Redistribution: Recent Developments and Research Perspectives. Paper presented at the meeting of the McArthur Foundation Costs of Inequality Project, Boston, May 3–5. http://piketty.pse.ens.fr/fichiers/public/Piketty1996b.pdf. Accessed Aug 2017.

———. 2014. *Capital in the Twenty-First Century*. Cambridge, MA: Harvard University Press.

———. 2015. *The Economics of Inequality*. Cambridge, MA: Harvard University Press.

Postill, John. 2010. Introduction: Theorising Media and Practice. In *Theorising Media and Practice*, ed. Birgit Bräuchler and John Postill, 1–34. Oxford and New York: Berghahn.

Prentoulisa, Marina, and Lasse Thomassen. 2013. Political Theory in the Square: Protest, Representation and Subjectification. *Contemporary Political Theory* 12 (3): 166–184.

Private Eye. 2010. Countdown to Cuts: Somber Mood Grips Nation. October 15.

Quinn, Ben. 2011. Anti-Cuts Groups Descend on Banks in NHS Protest. *The Guardian*, May 28. https://www.theguardian.com/uk/2011/may/28/uk-uncut-nhs-bank-protests. Accessed 10 Feb 2017.

Razsa, Maple, and Andrej Kurnik. 2012. The Occupy Movement in Žižek's Hometown: Direct democracy and a politics of becoming. *American Ethnologist* 39 (2): 238–258.

Reckwitz, A. 2002. Toward a Theory of Social Practices: A Development in Culturalist Theorizing. *European Journal of Social Theory* 5 (2): 243–263.

Rheingold, Howard. 2002. *Smart Mobs: The Next Social Revolution*. Cambridge, MA: Basic Books.

Rolfe, Brett. 2005. Building an Electronic Repertoire of Contention. *Social Movement Studies* 4 (1): 65–74.

Romanos, Eduardo. 2013. Collective Learning Processes Within Social Movements: Some Inights into the Spanish 15-M/Indignados Movement. In *Understanding European Movements: New Social Movements, Global Justice Struggles, Anti-Austerity Protest*, ed. Cristina Flesher Fominaya and Laurence Cox, 203–219. London: Routledge.

Rucht, Dieter. 2004. The Quadruple "A": Media Strategies of Protest Movements Since the 1960s. In *Cyberprotest: New Media, Citizens, and Social Movements*, ed. Wim van de Donk, Brian D. Loader, Paul G. Nixon, and Dieter Rucht, 29–58. London: Routledge.

———. 2013. Protest Movements and Their Media Usages. In *Mediation and Protest Movements*, ed. Bart Cammaerts, Alice Matoni, and Patrick McCurdy, 249–268. Bristol: Intellect.

Ryan, Charlotte. 1991. *Prime Time Activism: Media Strategies for Grassroots Organizing*. Boston, MA: South End Press.

Saunders, Clare. 2008. Double-Edged Swords? Collective Identity and Solidarity in the Environment Movement. *British Journal of Sociology* 59 (2): 227–253.

Scalmer, Sean. 2002. *Dissent Events: Protest, the Media and the Political Gimmick in Australia*. Kensington: University of New South Wales Press.

Schmitt, Carl. 1996 [1927]. *The Concept of the Political*. Chicago, IL: Chicago University Press.

Schrøder, Kim C. 2000. Making Sense of Audience Discourses: Towards a Multidimensional Model of Mass Media Reception. *European Journal of Cultural Studies* 3 (2): 233–258.

Schumpeter, Joseph A. 1973 [1942]. *Capitalism, Socialism, and Democracy*. New York: Harper & Brothers.

Semetko, Holli A. 2004. Political Communication. In *The Sage Handbook of Media Studies*, ed. John D.H. Downing, Denis McQuail, Philip Schlesinger, and Ellen Wartella, 351–374. Thousand Oaks, CA: Sage.

Seymour, Richard. 2014. *Against Austerity: How 'We' Can Fix the Crisis 'They' Made*. London: Pluto Press.

Shoemaker, Pamela J. 1984. Media Treatment of Deviant Political Groups. *Journalism Quarterly* 61 (1): 66–82.

Siebert, Fred S., Theodore Peterson, and Wilbur Schramm. 1956. *Four Theories of the Press: The Authoritarian, Libertarian, Social Responsibility, and Soviet Communist Concepts of What the Press Should Be and Do*. Urbana, IL: University of Illinois Press.

Silverstone, Roger. 1994. *Television and Everyday Life*. London: Routledge.

———. 1999a. Domesticating ICTs. In *Society on the Line. Information Politics in the Digital Age*, ed. William Dutton, 251–253. Oxford: Oxford University Press.

———. 1999b. *Why Study the Media?* London: Sage.

———. 2002. Complicity and Collusion in the Mediation of Everyday Life. *New Literary History* 33 (4): 761–780.

———. 2005. The Sociology of Mediation and Communication. In *The Sage Handbook of Sociology*, ed. Craig Calhoun, Chris Rojek, and Bryan Turner, 188–207. London: Sage.

———. 2006. *Media and Morality: On the Rise of the Mediapolis.* Cambridge: Polity.

Simpson, Sean. 2012. *Credibility Intervals for Online Polling.* Toronto: Ipsos Public Affairs.

Sinclair, Mark. 2012. A Newspaper for the Times. *Creative Review*, January 6. http://www.creativereview.co.uk/a-newspaper-for-the-times/. Accessed 10 Feb 2017.

Smith, Jackie. 2001. Globalizing Resistance: The Battle of Seattle and the Future of Social Movements. *Mobilization: An International Quarterly* 6 (1): 1–19.

Smith, Jackie, John D. McCarthy, Clark McPhail, and Boguslaw Augustyn. 2001. From Protest to Agenda Building: Description Bias in Media Coverage of Protest Events in Washington, D.C. *Social Forces* 79 (4): 1397–1423.

Snow, David A., and Robert D. Benford. 1988. Ideology, Frame Resonance, and Participant Mobilization. *International Social Movement Research* 1: 197–217.

Snow, David A., Burke E. Rochford, Steven E. Worden, and Robert D. Benford. 1986. Frame Alignment Processes, Micromobilization, and Movement Participation. *American Sociological Review* 51 (4): 464–481.

Sreberny-Mohammadi, Annabelle, and Ali Mohammadi. 1994. *Small Media, Big Revolution: Communication, Culture, and the Iranian Revolution.* Minneapolis, MN: University of Minnesota Press.

Steinberg, Marc W. 1998. Tilting the Frame: Considerations on Collective Action Framing from a Discursive Turn. *Theory and Society* 27 (6): 845–872.

Tarde, Gabriel. 1903. *The Laws of Imitation.* Trans. Elsie Clews Parsons with Introduction by Franklin H. Giddings. New York: Henry, Holt and Co.

Tarrow, Sidney. 1994. *Power in Movement: Social Movements and Contentious Politics.* Cambridge: Cambridge University Press.

Taylor, Verta, and Alison Dahl Crossley. 2013. Abeyance. In *The Wiley-Blackwell Encyclopaedia of Social and Political Movements*, ed. David A. Snow, Donatella della Porta, Bert Klandermans, and Doug McAdam, 1–2. Malden, MA: Wiley-Blackwell.

Thompson, John B. 1995. *The Media and Modernity: A Social Theory of the Media.* Cambridge: Polity Press.

———. 2005. The New Visibility. *Theory, Culture and Society* 22 (6): 31–51.

Thumim, Nancy. 2009. 'Everyone Has a Story to Tell': Mediation and Self-Representation in Two UK Institutions. *International Journal of Cultural Studies* 12 (6): 617–638.

Tilly, Charles. 1986. *The Contentious French: Four Centuries of Popular Struggle.* Cambridge, MA: Harvard University Press.

———. 2000. Violent and Nonviolent Trajectories in Contentious Politics. Paper presented at the Symposium on States in Transition and the Challenge of Ethnic conflict at the Russian Academy of Sciences/US National Academy of Sciences, Moscow, December 29. http://130.203.133.150/viewdoc/summary?doi=10.1.1.8.6842. Accessed 10 Feb 2017.

Torfing, Jacob. 1998. *Politics, Regulation and the Modern Welfare State.* Basingstoke: Palgrave.

Touraine, Alain. 1981. *The Voice and the Eye: An Analysis of Social Movements.* Cambridge: Cambridge University Press.

Townsend, Mark. 2011. UK Uncut Accuses Police of Politically Motivated Arrests. *The Guardian*, April 2. http://www.guardian.co.uk/uk/2011/apr/02/uk-uncut-fortnum-mason-protest. Accessed 10 Feb 2017.

Treanor, Jill. 2012. How Much Profit Will Northern Rock and Bradford & Bingley Make for the Taxpayer? *The Guardian*, February 28. http://www.theguardian.com/business/blog/2012/feb/28/northern-rock-bradford-bingley-profits. Accessed 10 Feb 2017.

Trottier, Daniel, and Christian Fuchs, eds. 2015. *Social Media, Politics and the State: Protests, Revolutions, Riots, Crime and Policing in the Age of Facebook, Twitter and YouTube.* New York: Routledge.

UK Uncut. 2010a. Flyer for Workers. https://ukuncut.files.wordpress.com/2010/10/workers.pdf. Accessed 10 Feb 2017.

———. 2010b. Bust Card. https://ukuncut.files.wordpress.com/2010/10/bust1.pdf. Accessed 10 Feb 2017.

———. 2010c. Tax Dodgers. Flyer. https://ukuncut.files.wordpress.com/2010/10/vodafoneflyer2.pdf. Accessed 10 Feb 2017.

———. 2015a. About. http://www.ukuncut.org.uk/about/. Accessed 10 Feb 2017.

———. 2015b. Organise an Action. http://www.ukuncut.org.uk/organising-an-action/. Accessed 10 Feb 2017.

UK Uncut Brighton. 2011. Twitter Direct Action Training. January 18. http://www.ukuncut.org.uk/blog/twitter-direct-action-training---saturday-22nd/. Accessed 10 Feb 2017.

Vale, Paul. 2011. Occupy London: The First Edition of The Occupied Times Hits the Presses. The Huffington Post, October 26. http://www.huffingtonpost.co.uk/2011/10/26/occupy-london-the-first-e_n_1032909.html. Accessed 10 Feb 2017.

Van Dyke, Nelle, Sarah A. Soule, and Verta A. Taylor. 2004. The Targets of Social Movements: Beyond a Focus on the State. *Research in Social Movements, Conflicts, and Change* 25 (1): 27–51.

Van Laer, Jeroen, and Peter Van Aelst. 2010. Internet and Social Movements Action Repertoires: Opportunities and Limitations. *Information, Communication & Society* 13 (8): 1146–1171.

van Zoonen, Elizabeth A. 1992. The Women's Movement and the Media: Constructing a Public Identity. *European Journal of Communication* 7 (4): 453–476.

Walker, Peter, and Paul Owen. 2011. Occupy London Protesters Take over Empty UBS Bank Offices. *The Guardian*, November 18. https://www.theguardian.com/uk/2011/nov/18/occupy-london-protesters-ubs-bank

Walker, Peter, Paul Lewis, Matthew Taylor, and Patrick Wintour. 2010. Student Protests: School's Out Across the UK as Children Take to the Streets. November 24. http://www.theguardian.com/education/2010/nov/24/student-protests-school-children-streets. Accessed 10 Feb 2017.

Warf, Barney. 2011. Geographies of Global Internet Censorship. *GeoJournal* 76 (1): 1–23.

Wilks-Heeks, Stuart, Andrew Blick, and Stephen Crone. 2012. *How Democratic Is the UK? The 2012 Audit*. London: Democratic Audit.

Williams, Robin. 1997. The Social Shaping of Information and Communications Technologies. In *The Social Shaping of Information Superhighways: European and American Roads to the Information Society*, ed. Herbert Kubicek, William H. Dutton, and Robin Williams, 299–338. New York: St. Martin's Press.

Wilson, John. 1973. *Introduction to Social Movements*. New York: Basic Books.

Zamponi, Lorenzo, and Priska Daphi. 2014. Breaks and Continuities in and Between Cycles of Protest. Memories and Legacies of the Global Justice Movement in the Context of Anti-Austerity Mobilisations. In *Spreading Protest: Social Movements in Times of Crisis*, ed. Donatella della Porta and Alice Mattoni, 193–225. Colchester: ECPR Press.

Zukin, Cliff. 2015. What's the Matter With Polling? New York Times, June 20. https://www.nytimes.com/2015/06/21/opinion/sunday/whats-the-matter-with-polling.html

Index[1]

[1] Note: Page number followed by 'n' refers to note.

B. Cammaerts, *The Circulation of Anti-Austerity Protest*,
https://doi.org/10.1007/978-3-319-70123-3

V

The manufacturer's authorised representative in the EU is Springer Nature Customer Service Centre GmbH, Europaplatz 3, 69115 Heidelberg, Germany. If you have any concerns regarding our products, please contact ProductSafety@springernature.com

Printed and bound by CPI Group (UK) Ltd, Croydon, CR0 4YY
30/09/2026
02225653-0004